MARY RITTER BEARD

MARY RITTER BEARD: *A Sourcebook*

Edited by ANN J. LANE

STUDIES IN THE LIFE OF WOMEN

GENERAL EDITOR: Gerda Lerner

SCHOCKEN BOOKS · NEW YORK

Library of Congress Cataloging in Publication Data

Beard, Mary Ritter, 1876–1958.
  Mary Ritter Beard: a sourcebook.

(Studies in the life of women)
  Bibliography: p. 240.
  Includes index.
  1. Feminism—United States—Addresses, essays, lectures. 2. Education of women—
United States—Addresses, essays, lectures. 3. Beard, Mary Ritter, 1876–1958. 4.
Women—Suffrage—United States—Addresses, essays, lectures. I. Lane, Ann J., 1932–
HQ1426.B424 1977   301.41'2'0973   77–3135

Manufactured in the United States of America

Acknowledgments

I wish to thank the following publishers, institutions or persons for granting me permission
to quote from works by Mary R. Beard cited below.

On Understanding Women, Greenwood Press, Inc., reprint edition; copyright 1931 by
Longmans, Green & Co.; copyright renewed by William Beard and Miriam Beard Vagts.
  "American Women and the Printing Press," The American Academy of Political and
Social Science.
  "University Discipline for Women—Asset or Handicap?" and "The College and
Alumnae in Contemporary Life," the American Association of University Women.
  "The Direction of Women's Education," Mount Holyoke College.
  Woman as Force in History: A Study in Traditions and Realities, Macmillan Publishing
Co., Inc.
  "A Changing Political Economy as It Affects Women," William Beard and Miriam
Beard Vagts.
  "The Economic Background of the Sex Life of the Unmarried Adult," Vanguard Press,
Inc.

William Beard and Miriam Beard Vagts hold their mother's literary property rights and granted me permission to quote from her letters and any other documents to which they hold the copyright.

My thanks to the Library staffs of the Schlesinger Library, Radcliffe College; the Sophia Smith Collection of Smith College; and the University of Wisconsin Library. I am particularly indebted to David E. Horn, archivist of the Roy O. West Library at DePauw University, for his help. Stephen Fox and Leo Ribuffo called my attention to letters of Mary Beard I was not familiar with.

The Leopold Schepp Foundation gave me a grant which provided me with a year free from normal academic obligations. A summer stipend from the National Endowment for the Humanities, a grant-in-aid from the American Council of Learned Societies, and a City University of New York Faculty Research award supplemented that grant and provided me with funds for travel.

Without a sizable body of papers, it became necessary to rely upon many individuals to provide me with a sense of Mary Ritter Beard and the world she knew. Merle Curti read the manuscript and offered me both his criticisms of it and his memories of Charles and Mary Beard. Patricia A. Graham gave me vivid descriptions of life in central Indiana, based upon her own family's history, and in so doing helped me understand in very important ways the kind of world in which Mary Ritter developed. Mary Beth Norton, happily for me, grew up on the DePauw University campus, as the child of a member of the faculty, and she reconstructed for me, in very personal and meaningful ways, the quality of life there in the recent past. Dora Edinger, a longtime co-worker of Mary Beard, on the *Encyclopaedia Britannica* project as well as others, spoke to me at length about her recollections and gave me all the pertinent documents in her possession. Catherine McCord of Greencastle, Indiana, who graduated from DePauw University two classes after Mary Ritter, was a member of the same sorority, and has been intimately connected to the University ever since, was a source of enormously important descriptions of life on the college campus; she also was able to locate an early photograph of Mary Ritter. Dorothy Ritter Russo, Mary Beard's niece, a resident of Indianapolis, gave me many delightful hours of nostalgic recollections of her family. Clifton J. Phillips, whose effort to write a biography of Charles Beard was ultimately abandoned, as were attempts by others, provided me with materials he had accumulated. Reverend Arthur Neuerman, of the Central Avenue United Methodist Church of Indianapolis, graciously opened the church's archives to me.

As the children of Charles and Mary Beard, William Beard and Miriam Beard Vagts brought a singular kind of perspective to their reading of the manuscript. As scholars, they were also able to examine and comment upon the study from the viewpoint of trained historians. While I did not always accept their advice, I always paid careful attention to it. Their assistance and cooperation greatly helped me.

I also relied upon many friends. Warren I. Susman, Barbara Sicherman, Claire Sprague, and Dolores Kreisman read the entire manuscript and provided valuable criticisms and suggestions.

Gerda Lerner, friend, colleague and the editor of this series, spent many hours, often on Sundays, reading the manuscript at every stage and commenting closely on it. I am very grateful to her for the time she gave to me and for the high quality of her criticisms. I benefited greatly from her long-standing interest in Mary Ritter Beard.

Rolando R. Lopez brought his special skills as an investigator and his talents as a writer to help me re-create the form of Mary Beard's personality and thought from tenuous and shadowy clues. He generously took time away from his own writing to work with every draft and every idea until he became as much a part of Mary Ritter Beard's life and world as did I.

For my children,
Leslie and Joni

Contents

Part One.

**Mary Ritter Beard:
An Appraisal of Her Life and Work**

Chapter I

In 1946 Mary Ritter Beard published her most famous book, *Woman as Force in History*. Her thesis that women have always been a very real, although unrecognized, force in society grew from her own experience. It was stated in her earliest articles and books, and restated, extended, and illustrated, essentially unchanged, for four decades. She vigorously rejected the notion that women have been an oppressed and subject group. Women have been active, assertive, competent contributors to their societies. The myth that women were or are a subject sex is not only wrong, she argued, but counterproductive, because as women accept that designation of themselves and their pasts, their collective strength is undermined. The very idea of oppression takes hold of women's minds and oppresses them. But women could be freed from that ideological bondage by discovering their own powerful, creative history and using that knowledge to create new social relations.

Women are left out of history, are made to seem invisible, she said, not because history has been written by men who are evil or because women have been without power, but because these men, as well as most professional women and radical feminists, focus their attention on those areas of the community in which men predominate.

Simple-minded slogans calling for equality, she insisted, deny the power and force of the total community of women, a community so binding that Mary Beard could write of a separate male and female language, of a shopping list as an important fact for the social historian, of the history of bathing and laundering as a useful way to examine society.

The militant call for absolute equality, Beard said, denies the existence and value of female culture.

Mary Beard devoted her life to reconstructing women's pasts in an effort to end that invisibility. Yet is as if she herself—her life and her work—were a demonstration of her thesis. She still remains largely neglected or relegated to the status of Charles Beard's wife and collaborator, a true but hardly adequate designation. She was a political activist identified with the most radical wing of the American suffrage movement; she was a committed feminist, despite her criticisms of the militants; and she was a highly productive scholar. Her intellectual work—she wrote six books alone and collaborated with her husband on seven others—is sufficiently important to warrant serious assessment. She is also a prototype, a model, of a particular kind of extraordinary woman who was able to combine scholarship and activism while maintaining a traditional commitment to home and family. An examination of her life and work provides a way of studying the nature of and the problems facing women as scholars-activists-wives-mothers.[1]

Mary Beard was of the generation that came of age at the turn of the century, when reform movements were undergoing change, when the New History was beginning to emerge, when, as Richard Hofstadter said, "the critical intelligentsia in the United States" was formed.[2] The environment of the Progressive era stimulated outcries against abuses by big monopolies, concern for the survival of democratic government, and efforts to institute municipal reforms. From that period came the literature of exposure by muckrakers such as Upton Sinclair and Lincoln Steffens, the school of naturalist writers such as Theodore Dreiser and the settlement house movement led by reformers like Jane Addams. In the academic community traditional, formalist approaches were smashed: by Thorstein Veblen in economics; by Roscoe Pound in legal theory; by John Dewey in philosophy; and by James Harvey Robinson, Frederick Jackson Turner, Arthur M. Schlesinger, and Charles and Mary Beard in the New History. The writers of the New History were determined to stress the needs of the contemporary world, to challenge the primacy of military and political explanations by including the significance of economic and social factors, and to show new respect for the history of ideas. They wished to expose the realities and describe the world as it was.

Mary Beard belongs with this new breed of critics and writers. Her work deals with the fundamental matter of writing history, any history.

She devoted her life to asserting and demonstrating the centrality of women in history and the need to incorporate that conception of women in history into the mainstream of historical writing.

*   *   *

This book is about Mary Ritter Beard. But her life was so intimately intertwined with that of her husband and collaborator, Charles Austin Beard, that to isolate her work and her life inevitably distorts both. They shared a life for almost fifty years, raised two children, and established a warm, loving, and exciting home. They shared a political commitment that carried them into the public arena—sometimes working for the same cause, as they did for woman suffrage, sometimes going in different but always compatible directions. They served as models—as "foster-parents"—their daughter, Miriam Beard Vagts said,[3] to unending numbers of younger scholars, reformers, and activists of all kinds who crowded around them.

And they collaborated on major works. The Beards' first joint venture, *American Citizenship*, appeared in 1914. In 1920 they issued *The History of the United States*. The first two volumes of their monumental history of the nation appeared in 1927. The total work is titled *The Rise of American Civilization*, but the world has designated these first two volumes, actually subtitled *The Agricultural Era* and *The Industrial Era*, with the full title. In 1939 appeared another two volumes of *The Rise*, known by their collective subtitle, *America in Midpassage*. In 1942 came the concluding volume, titled *The American Spirit: A Study of the Idea of Civilization in the United States*. The first two volumes end in the middle 1920s; *America in Midpassage* goes to 1939; and the last of the five-volume work sees the idea of civilization as the unifying force in American history. "Bibles to thousands of us in the 1930s," said Eric Goldman in describing the impact of *The Rise*.[4]

As much as any book can change people, *The Rise of American Civilization* shaped the thinking of generations of Americans. Later editions became Book-of-the-Month selections and were widely read outside academic circles. It is probably still the most popular work in American history written in the twentieth century. While it is not possible to determine who wrote which lines, it is also not necessary. Their writings were genuinely collaborative efforts that reflected the thinking of both, although the inclusion of material on the significant role of women in American life and the sizable slice of cultural and literary history were Mary Beard's contributions. *A Basic History of the United States*, their "last will and testament to the American people," said Charles Beard, was published in 1944.[5]

The work she produced alone, the work he produced alone, and the work they produced jointly reflect important shared conceptions. They were determined to make both history and politics accessible to the ordinary reader without demeaning the demands of critical scholarship. Their books have a scope and a vision that repudiates the academic's usual concern for specialization. Above all, they sought to use their intellectual gifts in the service of humanity.

* * *

During their years together, Charles and Mary Beard spent a good part of their life in New Milford, Connecticut, dividing their time between an active social and intellectual life and their demanding work. Resident housekeepers provided Mary Beard with the time for her activities in the years when the children, Miriam and William, were young. Still, her most productive years did not occur until her children were adults, a pattern characteristic of women. Their sixteen-room house, a former boys' school, was "too big for an ordinary household," said their daughter, "but not for *their* household, *their* weekend guests; their house was like Grand Central Station, filled with people coming and going, and father letting out his enormous voice from dawn to dusk."[6] Winters were spent in Washington, in New York, in travel, and, during their later years, in the South, frequently in North Carolina. While associated with Columbia University, the Beards lived near the school in an apartment on West 118th Street in Manhattan. Some time later they moved to a cooperative apartment in the West Sixties, which had for two working people the advantage of housing a restaurant in the building; it was a great benefit because, said their daughter, "the Beards did not know how to keep house."[7]

Miriam Vagts here captures the quality of life in her parents' home:

> My parents were very gregarious, and so were most of their contemporaries. . . . how draining life with a man like Beard was. His vast energies, his tremendous voice (he let it out in the country but tried to hold it down in town), his thousand ideas and projects, his pupils and friends, engineers, professors, firemen and policemen and municipal experts,

visiting Orientals, Albanian archbishops, German refugees, and all the Beards' relatives and neighbors—Mattie and Hannah Josephson, the Cowleys, the Schuyler Wallaces, the Alfred Cohns and Felix Frankfurters and the local New Milford people, the Dairymen's League. Their house witnessed pandemonium; the places in New York, Washington and elsewhere, were also a sea of faces.

And those people were so bursting with zeal, you can't imagine, they all *believed* in things in those days. Mother's myriad suffragette friends who came for the weekends, and father's municipal experts, all shouted at the top of their voices.

. . . that tiny demoniac wasp-like Emmeline Pankhurst . . . or the young Alice Paul, a martyr born, or Rose Schneiderman, tall and raw-boned epitome of mass-suffering, whose woeful voice could shake you with the miseries. . . . It was . . . argue all day, every day.[8]

These assorted friendships produced complications, she observes:

It was a problem, knowing so many different types that could not be harmonized. Father's lawyers and sewage engineers might not mesh with his historians; none of them went very well with the . . . suffragettes or fiery personalities like Rosika Schwimmer. And [my] parents had some trouble making up houseparties. Father's municipal experts bored mother; her wild women got on father's nerves. So they both saw their difficult chums in town.[9]

All signs suggest a good marriage—a marriage built on mutual dependence, respect, affection, and trust. He depended on her at least as much as she did on him. She relied on him to work out some of the legal history in her books, and she regularly gave up her work of the moment because he needed her collaboration in some new interest of his. They learned from each other.

In certain ways the Beards were very public people. Subsequent pages will describe Mary Beard's rich and varied career. A brief sketch will have to suffice for Charles Beard's career. He received his Ph.D. in 1904 from Columbia University, where he joined the faculty and in 1907 was named adjunct professor of politics. He resigned from that position in October, 1917, to protest what he described as an arbitrary dismissal of three antiwar faculty members by Columbia President Nicholas Murray Butler. Charles Beard, who himself supported the U.S. involvement in World War I, denounced the trustees of the University for being "reactionary and visionless in politics, narrow and medieval in religion." It was many years before he returned to university life, and then not permanently.

In 1915 he affiliated himself with the Bureau of Municipal Research in New York, and from 1917 to 1922 he organized and directed New York City's Training School for Public Service. In 1918 he, together with Dewey, Veblen and Robinson, founded the New School for Social Research. In 1921 he became an active member of the Workers' Education Bureau. In 1922 he went to Japan (Mary Beard accompanied him) to consult with the Institute of Municipal Research on its consolidation of greater Tokyo. After the 1923 earthquake there he returned to help in the rebuilding of the city. He spent 1927 and 1928 in Yugoslavia making a study for two private American organizations. In 1940–1941 he joined the faculty at Johns Hopkins University. He also served as president of the American Political Science Association in 1926 and of the American Historical Association in 1933.

In certain ways the Beards were very private people and very much wished to remain unknown to the public, except through their published writings and their public activities. There was neither a radio nor a telephone in their Connecticut home. They gave few interviews, and when they did, they dealt essentially with their public lives. Only rarely did they discuss their collaboration and only in general terms. To protect their future privacy, they apparently destroyed most of their papers, letters, and manuscripts, causing great grief to subsequent biographers. Some files of correspondence exist in small depositories, but generally they succeeded, as trained historians could, in erasing their personal histories.

The vehement attack by former supporters and friends that Charles Beard sustained in the last decade of his life may have reinforced their earlier decision to destroy their papers. Although he thrived on controversy, especially if he had provoked it, the intensity and quality of some of the assaults must have offended him. He supported U.S. involvement in World War I, but "then I slowly awoke" when "I learned what war could do," he said years later. An early defender of Franklin D. Roosevelt and the New Deal, he became increasingly critical of the President for establishing the right of "limitless authority publicly to misrepresent and secretly to control foreign policy, foreign affairs and the war policy."[10] As Woodrow Wilson had abandoned the New Freedom when the U.S. entered the First World War, so FDR would scrap the New

Deal for the Second, predicted Charles Beard long before 1941. Just as his heretical suggestion in *An Economic Interpretation of the Constitution of the United States* that the framers of the Constitution had economic and political motives initially aroused fury but in time came to be appreciated and accepted, so his criticism of FDR, seen by some at the time as bordering on treason, has in many ways been vindicated by recent revisionist writings.

Charles Beard's public personality is known: he was puckish, hard-headed, zestful, roaring, kind, eloquent. His was a commanding personality.

Mary Beard, "quick, incisive and camera-shy,"[11] is harder to recapture. What appears in these introductory pages, therefore, is a tenuous reconstruction of the life of a very private woman. Her desire to remain elusive is itself a statement about her personality. Did she strike her friends as dowdy—unlike the electric and scintillating Charles—as a considerably younger niece remembers her? Her photographs, from college days on, confirm such a view. Was she a gentle, benign, matronly presence—recognizing, accepting her role in the shadow of her outgoing husband—as historian Merle Curti remembers her?[12] She was, as she said many times, not a career woman, just a woman who wrote—and not well, but crudely, clumsily, as she said again and again to her intimates in her letters. "No photographs," she cautioned in a letter to a friend, "I would break the camera." Did she demur, defer, at least verbally and in public, to Charles, as a co-worker remembers?[13]

But what of the "mysterious" woman, as her daughter described her?[14] What of the elusive, evasive, indirect, withholding woman? Why did a scholar and feminist who devoted decades of her life to collecting the papers of women destroy her own?

For all of her practicality and reserve, she had a tenacious, persistent, dogged, unyielding, evangelical passion that would not be silenced. Often faced with the most devastating response of all—none—she went on and on and on. At some point early in her life she developed a belief that women were now and always had been active and engaged participants in the human story. She was so certain of her truth that—regardless of responses from men or women, students or university faculty, administrators or college alumnae—she would not waiver. The tactics would alter, the strategy would change, the audience would not always be the same, but the message remained, in whatever form.

How does such a woman develop? Surely her father, Eli Foster Ritter, mattered a great deal. He was a zealot, an active Methodist, a passionate temperance man, a true believer. Of her mother, Narcissa, there is more speculation than documentation, but indications of a spirited, cultured, dynamic woman make one wonder if she was the model for Mary Beard's unrecorded but powerful female force.

And, of course, Mary Ritter married Charles A. Beard. By conventional standards he was a catch, for he came from a wealthy, respectable family and was assured of a solid future. Or was it the sparkle that captured her—the hours of rapid talking, the ambition that fired him, the need to grab-it-all and fly. And he did fly: to London, to Japan, to New York, to Albania, to Yugoslavia, to Mexico. Perhaps she in some way knew that he was her way out of Indiana, out of a place that could not offer a woman of her talents and ambitions a rich future. If she had married a less driven and determined man, one who would have been content to settle into a tranquil, academic life in some Midwestern university, how different Mary Ritter's life would have been! Perhaps Charles Beard— aggressive, energetic, demanding—recognized in Mary Ritter, under that surface of gentle calm, a similar restless spirit that also wanted to be off and running.

There were not many people who had such strong ties, as she did, in the intellectual-scholarly world and in the political-activist world. There were very few who were so determined to link them up to demonstrate the value of history to politics and politics to history. She had a mission, as her ancestors had, only this one had a different name. She called it "Women in Long History," and she was determined to be heard.

In the first fifteen years of their marriage, Charles Beard wrote several brilliant and provocative books that established his reputation with the intellectual community. Mary Beard was thirty-nine years old when her first book was published. By that time she had reared two children and worked for years at the politics of her commitment. She was quite right when she denied having a career. She had a calling. Her plan was to reach every woman and arouse each to a new and vital sense of self-worth through an understanding of the past. It was a large and very lonely task. The anti-feminists saw her as one of the enemy, and the feminists denied her a place in their ranks because her line was not theirs.

Although she found and nurtured several women along the way in each of her many projects, the work was primarily her own; their contributions were valuable, but essentially supportive. For all her belief in the strength of the community of women, she was ultimately a loner. In a letter to William Beard after his mother's death in 1958, Marjorie White, longtime friend and associate, remarked on how strange it was that plans for a memorial volume were being abandoned because there were not a sufficient number of contributors.[15] Sad, but not surprising. When she left organizational activity, Mary Beard launched projects in which she operated alone or with a small staff. Unlike Charles Beard, who maintained his ties with numerous faculties and professional organizations, she had no institutional base; whether it was because she did not want one, or was excluded, or a little of each, is not clear.

This volume began as a biography, but Charles and Mary Beard's efforts to elude a full portrait have thus far succeeded. The absence of an adequate body of papers dooms any effort to create a biography. As I put together the material for this collection, I began to realize that ultimately such a book as this may be the best way to reintroduce Mary Ritter Beard to the public and provide her ideas with the recognition she sought and should have had in her lifetime.

NOTES

1. Lucy Sprague Mitchell, in her impressive but overlooked book, *Two Lives: Wesley Clair Mitchell and Me*, suggests a comparable life.

2. Richard Hofstadter, *The Progressive Historians: Turner, Beard, Parrington*, New York: Vintage Books, 1970, p. 184.

3. Letter from Miriam Beard Vagts, undated, received January 2, 1977.

4. Eric F. Goldman, "Charles A. Beard: An Impression," in *Charles A. Beard: An Appraisal*, ed., Howard K. Beale, Lexington: University of Kentucky Press, 1954, p. 5.

5. Comment by Charles A. Beard to George S. Counts while reading proofs of *A Basic History*. Quoted by Counts in *Charles A. Beard: An Appraisal*, p. 239.

6. Letter from Miriam Beard Vagts, undated, received January 2, 1977.

7. Letter from Miriam Beard Vagts, January 11, 1977.

8. Letter from Miriam Beard Vagts, undated, received January 2, 1977.

9. Letter from Miriam Beard Vagts, January 11, 1977.

10. Charles A. Beard, "President Roosevelt and the Coming of the War, 1941," quoted by H. K. Beale in *Charles A. Beard: An Appraisal*, p. 135.

11. *Current Biography: Who's News and Why*, ed., Maxine Black, New York: The H. W. Wilson Company, 1941, p. 53.

12. Merle Curti, in private conversation with the author.

13. Recollections of Dr. Dora Edinger.

14. Letter from Miriam Beard Vagts, March 29, 1974.

15. March 23, 1959. Beard Papers, DePauw University Archives.

Chapter II

On a Sunday morning in Indianapolis, on June 17, 1877, Reverend Reuben Andrus delivered the first sermon in the newly built Central Avenue Methodist Church.

> God has so constituted man that he finds in all things a material element and a spiritual element. . . . All our industry may be taken as proof . . . [that] the manufacturer, tradesman, speculator, banker, capitalist, builder, all these men of wealth and energy and business power who spread commerce, build railroads, palaces and cities, and give employment to millions . . . are at the foundation of progress of the nation. . . . This means the regeneration of the inferior races, the abolition of the antipathies of races, cessations of wars, diminution of poverty, better clothing, better shelter, better food for the people, enlarged securities for health, more efficient schools, wiser preaching, more social morality.[1]

Mary Ritter was born in Indianapolis on August 5, 1876, not far from the church where Dr. Andrus extolled the leaders of the nation. His sermon captured the attitudes and interests of the social class into which she was born.

Today an inner-city ghetto, that part of Indianapolis during the years that Mary lived on Central Avenue was considered an exclusive suburb. It was where the growing, prominent middle class lived in comfortable prosperity. Their church, with six or seven thousand members and a huge Sunday attendance, was a testimony to their solidity.[2] Church records indicate that her father, Eli Foster Ritter, was on the church's board of trustees and that in 1877 he was in charge of the Sunday school. In fact, on the evening of Reverend Andrus' sermon, Ritter made a short speech in honor of the Sunday school's opening.[3] How much contact Mary had with the church cannot be gauged directly, for her name does not appear on available church records, but social and church activities must have been a part of the Ritter household scene, because "previous to 1890, the Central Avenue young people met in various homes like the Hereth's and Ritter's for devotional and social activities . . . In October 1892 the Epsworth League [a youth group] was chartered with Halstead and Dwight Ritter as the first Presidents."[4]

All the members of the congregation from infants to adults were integrated into church activities. There was, for example, a nursery run by churchwomen which served a dual purpose: to care for infants and toddlers, thus leaving their mothers free to participate in other church functions; and to operate as a preschool indoctrination program to make the very young children familiar with religious concepts.

Another example of this integration was the "Sunday pageant," in which all groups, regardless of sex or age, participated both as performers and audience to celebrate their religion. The pageant used various forms to present the Methodist doctrines. Songs, readings, possibly short morality plays, all served multiple functions: first, to convey religious dogma in a dramatic, palatable way; second, to create a sense of unity and common belief, thus strengthening the bonds among the people in the congregation; third, to serve as a social outlet that conformed to strict Methodist rules. This Sunday evening pageant seems to have been, outside of the regular Sunday services, the only instance where the entire congregation merged socially within the church.

Each sex had its own separate organizations within the framework of the church. For example, women had their own Bible classes, tea circle, and sewing circle—the latter two having much to do with organizing church functions and fund-raising for the church, and also, in later years, for public services, such as hospital building and missionary work locally and abroad.

Adult males had such organizations as the Businessmen's Bible Class, but the younger, unmarried men had their own Bible class and a youth group which was first known as the Epsworth League, but later affiliated with the Y.M.C.A. The youth organization served to channel young men's interests into positive outlets by way of devotional programs, sports, and during the 1890s, through public works. Charles Beard went to Chicago under the auspices of the Epsworth League and was exposed for the first time to urban social problems, an experience that made a great impact on him.

One can assume that Mary Ritter grew up within the safety of an entrenched, conservative Republican, upper-middle-class society—one where social, political, and religious values were all combined so that all activity would buttress the established order of things. Even when she left home to attend DePauw University in 1893, Mary was still sheltered by the church, family, and political ties that joined the school to the other institutions that made up Mary Ritter's world.

Her family, the Ritters and Lockwoods—the former from North Carolina, the latter from Kentucky—was of old American, Protestant stock. Mary's paternal grandparents, James Ritter and Rachel Jessup, were Quakers. In 1822, when the state was still a frontier, they took up residence on a farm near Indianapolis and remained there until the end of their lives. There is no indication that the Ritters were prominent or wealthy.[5]

On the other side of the family were Benjamin Lockwood and Rebecca Smith, her mother's parents, who migrated from Bourbon County, Kentucky, and settled in Greencastle, Indiana, the home of Asbury, now DePauw, University. Through marriages, the Lockwoods linked themselves with the Town family, each family having many eminent Methodist churchmen and educators in their ranks, each family having strong ties with DePauw.[6]

Eli Foster Ritter remained on his parents' farm until he left for Indianapolis in 1859 to attend Northwestern Christian College and then Asbury University in 1861.[7] Ritter was at Asbury when the Civil War erupted. Turning away from the Quaker precepts taught him from childhood, he joined the Union Army. He went back to Greencastle in 1863 to marry Narcissa Lockwood, then returned to the army and was involved in active fighting for the duration of the war, at one point even as a private citizen.[8]

Returning to civilian life at war's end, he received his bachelor's degree from Asbury and entered into law practice in Indianapolis. Inflexibly principled, Ritter became a reformer and an advocate of the Temperance movement. In his zeal he fought the local political machine and prosecuted some of its people for tampering with elections. His belief in Temperance was so great that he became disillusioned when his own party seemed reluctant to stamp out or even restrict the liquor combines within the state. Because of this reluctance, Ritter eventually became an Independent, a Republican still, but independent of the mainstream of the Indiana Republican Party.[9] Perhaps his adamant convictions hurt his professional career, for in 1904 the Ritter household moved around the corner from Central Avenue into the "flats," a row of look-alike, unimpressive, frame houses, a material comedown and a world apart from the large, comfortable house in which Mary grew up.[10]

Narcissa Lockwood, Mary Ritter's mother, was the second of three sisters. The nostalgic recall of her granddaughter, Dorothy Ritter Russo, evokes the image of an elegant lady who "liked nice things," and who could be quite formidable. Born in Paris, Kentucky, Narcissa Lockwood graduated from the Brookville Academy and taught for a time.[11] Mary Beard, reflecting on this period of her mother's life, commented that "Narcissa Lockwood . . . taught boys and girls in a cottage on her father's land. [She never] thought of herself as a 'careerist.' . . . I don't know whether my mother was paid a cent but I doubt it. My mother had the kind of education which enabled her to read law to my father when his eyes were too weak from exposure in the Civil War to read for himself. Through her aid to him, he passed the examination for the bar and with the rest his eyes had he became a distinguished lawyer."[12]

All the Ritter children followed their father's footsteps and went to DePauw, as their father had. Mary, age sixteen, arrived there in 1893; her oldest brother, Halstead, had graduated in 1891; another, Roscoe, finished in 1895. Her brother, Dwight, and the youngest of the Ritter brood, Ruth, graduated from the same school. One brother, Herman, died while a senior there.

DePauw University was one of the first Methodist educational institutions established in the West. Franklin College was the Baptist school, and Hanover was the Presbyterian college. It was considered more prestigious to attend one of these schools than to go to the state university. The educational level was nearly comparable to those Eastern colleges with good reputations. The curricula of even the more recognized schools was so limited (the influx of German Ph.D.s not having yet begun) that places like DePauw could compete educationally with institutions such as Amherst or Williams or Harvard or Yale. Asbury (DePauw) was also coeducational, the first four women graduating in 1871. Many colleges in central Indiana had become coeducational even before the Civil War, largely to offset low enrollment and the inadequate tuitions that resulted.[13]

Asbury, like all the rest of the colleges, suffered from financial worries, but the decision to admit women probably had no connection to money. Asbury tuitions, which had always been small, were eliminated in 1874. Students entering after that year had only to pay a small "janitor's fee" and buy miscellaneous items related to their studies. The outlay was small. The money that ran the school came from subscriptions pledged by the Methodist residents of the town of Greencastle and of Putnam County and by the Indiana Conference of the Methodist Church. It had also been a practice, nearly from the inception of the school, to sell scholarships as advance payment for a student's college education for varying prices and time limits; this last source of revenue was one that subsequently did not work to the advantage of the university.[14]

Asbury may have decided to admit women because all the neighboring schools had already done so, or it may have responded to pressure from Methodist families that wanted their daughters to be college-educated and to make social contacts.

Social contacts were an important element in maintaining the homogeneous quality of the middle-class, Methodist, central Indiana community. The college, an institution that combined scholarly development and a "program of preparing students for a spiritual and religious life,"[15] was an ideal place for the children of the more substantial members of that community to meet, and if a marriage resulted, what better way of solidifying and insuring stability of family and clan? What better way to build dynasties of those people whom Dr. Andrus praised in his sermon at the Central Avenue Methodist Church? (Andrus, incidentally, had been president of Asbury for three years before becoming pastor at the church attended by the Ritter family.) Within Mary Ritter's own family, "each member of the Ritter family met his wife or husband while attending DePauw University."[16] Many families, through intermarriages of alumnae, have sustained four or five generations of family to be represented at the university. A "family school," one DePauw president called it.[17]

With the severe depression of 1893, enrollment at DePauw went down to 803 from 1,015 in the previous year; it declined again the following year. The faculty of 1894 consisted of fifty-two members; fourteen were women, ten of whom taught either music or art. For the most part, the faculty was comprised of DePauw graduates.

In 1890, the DePauw curriculum had been modified to incorporate the major-minor course concept. Required courses at that time included Mental and Moral Science (later titled Philosophy), History (in 1895 eliminated as a required subject), Political Science, English, a science requirement, Greek, Latin, French or German, and a mathematics requirement. This curriculum remained substantially the same until the turn of the century. In many ways, it continued the kind of study established in the secondary school system, which still retained classical studies as an item of importance in young people's education.[18]

Not much is known about Mary Ritter during her college years.[19] She was undoubtedly a highly competent student, for she was retroactively elected to Phi Beta Kappa in 1939. She arrived at DePauw as a rather sheltered young girl, a bit over sixteen. She spent four years in college, and for the first time, made contact with a world outside the safety of her Indiana home. One senses an intelligent, concerned, sensitive young woman, attracted to those people and those forces that would help to remove the limiting walls of her narrow world in central Indiana.

She was a member of Kappa Alpha Theta, the first sorority established at DePauw in 1870. Many years later she reflected upon her feelings regarding the impact on her of other DePauw sororities.

She says of the two young women who had the greatest impact on her that one allowed her to "understand that even a young woman could really break the social conventions which inclined girls to study the 'belle lettres' and boys to study politics." This young woman took the courses she felt she was most interested in—political science for one—and the way she maintained herself allowed her to be "accepted by the men in her class at her own value." The second young woman led Mary to understand that a woman "could really break the social conventions which called for pseudo-patrician or genuinely bourgeois manners and be guided in her human relations by a more creative sense of values. She too did the things that were 'not done' by her clan sisters." As for Mary Ritter herself, "I too was a 'sport' in that I responded to such innovators beyond the conventions of a clan . . . the thing that lingers with me in this connection is not the thought of clannishness itself and its tendency to standardize and defeat creative intelligence, for after all, the . . . clans involved . . . protected their errant sisters. It may be that the freedom to dare sprang from that very protection.''[20]

Women protecting women. From what? Within the structure of DePauw, there had been, from the very beginning, a male resistance to the admission of women students into the school. Women were, for example, barred from the existing male discussion clubs, including the philosophical club. They reacted by forming their own organizations and gaining recognition for their ability to make an equal place for themselves on campus. Jean Nelson (Penfield), a young woman who was at DePauw when Mary Ritter arrived, was a Kappa Kappa Gamma sorority member; in 1892 Nelson became the first woman to win the Indiana and interstate oratorical awards, a much coveted prize in a time when rhetoric and oratory were valued as academic and cultural assets. After leaving De-Pauw, Nelson studied at Brooklyn Law School, the Sargeant Dramatic School, and the Metropolitan Conservatory of Music; she practiced and taught law, lectured, wrote poetry, and was an active leader in the woman suffrage movement. She and Mary Ritter worked together in 1911 to present a woman's suffrage platform in New York City.[21] Undoubtedly a convention breaker, she must have greatly impressed many young women around her, as she did Mary Ritter.

Two photographs taken while Mary Ritter was a student at DePauw show her with a group of other young women (possibly sorority sisters) and posing with another young woman and two young men, one Charles Beard, after an afternoon bicycle ride. In these photographs from her late teens, she seems rather matronly. Her face has a serious expression, her mouth is set, and her posture is stiff, nearly rigid. Is this an indication of "uptightness" or righteous determination, or is it simply the discomfort that an extremely shy person suffers when in front of the camera?

Charles Austin Beard began his studies at DePauw in the spring of 1895. He, like Mary Ritter, came from a family background of mid-Southern origins. Both his maternal and paternal ancestors came from the same area in North Carolina; they shared the same Whig-Republican views, and both gave importance to religion in their private and public lives.

Charles' father, William Henry Harrison Beard, was a latecomer to Indiana, having left the South in 1861, not long after the outbreak of the Civil War. He initially worked as a carpenter and rural teacher, but by the time of his death in 1907, he had become a bank president. In between, he had been a successful farmer and a substantial contractor, building houses, churches and bridges; he also speculated in land, which in the depression of 1873 made him a small fortune.[22]

Nathan and Caroline Beard, Charles' paternal grandparents, were brought to Indiana in 1865 by their only son. The elder Beards had been ostracized in their community when Nathan, a Quaker, married Caroline, a Methodist; yet they chose to remain on their land until the end of the Civil War, when most of their property had been destroyed by the fighting. After being ousted by the Quakers, neither Nathan or Caroline affiliated themselves with a formal church.

Mary J. Payne, Charles' mother, was one of twelve children born to John Payne and his wife, Sarah Wilson. Payne arrived in Indiana in 1829, met and married Sarah, who had been raised in the Indiana Territory when it was still a wilderness. According to family recollections, the Paynes began their marriage with seventy-five cents, but by the time of Payne's death, his estate was estimated to be worth about $150,000.[23] Both John and Sarah's religious beliefs had moved from Methodism toward spiritualism by the end of their lives. A photograph album, donated to DePauw by the Beards' children, notes that Charles maintained a warm, close tie with his grandmother, Sarah, and always kept a picture of her on his desk.[24] John probably died in the late 1870s, and Sarah died in 1882, when Charles was eight years old.

Charles Beard, while a student at DePauw, was an active, intensely interested, rather loud young man, one who was fully enjoying his life. There was a gamesman quality about him that one gleans from his letters and articles, but there was also an underlying sense of serious intent, which is a very important part of his development. It was as if he were trying to absorb as many experiences as he could—and probably vigorously rejecting those things which did not conform to his personal truths, to his intellectual awareness. He was also a convention breaker.

Very little is known about the courtship of Charles and Mary Beard. They met and fell in love while students at DePauw. After she graduated in 1897, she stayed in Greencastle, near her college, her sorority, and Charles, who graduated the following year. He then went off alone to England in August, 1898, to study English and European History. Perhaps they had agreed to wait to marry until his English studies were over, but the long separation became too painful. The following year Charles did return to Mary Ritter, who was teaching German in a local school. In 1900 they married, and "with my young bride," Charles "returned to Oxford."[25]

NOTES

1. C.A.M.C. pamphlet: *75th Anniversary, Central Avenue Methodist Church, 1877–1952*, Indianapolis.
2. Information from conversation with Dr. Arthur Neuman, pastor, C.A.M.C., 1974.
3. C.A.M.C. pamphlet.
4. *Ibid.*
5. Jacob Pratt Dunn, *Indiana and Indianans*, Chicago and New York: The American Historical Society, 1919, Vol. 3, p. 1262.
6. George B. Manhart, *DePauw Through the Years*, Greencastle, Ind.: DePauw University, 1962, Vol. 2, p. 512.
7. Septima Snowden, "Eli Foster Ritter," unpublished article.
8. Dunn, *op. cit.*, p. 1262.
9. "Eli Foster Ritter," unpublished article solicited by members of the George H. Thomas Post 17, Department of the Indiana Grand Army of the Republic. Beard Papers, DePauw University Archives.
10. Recollections of Dorothy Ritter Russo. General information regarding the relocation of Eli and Narcissa Ritter was confirmed through the Indianapolis Telephone Directory for the years involved.
11. Newspaper article on the Ritters and their Central Avenue house. *The Indianapolis Sunday Star*, August 10, 1930.
12. Letter from Mary Ritter Beard to Margaret Grierson, January 25, 1951, Smith College Library.
13. I am grateful to Dr. Patricia Graham, Director of the Radcliffe Institute, for information about education and institutions in Indiana and for many insights into the cultural and social life of central Indiana in the early twentieth century.
14. Manhart, *op. cit.*, Vol. I, p. 119.
15. *The Indianapolis Sunday Star*, August 10, 1930.
16. Manhart, *op. cit.*, Vol. II, p. 512.
17. Manhart, *op. cit.*, Vol. II, p. 512.
18. Conversation with Dr. Patricia Graham.
19. Unfortunately, Merle Curti's description of Charles Beard's teacher,

James Riley Weaver, in his article, "A Great Teacher's Teacher," *Social Education*, Vol. XIII, October 1940, pp. 263–267, is not relevant for Mary Ritter, who was not one of Weaver's students.

20. Mary Ritter Beard, "Memory and Human Relations," *The Key of Kappa Kappa Gamma*, December 1, 1936, pp. 308–311.

21. Manhart, *op. cit.*, Vol. I., p. 302.

22. Richard P. Ratcliffe, *Charles A. Beard, 1874–1948: A Native of Henry County, Indiana (With Emphasis on His Boyhood and Accomplishments)*, 1966, p. 9. Deposited in Beard Papers, DePauw University.

23. Letter from Miriam Beard Vagts, received January, 1977.

24. Note by Beard children on a family picture album. Beard Papers, DePauw University Archives.

25. Burleigh Taylor Wilkins, ed., "Documents: Charles A. Beard on the Founding of Ruskin Hall," *Indiana Magazine of History*, Vol. III, September 1956, No. 3, p. 283.

Chapter III

After a bicycle trip through the French countryside, the young couple set up housekeeping in Manchester, England, a center of labor and feminist ferment. Both movements absorbed their energies. Charles Beard became actively involved in helping to found Ruskin Hall in Oxford, a college designed for working-class men. The atmosphere undoubtedly was heady stuff for the young Indianan, but he was up to it, for his activities brought him to the attention of the new Labour Party in England, which marked the young man "as a coming leader."[1] Meanwhile, Mary Beard discovered the militant woman's movement, and through her active participation she met and worked with the leading English radical suffragists.

Everything they experienced must have been exciting and gratifying for the Beards, newly arrived from America and only recently separated from their Midwestern roots. Up to this point they had only brief glimpses of another world that was denied those qualities of life cherished in their middle-class community. Now they were part of experiments that were considered radical, experiments that moved through and out of the bounds of Victorian conventions, activities that involved meeting and dealing with a wide constituency of people on many levels of British society. Mary Beard's later concern for working-class women, a concern shared by very few American suffragists, undoubtedly was forged in this period.

Mary Beard's political activities were curtailed for a time by the birth of a daughter, Miriam, in 1901. The following year the family returned to

New York City, where both Charles and Mary Beard entered Columbia University as graduate students. It was unusual, but not startlingly so, to find a woman in graduate school. It was extraordinary to find a woman with a year-old baby in graduate school in 1902.

Although Charles Beard's prolific writing career and his reputation as a social critic were launched at Columbia University, their roots were in England with his affiliation with Ruskin Hall and the persons he had met at Oxford. He wrote many articles for *Young Oxford*, the magazine of the Ruskin Hall supporters, which reveal him "as much in the role of spiritual teacher as social agitator."[2] His first book, *The Industrial Revolution*, all but forgotten today, was published in England in 1901 to sell for a shilling "as an aid in adult education."[3] While on the faculty at Columbia University, he wrote nine books alone, including his controversial *An Economic Interpretation of the Constitution of the United States*, collaborated on two four-volume textbooks, collaborated in editing another textbook, collaborated with his wife in writing *American Citizenship*, wrote ten articles for the *Political Science Quarterly*, and reviewed approximately sixty-five books.[4] By the time he left his teaching position in 1917, his reputation was enormous, and his career was well established.

Mary Ritter Beard dropped out of Columbia, where she was doing graduate work in Sociology, and after 1904 her affiliation with the University was only as faculty wife. In later years she was to express a peculiar hostility toward college education for women and toward academics. One wonders how her venture into academia was greeted at a time when women rarely sought advanced university degrees. She must have been as excited as her husband was during the lively years in England, exposed to the labor and feminist agitation. Was Columbia, perhaps, too stultifying for her restless spirit? Did her growing feminist consciousness, nourished by the impassioned English feminist leaders she had met, find the atmosphere of Columbia uncongenial?

In 1907, when their daughter was six, another child, a son, William, was born. However, family duties did not absorb all Mary Beard's energies. In 1911 both Beards were ringing doorbells to raise money to defend the McNamara brothers, who were accused of conspiracy involving labor violence.[5] A 1915 issue of the *National Municipal Review* describes her as "the wife of Professor Charles A. Beard of Columbia University and . . . well known for her active work along social and industrial lines, especially in connection with the shirtwaist strike and the Triangle fire.''[6] Mary Beard was an active member of the National Women's Trade Union League (NWTUL) in 1909, when that group supported the shirtwaist makers' long strike. The NWTUL raised money for bail fees and the strike fund as well as propagandizing in behalf of the strikers. The Triangle Shirt Waist Fire in 1911 was a factory fire in which 147 workers, mostly girls and young women, lost their lives. In this instance the NWTUL pressured for legislation for stricter fire regulations in New York.

By 1910 Mary Beard was involved in the affairs of The Woman Suffrage Party, led by Carrie Chapman Catt. (One of the party's chairs was held by her friend from the DePauw years, Jean Nelson Penfield.) In June, 1910, Beard was one of many fund-raisers for the organization; in November she was vice-chairman of the Manhattan branch of the party; a year later she was editor of *The Woman Voter*, the official organ of The Woman Suffrage Party of New York. During her brief tenure as editor of the magazine, she published an article entitled "Mothercraft."[7] It is a classic, Progressive statement, answering the anti-feminist implications of the Mothercraft Institutions that were sprouting up throughout the country during the early part of the century. She wrote angrily, disdainfully, describing not the ideal but the real. To the Progressive mind, as Hofstadter said,

> Reality was the opposite of everything the genteel traditon had stood for in literature and the formalistic thinkers in social philosophy. . . . Reality was the bribe, the rebate, the bought franchise, the sale of adulterated food, the desperate pursuit of life in the slums. Reality was what one did not find in the standard textbooks on constitutional law, political science, ethics, economics or history.[8]

Mary Beard was not concerned with textbook descriptions; she wrote of the world in which working women struggled to raise their children. She was thirty-five when she wrote this article, and through her activist experiences in England and in the United States, she had learned about the sweatshops and slums in which women worked and lived. But she went beyond the indignation of the Progressive reform mentality to pull out of the world around her the ideal of complete unity of women, as a force, as a positive power in world motion. It is an ideal that she nurtured and developed all her life, and it ultimately was widened to encompass all people, both men and women. Critical of those with a "narrow concept of human life,"[9] time and again she attacked college-trained "professional" women and academics, entrenched within the walls of convention and pseudo-intellectualism, who speak with authority of worlds that she knew they had never seen outside of a book. To persuade these people, to make them understand, be aware, she approached her most precious topic—women—from such a broad range that her work often seems to be a compilation of "evidence" and not a personal statement. But it is a very personal statement.

Mary Beard resigned from her editorial position in June, 1912, to work for the Wage Earner's League, an affiliate of The Woman Suffrage Party designed for workingwomen. Soon after, she published another article, a short, easily read history of the enfranchisement of workingmen and a critical analysis of the male-dominated tradition that refused women the vote.

In April, 1913, Mary Beard received a letter from Alice Paul, who had recently been named Chairman of the Congressional Committee of the National American Women Suffrage Association (NAWSA), congratulating her on her appointment to the committee and asking her to lead the committee procession in a New York Suffrage parade. In the letter Paul also informed her that the Congressional Union, "made up of members who want to help in Congressional work," had been formed.[10] The Congressional Union, which later became the Woman's Party, was headed by Alice Paul. In less than a year after its founding, it came into conflict with the conservative leadership of NAWSA.

During this period there was little official interest in the federal amendment for woman suffrage. Indeed, the yearly Congressional hearings on the bill "had become routine," according to Eleanor Flexneor's history of women's rights, "since nothing was expected to come of them."[11] The National Board of NAWSA was directing most of its energies toward woman suffrage referenda within individual states and offered minimal support for pressure at the federal level. In 1912, young, tenacious Alice Paul, who from 1907 until 1910 had "undergone a vigorous apprenticeship in the militant wing of the British suffrage movement," joined the ranks of NAWSA. After meeting with the national president, Anna Shaw, and its first vice-president, Jane Addams, Paul took the initiative in creating the Congressional Committee to begin a drive for a federal amendment "with the understanding that the Committee was to raise its own funds.''[12] The Committee received only moral support and the use of the organization's name as a means of achieving its goal. As the other members of the Committee Alice Paul chose Lucy Burns, who was also a veteran of the British feminist movement, Crystal Eastman, Mrs. Lawrence Lewis, Jr., and Mary Beard. The Committee was quick to act. It organized a march in Washington, D.C., in March, 1913, on the day before the Presidential Inauguration of Woodrow Wilson. The march, which was nastily attacked by many male hecklers, drew immediate publicity that placed the NAWSA members into nation-wide view. Then the push was on. The Committee was clamorous, persistent, bold, using any means to draw attention to the single-minded goal of the Committee and the Congressional Union.

"The national situation," wrote Mary Beard in June, 1913, "at this moment is unique in the history of women suffrage. . . . In the first place, one-fifth of the Senate and one-eighth of the House are elected by the aid of women's votes. . . . We have never had so many supporters from non-suffrage states. . . . Thus the Democrats in power are face to face with the political possibilities before them in 1916. These they must take into consideration immediately."[13] This was the stick that the tiny organization shook at the Democrats in Congress and the White House.

And Mary Beard's part in all of this? She wrote articles, spoke whenever and wherever she could, organized deputations to appear before Congressional hearings, used her ties to the labor movement for these deputations, made contact with women leaders in other areas of public life to urge support for the Committee's goals, searched for financial supporters, and tried to get as many women as possible committed to the organization's goals. When the break occurred between the militant section, led by Alice Paul, and the National Board, now led by Carrie Chapman Catt, in February, 1914, Beard sided with the Congressional Union and remained there, doing the same work as she had in the Congressional Committee.

Mary Beard's seemingly staid career as a writer and historian and her later outspoken criticism of the "intransigent" feminists obscures her radical political commitment in this period. She chose to identify herself with the most extreme militant faction of the woman's movement. When she left this movement, it was not to seek a more moderate alternative, but to find a vastly different, but no less radical, way of approaching her goal.

Much occurred in her personal life during these early years. Both of her parents died in 1913, her mother, Narcissa Ritter, dying at the Beard home in New Milford, Connecticut. Nevertheless, the Beards prepared their first joint effort, *American Citizenship*, and Mary Beard probably started work on her own book, *Woman's Work in Municipalities*, which appeared in 1915.

In several letters to Alice Paul, Mary Beard speaks of her obligations to her husband and children; she writes of her guilt at not being able to meet the demands of the organization. Was she becoming disillusioned by the organization's narrow view, a necessary view, perhaps, but one that was too limited in its goal? She hinted at her inner feelings in this observation to Alice Paul in a letter dated July 26, 1916:

> I can do much better when I stay in the daily fight than when I get away for a time and look at things with a more distant perspective. I am so much more radical than either of the old political parties that, when I get off and think, I lose my whole absorption in the one fight for enfranchisement. I keep that absorption in town when I am at the office every day and have responsibilities that are heavy.[14]

What she observed around her were formidable women, women like Alice Paul, Carrie Chapman Catt, Lucy Burns, Crystal Eastman, Rose Schneiderman, and the many workingwomen she had seen come from the sweatshops to become leaders in the suffrage movement—women with enormous talents, devotion, strength, and commitment, who were struggling to achieve the vote for women. At some point, perhaps, she discovered that it was not the goal that was so extraordinary; it was the women working toward it. Women without traditional power had access to resources of strength and pressure that had little to do with votes and more to do with petitions, protests, strikes, and organization. It was their community that gave them strength, not the formalities that society conferred upon them. Obviously women should have the right to vote, but it was the community that created the power.

She had stayed with both trade union organizations and the woman suffrage movement for years, believing, writing, speaking, propagandizing for what was evolving as the militant feminist position: namely, that women have been oppressed for eons, and it is their time to demand justice and equality, first in the form of the vote.

Beard was becoming detached from the role of activist and was beginning to move toward the role of analyst and critic, as her books would demonstrate. There was no sudden, definitive break, merely a drifting away from political action. It is not clear why she changed after a decade and saw the feminist demands as shrill and her contribution to militant feminism as "trash," as she later said in a private letter. It is not hard to understand why she went with these feminists initially. There was no alternative for a woman like her. It is her eventual rejection of that feminist doctrine, it is her development of her own particular feminist position, quite alone, that is fascinating.

The break came with the battle for the Equal Rights Amendment, undertaken by the Woman's Party after the suffrage amendment was won. It may seem difficult to understand how it was possible that many determined feminists opposed so strenuously and consistently the passage of the ERA. Mary Beard's opposition to the amendment was shared by women such as Florence Kelly, Mary Anderson of the Women's Bureau, Frances Perkins, Sophie Loeb, Rose Schneiderman, Alice Hamilton, Lillian Wald, and other distinguished and committed feminists in many fields, but particualrly in the labor sector. In general, the activist women who were closest to the concerns of the workingwomen and trade union problems were in earnest opposition to the amendment. In the words of Irene Osgood Andrews, of the American Association of Labor Legislation, "equal treatment of unequals is the greatest inequality."[15]

The feminist anti-ERA forces argued that, while all working members of society were exploited inhumanely, women were the most victimized. They saw the mass of the nation subjected to unconscionable treatment, especially in their work lives. They believed that protection of children and women was the first step toward a more humane reformation of the total society. They also believed that women, most of whom were mothers or would-be mothers, required different treatment, that a special set of conditions had to be granted to women for their protection. Many feminists had struggled for years to bring about protective labor legislation and, if they were not entirely satisfied, they were convinced that the gains they had achieved were better than none. They would settle for small victories while the larger struggle continued.

The alliances that emerged on both sides of the ERA issue were curious and awkward. The militant feminists, most of whom supported the amendment, found themselves applauded from the sidelines by those elements of society that would have been delighted to remove protective legislation to make easier the return to openly abusive, exploitative conditions in the marketplace. In the name of a return to the ideals of laissez-faire—in the name of free enterprise, unhampered by legal restrictions affecting working hours and working conditions—these forces happily embraced the pro-ERA push.

On the anti-ERA side, the well-meaning supporters of special protection for workingwomen were also part of an uncongenial coalition. Legal devices that distinguished men from women in the work world could easily be turned into sanctioned ways of discrimination. For instance, from her perspective as a physician concerned with industrial medicine, Alice Hamilton observed the effects of lead poisoning on the female reproductive organs and struggled tirelessly for legislation to protect women from jobs that would expose them to lead. But others, citing such protective legislation as precedents, could use disreputable "scientific" data to prevent women from working in areas where they could work equally well with men.

There were no easy answers, in spite of the slogans that made the issue seem simple, but then Mary Beard's view of history had taught her that there were no easy answers anywhere. She knew that, even on an individual level, the complex relationship between men and women made simple-sounding solutions suspect.

Unlike many feminists, and reformers in general, she examined the problem from the perspective of workingwomen. In that world, where mothers had not only to work long hours but were also responsible for the care of children, protection from abuses in the sweatshops and from their men at home was vitally important. On these grounds, Mary Beard did not support the ERA when it was first proposed by the Woman's Party in the twenties, and she continued to oppose it for years each time it was proposed again. "I ought to be interested in suffrage first and labor second but I am frankly not," she had said in a letter to Alice Paul in 1914, thus expressing her overriding concern with the hard-earned labor achievement of the first portion of the 1900s. She saw passage of the blanket ERA as endangering the laws that so many had worked for to gain protection for the wage-earning woman worker. Her opposition was expressed privately, but to those interested she wrote lengthy objections. There was no public action on her part, for she moved away from confrontation, determined not to permit the issue to split feminist ranks. She had seen the disastrous effect of splits within the movement.

To Alice Paul, the principle of absolute equality was a necessary ideal around which to organize and struggle; concessions along the way would only hinder ultimate success. To Mary Beard, the world was imperfect, and survival for the moment required the recognition that men and women had different social roles and, therefore, had to function differently. Whatever the ultimate goal, people live one day at a time. To Alice Paul, keeping an eye on day-to-day needs crippled one's long-range goals. These conflicting approaches to issues were hardly new, for they had divided radical and reform movements for generations. But they were new in feminist circles, where splits had previously been along lines that separated radicals from conservatives—where it had been easier to make a satisfying choice, to separate right from wrong, depending on one's definition of right. In this split the pro-ERA faction also cast the division as militant-versus-conservative, but unfairly.

Mary Ritter Beard's opposition to the Equal Rights Amendment marked her transition from feminist activist to feminist historian seeking a new way toward her vision of unity among women.

NOTES

1. Hofstadter, *The Progressive Historians: Turner, Beard, Parrington*, New York: Vintage Books, 1970, p. 179.

2. *Ibid.*, p. 176.

3. "New and Notes," *The American Political Science Review*, Vol. XLII, No. 6, December, 1948, p. 1209.

4. Hofstadter, *op cit.*, p. 480.

5. George S. Counts, in *Charles A. Beard: An Appraisal*, ed., H. K. Beale, Lexington, Ky.: University of Kentucky Press, 1954, p. 237.

6. *National Municipal Review*, 1915, p. 204. (Miriam Beard Vagts called this item to my attention.)

7. Mary R. Beard, "Mothercraft," *The Woman Voter*, Vol. 1-2, January, 1912.

8. Hofstadter, *op. cit.*, p. 184.

9. Beard, *op. cit.*, p. 12.

10. Letter from Paul to Beard, dated April 24, 1913, Woman's Party papers, Library of Congress.

11. Eleanor Flexner, *Century of Struggle: The Woman's Rights Movement in the United States*, New York: Atheneum, 1971, p. 264.

12. Flexner, *op. cit.*, p. 265.

13. *The Woman Voter*, Vol. 14, June, 1913, p. 17.

14. Letter from Beard to Paul, July 26, 1916, Woman's Party papers, Library of Congress.

15. Statement presented at a luncheon at the Cosmopolitan Club, October 10, 1922, to mobilize opposition to the ERA. League of Women Voters papers, 1922, Library of Congress.

Chapter IV

In response to the trauma and anguish of the Great Depression of the thirties, certain features of American society regressed. What remained of the women's movement went underground as "all devices of media, the energies of psychology and social science, were enlisted in a major effort to . . . reassert the primary importance of the family. . . . the role of women was again to be found in the home primarily and not outside it."[1] The sense of community Mary Beard had long hoped the world would embrace was, for a time at least, beginning to emerge, but it was not based on a new and revitalized recognition and understanding of the real relationships between men and women, culture and community, government and citizen. Instead, it was an effort to reinforce the traditional network of relationships and institutions that she had spent years trying to analyze and alter.

Her activist part in the suffrage movement was behind her now. Women had succeeded in acquiring the vote, but with that victory came the incredible belief that women's history began with the suffrage struggle. To Beard, such an assertion was a denial of all the pasts of women and, therefore, a denial of self in the women who were living in the present.

Mary Beard had published two books alone while she was still involved in activist politics. The first, *Woman's Work in Municipalities*, was a lengthy essay in the tradition of muckraking literature demonstrating, as its title indicates, the varied and essential work of women in cities.

In 1920 she produced *A Short History of the American Labor Move-*

ment. Simply written and pro-labor, it was designed for readers with little knowledge of the working-class struggle in the United States. She wrote it, she said, because "there are many special studies, [but] there is no single, comprehensive volume of moderate size for the busy citizen."[2] The volume was published by the Workers Education Bureau of America and was written with a working-class audience in mind.

Mary Beard's only other book that did not deal with women was a long essay, *The Making of Charles A. Beard*, which was published in 1955, seven years after her husband's death.

In 1931 Beard's *On Understanding Women* appeared. She was fifty-five when this book was published. Most prominent men have reached success long before that time in their lives. She, as is characteristic of many women, moved into her most creative period in her middle years.

Beard moved away from the simple, straightforward style of her earlier works to use a method that layered statement upon statement as evidence to support her beliefs.

Her explanation of the order of things begins with primitive times, moves into the Golden Age of Greece, then to Imperial Rome, and into the Dark Ages of Europe. She presents her vision of the force of women from many views, sometimes from such a broad view that one must stop and read again, for she catches the complexities of a living people too well. Sometimes there is so much evidence to buttress her argument that it becomes tedious, and one wants to put the book down, but not quite. One can nearly sense this woman's mind moving into those ancient periods of history—observing, touching, listening, analyzing with such ease that one begins to understand why she sees the historical past as the key to understanding the rich potential of the future. Her vision provides a framework far larger than a restricted view of feminism or male dominance.

In writing of these early periods, Beard is most comfortable and secure, and she captures the essence of historical process. She seems to remove herself—by a tone, by way of a phrase—as she approaches the eighteenth century, and seems even more remote as she nears contemporary history. She said many things during the course of her lifetime, but on close study, never directly. Her indirection is a problem in her later books, for in many instances one is impelled to read between the lines to try to reach her answer, her solution, only to discover that she did not have an answer or solution but a goal, an idea.

The 1930's were productive years for her. After *On Understanding Women*, she wrote, in 1934, an extraordinary fifty-page pamphlet entitled "A Changing Political Economy As It Affects Women,"[3] which was, in effect, an extensive syllabus for a Women's Studies Program. In 1934 she also edited a reader, *America Through Women's Eyes*, which she used to show that American women were an integral part of the development of the United States from colonial to contemporary times, a power equal to, if not surpassing, men. Also in 1934, she co-authored with Martha Bruère, *Laughing Their Way: Women's Humor in America*.

The Rise of American Civilization may have been a pathbreaker, but what she was trying to do on the subject of women seemed not to be understood. By the time the later volumes were being written, women had had the vote for a decade and a half. Undoubtedly changes were in the making, but the state of women's consciousness, the recognition of their own vital history and active past, was as distant as ever. There had previously been, at least, a vigorous, vociferous woman's movement, one which Mary Beard could rail against and challenge, but suddenly there was not even debate.

Characteristically, she lamented a little, deplored the meager impact her work had made, and then began a project aimed at confronting the abysmal ignorance that still overwhelmed women. Her own books had not sufficiently engaged the imagination and activity of women. Perhaps women needed some active, real demonstration of their importance and the value of their history. Believing that knowledge derives from our actions upon the world, she moved to the idea, apparently influenced by the Hungarian feminist-pacifist, Rosika Schwimmer, of establishing a women's archive. For the next five years she tried to establish, finance, organize, structure, house, and publicize what became known as the World Center for Women's Archives.[4]

In January, 1936, after an initial meeting, Beard circulated a letter making the following announcement: "Aided and abetted by friends of the idea, I am calling a conference of women in and around Washington to consider the founding of a Center for Women's Archives." Later that year, a group of twenty women incorporated the World Center for Women's Archives (WCWA) in New York State, established an office in New York City's Rockefeller Center, and began to solicit material. The quotation from the French historian, Fustel de Coulanges, "No documents; No History" appeared prominently in early WCWA

literature. What documents did women have, asked the pronouncement?
Even influential women of the past had been forgotten. Only hints of their
existence survived. How could truth be established if women's history
were not known? What could social history signify if the social history of
women were not included? How could any interpretation of history be
valid if only men's lives were examined? How could the links between
the past and present, the present and future, be joined and understood if
women were omitted from the record? A circular bearing Beard's style and
substance represents a brief survey of the women's movement from the
end of World War I, when the achievements of women were at their peak,
until the economic crash, after which "women's political rights were
swiftly and sweepingly curtailed. Their business and professional
privileges diminished in nearly every country, including the United
States. Life and labor tended to revert to an archaic tooth and claw
struggle, with women as the major victims." Then, with the war spirit
beginning, "everything that woman holds precious in life and effort was
thrown in jeopardy." It was time for women to think about their culture
and their relationship to it; yet the materials upon which to do that type of
thinking were not available.

"In the furnace rooms, attics and cellars, in fading heaps crumbling
with age, source material pertaining to women's aspirations, struggles,
achievements, contributions and failures, remains hidden in large part."
The material was widely scattered; much of it was in private records,
which were frequently discarded. The object of the WCWA was to
assemble and preserve such source material, the guiding principle being
"the projection of woman's personality out of the shadows of time into
the living force which is woman in fact, into written history." All the
material, to be most dramatically presented, was to be housed in one
center, which was envisioned as a clearinghouse of information on the
history of women.

The ultimate goal was the recognition of the entire experience of
humankind, that is, the experience of both men and women. But until
woman discovered herself "in the shadow of time as half the human
race," the totality of experience was not possible. The concept of an
archive was viewed as a temporary measure, necessary for only so long as
the lives of women remained obscured and unexamined. The prevalent
theory that women's history began with the vote was persistently seen by

Mary Beard as "injurious . . . for men and women." It persisted largely because documentation of humanity's total view was not accessible.

No previous organization had shown any interest in a systematic collection of materials on or about women. Even women's colleges had neglected this responsibility. Many women cried out that the time had come to forget the separatism of women, but Beard argued vigorously against such a position. Carrie Chapman Catt, for instance, had given many NAWSA documents to the New York Public Library. When these papers were tracked down by a representative from the WCWA, they were located in the Economics Office, for lack of a better place to house them, "in about eight large drawers, crammed together, yellowing, covered with dust, rotting." The documents, in the library for twenty years, had remained untouched.

Mary Beard, in the initial stages of the organization, was named one of the thirteen board members, but later she was given the title of Director of the Archives, giving her recognition of the crucial role she played in the creation of the WCWA. As Director of Archives, she offered her ideas on the kinds of materials that would be desirable. A memo reflects her wide-ranging interests and her awareness of the varied types of activities that made up a collective woman's world. She called for women to forage in their basements and attics and send in all material, whatever little value they might put on it. It was a call to make visible the "invisible" women, by way of diaries, journals, letters, memos from leaders of community groups, mimeographed or pamphlet literature, anything relating to the handicrafts. Records were sought concerning women in the professions—that is, teaching, medicine, law, journalism, nursing, social work, science, the arts—or women in agriculture, as landlords or tillers, especially in situations demonstrating specific cultural adaptations, such as the Scandinavian cooperative customs, or Italians in truck-farming, or black and white sharecroppers and their efforts to unionize, or of women pioneering the virgin soils of the arid West, or of settled American Indian women farmers. The WCWA wanted written information about women as owners and workers in the factory system, as activists in the labor movement, and as entrepreneurs in the service industries and in finance. The center wanted details of all kinds, including household budgets, grocery lists, and even records concerning community gossip, for in "important gossip the substance of home life may be enclosed." The list did not finish there, and included women in domestic

and other personal services—for instance, companions and private secretaries. The WCWA wanted documents about women explorers and
adventurers, women in politics and government, in social movements, in
society, in religion. The full impact of what the information compiled
might do to the established contours of history was awesome.

The organization of the archives was a huge task that moved on a
limited amount of money. The estimated budget for each of the first three
years was modest, just a bit over $12,000, which covered the salaries of
the organization's director, the executive secretary, secretary, research
assistant, typist, and file clerks. The income for the first year was set at
$11,000, which included money from thirty sustaining members at $100
each, 100 contributing members at $25 each, and 200 active members at
$5 each, bringing in a little more than half of the allotted budget. It was
hoped that by the end of the third year there would be a provision, in the
form of some kind of endowment, which would insure the financial future
of the WCWA.

Money was not the only problem though. Interest in the project by the
intellectual world was limited; what this meant was that Beard was
working mainly with amateur personnel. With very few exceptions, such
as Dora Edinger, a refugee from Nazism with a Ph.D. in History from
Heidelberg, she dealt with nonprofessional women. Her memos and
outlines, some in great detail as to the kind of material she wished to
collect and what its purpose was, were in themselves an educational and
political statement. With limited resources, she was trying to teach a
group of women how to collect material for an archive. Appeals to
women librarians and others trained in manuscript collecting also were
made, but the act of reaching out to the masses of women was in itself an
act of consciousness-raising; women, by doing, learned the tools and
techniques of the social historian. To advance her notion of women's role
Beard demonstrated how the process itself was educational and part of the
achievement.

Beard, the Columbia dropout, was a teacher—in her books, articles,
radio scripts, lectures, and now in the WCWA but never in a college or
university. She envisioned the Center as leading to an Academy of
Women to stimulate research about women and to provide an institutional
base for women.

A partial list of the materials received during the short, harried life of
the Center are indicative of the scope that Beard had in mind.

There are the letters and papers of Catharine Beecher; documents and pamphlets in English, Hebrew, and Russian of Dr. Catherine Maryson, a member of the State of New York Infirmary at the turn of the nineteenth century; a pamphlet describing the Flotation Process, important in the development of metallurgy, which was invented by Carrie Jane Everson, an extremely gifted but unpublicized chemist; the original records, maps, and charts of Amelia Earhart's last flight; forty-four bound volumes of *The Woman's Journal*, presented by Lucy Stone's daughter, Alice Stone Blackwell, who donated the gift as "the most precious thing I have to give"; a copy in the original language of the memoirs of Gluckel von Hamelin, a German diarist of the seventeenth century; a copy of a speech delivered before a women's club in Indianapolis by Lois Grosvenor Hufford on her retirement after fifty years of service as a high school teacher; materials from Australia dealing with the Centenary Council of Melbourne in 1938; copies of the WPA Survey of Historical Records, marked "WH" (Woman's History); and a letter from Mrs. R. W. Rutherford to her son, in 1826, from Morrisania, New York, in which she described how women in her family were speculating in land values. There were sketches of Japanese women from the Mythological period until 1935, which were intended for publication in a projected *Encyclopedia of Women* being prepared in Vienna. After the Nazi takeover of Austria disrupted the project, the Japanese material was sent to Beard for safekeeping.

The WCWA files also held an assortment of letters from individuals describing the kinds of materials, letters, journals, diaries, that they had discovered in their family holdings—exactly the kinds of materials Beard was hoping to collect. There were also jottings of potential projects involving research on women of the old Spanish culture in California and the Southwest, on Spanish-Portuguese women of Old New York, on Jewish women, and on German-American women, including investigation of material collected on the German migration of 1848. The Guggenheim Foundation was asked to underwrite a project regarding "Women in Law"; the grant was denied, but one woman pursued the project part-time on her own initiative. Many such proposed projects were worked out in some detail and involved months of correspondence between Mary Beard and the person or persons involved in their preparation.

She was also working to establish individual state archives, to be coordinated with the national organization, and she sent out directives to individual state chairpersons on the archive committees. As always, she used the opportunity as an educational device; one three-page memo described the steps by which archival data was to be selected and collected. She advised the state leaders to familiarize themselves with the activities of the women in their respective areas, and to seek "women's words and visions" by finding their records of all their endeavors from politics to homemaking. She suggested organizational structure and urged the use of exhibits to induce men and women in the states to share in the fund-raising. She advised leaders not to turn away any material, but to accept everything offered, even if there were not sufficient facilities to house it immediately. In the event that the necessary financing for state centers was not found, the materials collected could be deposited in state libraries so "that your work will count anyway in developing the source materials for a wider and deeper study of women. The bigger and better aim of housing them in a Center is however one to which we must all cling."[5]

In a WCWA file dated July 18, 1940, there is a partial listing of projects under development. Marjorie White headed the first project to be launched, "Women in Science." Dr. Clare Lynch, of the Rockefeller Institute, was a consultant, closely supervising the section concerning "Women in Biology." Alice Andrews, a statistician, headed the section on "Women in Mathematics." The "Women in Music" project was run by Frederique Petrides, Mrs. Henry Drinker, and a German musicologist, Dr. Kathe Meyer. A specialist in international law, Dr. Fannie Fern Andrews, chaired the section on "Women in Diplomacy." Dorothy Porter, then librarian at Howard University, agreed to collect material for the "Black Women" project. Princess Te Ata, specialist in Indian folklore, was to pursue an "Indian Women" project. Rose Schneiderman agreed to coordinate the collection of materials regarding "Working Women," with the promised assistance of such others as Fannie Cohn, of the International Ladies' Garment Workers Union, and Mary Dreier.

Lists of prominent men and women in many areas of the public sector indicated the scope of the projects that Beard had in mind and the kind of devoted attention and energy she gave to developing the organization. That she viewed the act of collecting itself as a valuable function of the Center is suggested by another memo, entitled "The Educational Program," which calls for the following: expert archivist direction of student research; lectures by men and women on particular aspects of the materials collected; group discussions of "civilization and history-making as affected by men and women"; publications based on documentary findings; involvement of teachers and school administrators who "at present have no such opportunity to think about culture in the large."[6] In these ways, by developing archives that included the prominent and the unknown; by mixing archivists and non-specialists, students and working professionals; by having state branches and a national center in New York City, she was carrying out the principle of the WCWA in its very method of operation. It is the Beards' social history at work. It is her vision of the value of all humankind in the making of culture, a vision demonstrated in the process of establishing the Center.

Many responses to solicitations for the WCWA were supportive and promised materials of a varied nature, but apparently most of the promised records were never deposited because of the precarious and short-lived existence of the Center. There was the occasional satisfaction of having changed someone's attitudes: "I am becoming bewitched by your enterprise, though at first it left me cold, to be candid, because I am naturally indifferent to anything on lines of sex discrimination. But I have warmed up to your opportunities," one woman wrote.[7] Many expressed their concern about the value of an archive that was exclusively female. Mary Beard, writing to Mrs. Sue Bailey Thurman in March, 1940, said, "There will be objections on the part of many Negro women—perhaps a few on the part of Negro men—to separate Expositions, and/or to women's separate exhibition in such an exposition. But this is precisely the objection we meet with respect to our Women's Archive. Many women and many men deny the validity of a separate archive for women. I maintain however that only by dramatizing women can women be recognized as equally important with men. And I now maintain that only by dramatizing the hopes and achievements of Negro women per se can they be recognized as equally important with Negro men."

Dr. Alice Hamilton sent a check to Beard, but stated she was "not ready" to become a sponsor. "I have never seen the value of publicizing the work of women in men's fields . . . what we achieve is always so little compared to the record of men." Women's contributions were different, and, although as important, "so much more intangible." Beard returned the $5.00 check, wanting the contribution from Dr. Hamilton only when she would "want to give it." She was planning to persuade her old acquaintance that she, Beard, was indeed concerned with women's "feminine contributions" and not imitative work.[8] Meta Glass, president of Sweet Briar College, reluctantly sent $5.00, but expressed doubt that "this large effort to make the world conscious of what women have done in civilization" was worthy because "nobody has doubted it." She suggested that, when the new stationery was printed, perhaps her name be dropped from among the sponsors.

In September, 1940, almost five years after the first meeting that started the formation of the WCMA, Inez Hayes Irwin, chairperson of the Center, issued a statement dissolving the corporation. Financial problems were unending. Marjorie White, slated to be placed in a paying position as head of the science project, was, in early November, 1937, informed that "the most vital need" was the "actual raising of money," so that her project was postponed.[9] The following summer Beard wrote to Alice Stone Blackwell, who gave much material to the Center, that "with remarkable headway there is still a woeful lag in funds. . . . We could for instance now get valuable letters of Baroness von Suttner if we could find the necessary $3,000."[10] Added to the financial problems, the old splits between the Woman's Party sympathizers and the NAWSA sympathizers also opened up again. The WCWA leadership had representatives from all factions on their lists of sponsors and board of directors, on the premise that a women's community to accumulate archives could not legitimately make political discriminations, but there was discontent from some of the NAWSA women. Efforts to revise the board, partly with the hope of minimizing political differences, partly to increase efficiency, were undertaken in the summer of 1938.

But the very essence of the WCWA, the effort to engage the activities and commitment of non-specialists, pointed up a very serious flaw. The Center was without an institutional base, and, therefore, without the support services such a base could have provided. The prominent women who lent their names as sponsors spent most of their time elsewhere. The numbers of other women, largely without the credentials the world recognizes or the training that is involved, were unable to give the essential strength to keep the Center moving financially and professionally. The superintendent of the Minnesota Historical Society cautioned Beard to be sure "that you plan and administer the work with the highest degree of professional competence that can be found in the country in the domain of what the experts call manuscript economy."[11] Women were not accustomed to raising sums of money for a project like a women's archive, and during the process of learning the Center could not be financially sustained. The 1930s, with its restricted financial resources, its retrogressive assaults on the woman's movement, gave way to the Second World War, and the concern for a Center of Women's Archives appeared frivolous. The WCWA was dissolved, and most of the source material collected for it was distributed to various universities and libraries.

From the words of some of the women who directed the World Center, one senses sadness, more than bitterness and anger, at the project's closing. Inez Hayes Irwin, in her statement dissolving the Center, said "Mrs. Beard as our chief" had worked intensively to form the organization, raise money for it, collect archives, and "perhaps even more important, [try] to make the United States archive-minded." Surely a project of such magnitude would survive. "When the quiet days of peace and reconstruction come . . . there will be many such organizations as we have worked so hard to form and perhaps ultimately the big central one that was our dream."[12] Marjorie White, discussing the dissolution of the Center, referred to dissension among the board members, who had insisted that fund-raising must precede collection of sources; she pointed out that "one-half of the materials were sent to the Archives office without solicitation due to the name of M.R. Beard and other prominent women," and that Mary Beard "arose time and again, above personal jealousy and personal ambition." Beard herself wrote years later, "It is alive and lusty (she refers to the concept of the WCWA—AJL) . . . nothing can kill an idea, not even the Board."[13] In 1943, she admitted that she had tried to "drive the New York women faster than they could move intellectually and emotionally." She learned from that experience "the need for slower work, after lerning how much education has to be done among the promoters themselves."[14]

As the WCWA was nearing its end, she was cheered by the prospect of the immediate work ahead, a revised edition of *On Understanding Women*, which, she hoped, "will widen and deepen a foundation for thinking about women. . . . It is a high ambition, I am a low-brow, but if I can add a few stones to the understructure . . . I shall still be doing my bit for WCWA."[15]

NOTES

1. Warren I. Susman, *Culture and Commitment, 1929–1945*, New York: George Braziller, 1973, p. 16.

2. Mary R. Beard, *A Short History of the Labor Movement*, Workers Education Bureau of America, 1920, Preface, v. (This work was reissued by the Greenwood Press, Westport, Conn., in 1968.)

3. Excerpts from *On Understanding Women* and *A Changing Political Economy* appear on pp. 139–146 and pp. 204–209, respectively.

4. There is a file on the WCWA at the Schlesinger Library, Radcliffe College, which provided most of the source material for my account of the development of the Women's Archives.

5. From a Beard directive, entitled "Directives for State Chairman of the Archives Committee." Schlesinger Library.

6. Memo on "The Educational Program." Schlesinger Library.

7. Letter from Vida O. Scudder to Beard, October 31, 1940 [?], Schlesinger Library.

8. Letter from Alice Hamilton to Beard, June 18, 1938. Beard's answer is typed on the bottom of Hamilton's letter. Schlesinger Library.

9. Letter from Ruth Savord, secretary of WCWA, to Marjorie White, November 6, 1937. Schlesinger Library.

10. Letter from Beard to Alice S. Blackwell, July 12, 1939. Schlesinger Library.

11. Letter from Theodore C. Blegen to Beard, July 19, 1939. Schlesinger Library.

12. Letter addressed "To the Members of World Center for Women's Archives, Inc.," September, 1940. Sophia Smith Collection, Smith College Library.

13. Beard to Margaret Grierson, August 12, 1941. Smith College Library.

14. Beard to Margaret Grierson, November 9, 1943. Smith College Library.

15. Beard to Marjorie White, July 11, 1940. Schlesinger Library.

Chapter V

In an attempt to bring about immediate political and social change, Mary Beard had followed the direction of such acknowledged leaders of the feminist movement as Dr. Anna Shaw, Carrie Chapman Catt, and Alice Paul, but ultimately she felt unsatisfied with that kind of activity. It was in an arena detached from social action, the arena of her reality, the reality through an abstraction that touched *all* issues pertaining to women, that she best utilized her talents.

The World Center for Women's Archives had proven to be the wrong vehicle. Mary Beard, now in her mid-sixties, again sought a new project, a different way, to achieve her overriding goal. She and Marjorie White began to construct an outline for an encyclopedia of women. The impetus came initially from Marjorie White, but their ideas, they came to realize, were so similar that the project soon became a joint one.

The idea itself was not an original one, for a group of European women had assembled a great deal of material for a projected encyclopedia before World War II. All the files and papers had been destroyed, however, when the Nazis raided the home of Anna Askanzy, in Vienna, where the material was being collected and stored. In Japan, Baroness Ishimoto, working in conjunction with her European counterparts, realized that there was little chance of her material on Japanese women surviving the right-wing censorship of her government, much less being published, so that her work was sent to Beard to be stored in the WCWA. (This Japanese material, incidentally, formed the basis of the data compiled for Beard's book, *The Force of Women in Japanese History*, published in 1953.)

By the end of 1940, however, it became painfully clear to Beard and White that they were unable to overcome the obstacle of financing and would have to postpone the encyclopedia project indefinitely.

Very soon after, in the spring of 1941, Mary Beard was intrigued by a new and challenging prospect. Walter Yust, editor in chief of the *Encyclopaedia Britannica*, attracted by Beard's "persistent criticism of compilations of our sort," invited her to help rectify "any errors." She was delighted and wrote to Marjorie White of "the answer to your financial problem" and of cultivating "our mutual interest in widening the knowledge of women in history." If Yust would agree to hire her [White], she could then feed "much of your accumulated material into this exceedingly popular compilation . . . [which would] . . . certainly be one very fine way of getting women into public consciousness. . . . I am immensely excited by this receptivity at this long last to the justness of my criticism of its mannishness. . . . Are you also happy to know that our drives have counted in so many ways, this one included?" A meeting between Beard, Walter Yust, and the *Britannica* president brought positive results, and Beard set about to put together a research staff of three women.[1]

Dr. Dora Edinger was named to research "Women in Central Europe"; Janet A. Selig, "Women in Science"; and Marjorie White would be responsible for the remaining areas. Beard would function as an unpaid supervisor and editor. She did not wish to be paid "to assure that the present fund assigned for this enterprise will all go into your work. . . . Besides I have my own work of another kind and this provides my living."[2]

Working for the *Britannica* did not mean foregoing work on a separate women's encyclopedia. In the middle of the *Britannica* women's project, Beard returned to her "newest pipe dream," as she called the encyclopedia. A Chicago publishing firm, for whose *World Book* she was preparing an article, showed interest in a women's encyclopedia. She wrote to Marjorie White of her contact there, saying that the editor had "more understanding than our present boss of what the job of interpreting women is."[3] What problems existed with her "present boss", Walter Yust, are not exactly clear. The correspondence that exists between them, though limited, suggests a cordial working relationship.

Her move toward a separate encyclopedia was not one based on whimsy, or on ambition in the general sense, but on a rather pragmatic approach to a goal. She had been part of the political team that had worked simultaneously on the Congressional Committee of the NAWSA and the Congressional Union, two separate units with a single purpose, the Union insuring the continuation of the purpose in the event of a change in method.

It is difficult to reconstruct, from the data available now, how Beard planned to carry out the *Britannica* project. Soon after her staff began its work, she circulated a memo concerned with "Measurements for Inclusion" of new topics. One category of "women exercising direct power" included queens, feudal ladies, baronial nuns, merchants, bourgeois dispensers of great wealth, American planters, and cattle queens. A second category of "women exercising indirect power" included French court women under Louis XIV, Greek women, Oriental women, English noblewomen, religious creed makers, sect builders and promoters, Christian mystics, Buddhist leaders, the Levellers in England, American reformers, Russian nihilists, and Communists. The memo also suggested a line of investigation concerned with officeholders and legislators, contributors to the thought and practice of education, political science theorists, as well as artists, writers, historians and other "specialists, such as anthropologists, making major additions to knowledge."[4] Clearly an incomplete list, at best only a preliminary listing of suggestions, it reflected the breadth of her project, a large view consistent with her search for answers.

At the end of 1942, she and the three women on the research staff submitted a lengthy report summarizing their work. Yust was apparently impressed and reported that he and his staff were so influenced by it that "the long neglect of women in the compendium is to be rectified." He also planned to appoint a woman, to be named by Beard, to head a "Woman's Department" to advise him.

The report, entitled "A Study of the *Encyclopaedia Britannica* in Relation to its Treatment of Women," is a fascinating forty-two-page document, signed by the four women, undoubtedly written by Mary Beard.[5] It is filled with ideas for further research, many of them still largely undeveloped. Many of the notions that appeared earlier in *On Understanding Women* and later in *Woman as Force in History* are evident in the way she approached the revisions of the *Britannica*. There are numerous references to important women who had been neglected. The report reflects a recognition of the historical significance of sexual differentiation over time; for example, in the development of certain industries, such as spinning and weaving, and in the evolution of distinct male and female language patterns. It highlights new ways of looking at old material; for instance, the powerful role of women in medieval convents, and the creation, by those nuns, of the first hospitals. Among its most fruitful insights, the report suggests that earlier, traditional powers of women were reduced in modern civilizations, partly as a result of the development of institutions, such as univerisities and medical schools, that could, for the first time, exclude women.

The report also pointed out that the general selection of topics and their interpretation were based not only on obvious male but also Protestant biases. Although the document dealt with only the *Encyclopaedia Britannica*, and one particular edition at that, its analysis could still apply widely today.

Divided in three parts, the first portion of the report lists existing articles described as satisfactory. For example, the article entitled "Dress" recognized the significance for both sexes. "Illuminated manuscripts" was particularly fair to women in that it appreciated the "importance of the Ada-group." The "Shakers" article had a "good account of women in leadership." Sketches of Maria Theresa, Marie Antoinette, and Eleanor Duse were written with "impartiality and penetration." This portion of the report consisted of four and one-half pages.

The second part, the critical section, was twenty-eight pages long, and the language bristled. Since the report was not written for publication, Beard no doubt felt free from some of the restraints she ordinarily placed on her sense of propriety. Starting with A as in "Abbesses," the report condemns the article as unjust to the powerful role these churchwomen played in government and politics, as feudal lords, advisors to kings, and heads of hospitals. The discussion of "Abortion" was judged out-of-date and should have been "more than a moral question," embracing population, health, medical, and social issues. *Britannica* readers of "Academies" and "Academy, Greek" would never even "suspect that women were ever members or leaders," the report complained. The article on "American Frontier" had no "hint whatsoever that there were any women on the frontier and thus neglects . . . the civilizing domestic arts, mutual aid in community life, the cooperative enterprises." A reader of "Cookery" would "scarcely suppose . . . that woman was ever in a kitchen. . . . The illustration of medieval cookery reinforces that emphasis." If the article had begun with prehistoric times, "the purely creative first forms of boiling, broiling, baking," the report points out, it would be clear why "the weight of research credits women with starting this business."

"Education" represented women as uneducated "except as students in recent public institutions. Great definite harm is done to women and to the minds of men by assumption here maintained that women never had an education until recent times." The article on "Medicine" contained a "supercilious treatment of 'popular medicine' in respect of old women's remedies being tinged with magic." New material on the medicine man or priest doctor was available to permit a more penetrating treatment of old popular medicine, the report stated.

The enormous disparity in the treatment of women and men in some of the national histories was such that "a reader who studied these volumes might come to the belief that women played a more important part in Burmese life than they played in English or American life." The "Harem" article did not examine the internal politics, the political intrigues, and the "manipulations of social power" that went on. "Greece" discussed the status of slavery in detail, while the status of women was "not discussed at all," although women had been involved in all aspects of ancient Greek society, as members of all the Greek schools of philosophy, as teachers, healers, writers, and heads of philosophic academies. "Guerilla Warfare" totally ignored the participation of women. "Industry" did not even hint at women's part, for example, in the textile industry of the United States. "Labor, Primitive" was among the weakest of all the articles, for it ignored the "story of woman's original creativeness as inventor of the industries, arts, and as the first farmer by reason of her own concern with the soil—not her slavery."

The report criticized many of the articles that followed the anthropological school of Bronislaw Malinowski. "Magic" was "Malinowski's magic only. The subject is immense but made small here." "Marriage" followed Malinowski's belief that monogamy was the original sex relation, ignoring other historical judgments. "Matriarchy" was "fantastically absurd" in places. Its approach was "too biological and psychological and insufficiently historical and economic." "Medicine, History" was "utterly masculine in its assumption, for example, in its neglect of the original natural (non-magical) approach to healing by the old herb women," and there was a "nasty slur on midwives."

Dorothea Dix was not mentioned in the article on "Prison." "Reform Movement" omitted the woman suffrage activity in Great Britain, and the section on France made "Condorcet appear the sole sponsor of equality for women." There were no cowgirls in "Rodeo."

"Social Anthropology" again reflected Malinowski's "extremely masculine conceptual thinking combined with his dogma about monogamy as the first form of marriage." His particular functionalist interpretation was the only one permitted but "rules out history and evolution." From the article on "Song," one would conclude that "no woman sang in Europe—not the nuns in choir composition and singing, not Julia Ward Howe—and no woman sang madrigals although they were women's song."

The third section of the report suggested new articles or major revisions of old ones. The staff felt that the articles covering "Matriarchy," "Wealth," and "Land" were so bad that they should be wholly redone. A new article suggested was "Bathing and Laundrying"; and, if space was a problem, an article on "Bread-Making" could replace the existing one on "Pig-Sticking." The treatment of "Children" required an extended historical view dealing with the phenomenon of child sacrifice as a religious rite, colonial blue-laws, patriarchal powers, and the slow recognition of the need to understand and protect children. Discussions of goddesses were scattered throughout the *Britannica*, but the report suggested that the general topic was "a great subject in historical thought and merits a major article. It is an important way to study early religions and early history. Women were worshipped as goddesses of Health and Hygiene, Industry and Agriculture."

Toynbee Hall had a separate sketch; Hull House deserved one too, the report asserted. Midwifery also merited an article. The two lines dealing with nuns were not enough. A cross-reference led to "Monk," but no reference led from "Monk" to "Nun." As a result of "popular conceptions among Protestants . . . that women entered convents involuntarily," and the general ignorance of "their role as physicians and surgeons, the scope of their education, their 'spring into freedom' via the convent . . . and their dramatic and scientific writing," an extensive article was called for. The report suggested that there be a new article on "War, Women and" to counter "the ordinary assumption that women hate war because it demands their sons or because they abhor such violence in itself. The facts of history refute the assumption. . . . Women have initiated wars; participated in warring; and promoted both aggressions and defense from very early times to our own."

The report finished with a last swipe at the Index, which in relation to women was "so meager that it almost blots out the sex," even to the limited extent that women were represented.

The document was submitted to Walter Yust, who, according to a letter from Marjorie White to Mary Beard on December 15, 1942, received the recommendations quite well, and "while he had not read the STUDY *entoto*, he thought that there were moments when we must have had tongues in cheek!" He "apologized again for advertising your name in the Sat. Rev. of Lit., stated that it was an error, and that he had no intention of featuring our work or the new data on women until he had begun the inserting of sketches which he now thought would take place in 1943."

The "long neglect of women in the compendium," which Yust declared would be "rectified," was not rectified in 1943 nor in any later editions. The criticisms raised in the report are as pertinent today as they were thirty-four years ago.

In February, 1947, Mary Beard answered Anne Martin Grey, who inquired about an article she had written for the *Encyclopaedia*. Beard said, "I can't tell you a thing about it yet. Mr. Yust has never kept me in touch with one of the numerous sketches or anything else which he authorized me to collect for the compendium." She added that "his behavior is incomprehensible to me." It seems that when Yust asked Beard how long the project of gathering materials on women would take, she answered, "as long as the *Encyclopaedia* enlarges." Perhaps, as Beard said, "that ended the matter for him." In any event, said Beard, "I am asking no more women to write for it."[6] With unconcealed exasperation and disappointment, Mary Beard and her small staff finally understood that, after eighteen months of serious work, their recommendations would be ignored, and their hopes for change not realized.

A recent letter from the *Encyclopaedia Britannica*, dated October 8, 1976, concludes the story. "I'm afraid that we can provide very little information on Mary Beard's project. We do not have . . . a copy of the report she submitted, nor any of the correspondence relating to it."[7]

Despite repeated rebuffs, Mary Beard remained amazingly tenacious and resilient. Her vision of a central depository for women's archives was reawakened by the president of Radcliffe College, W. K. Jordan, in late 1943 when he wrote to her of a scheme for Radcliffe "to build within its library a strong research collection that would deal with the historical status and cultural contributions of women in this country and in England." Jordan had learned of Beard's earlier work through Walter Yust.[8]

She was enormously enthusiastic for a long while, but the correspondence with Jordan, sometimes effusive on her side, remained restrained on his, suggesting that his commitment to a new archival collection did not match hers. Beard did not notice, or chose to ignore, the reserve in Jordan, she was so thoroughly joyful at the prospect of the archives renewed, even if on a more limited scale.

The proposed project led to a long correspondence between the two that included advice from Beard to the Radcliffe administrator gleaned from earlier years. She urged him to get an advisory council to help collect material and raise money, but she warned him about "factionalism among women in respect of membership on the council. There has been a bitter warfare between ultra-feminists and middle-of-the-roaders. The intransigents can see nothing beyond the women's rights materials. . . . The 'protectionists' [referring to positions on the ERA issue] are apt to be just as extreme in their hostility to the National Woman's Party brigade. You will have to invite a representative of each faction to the Council I suppose." She also offered advice on personnel, and donated $1,000.[9]

Her fund-raising activities and shrewd assessments were valuable. The WCWA files and the later letters to Jordan hold numerous and extensive references to assortments of women in a variety of places, with jotted suggestions as to how to go about reaching them for fund-raising purposes and how much to expect. Her long-range scheme for approaching Elizabeth Arden is an illustration. Beard contacted Virginia Pope, a newspaperwoman and president of the Woman's Press Association, who advised Beard, who, in turn, advised Jordan on how to proceed. A written statement should be submitted to Arden in advance, asking her to head a group of women financial backers, but Arden's publicity man should be approached first, and Jordan should be brought to the Arden home after these preliminary steps were completed. In that way the Radcliffe fund will "get a largish sum instead of a tiny check which would have no importance."[10]

Mary Beard described Jordan as "an amazingly enlightened man," but in a memo to the Radcliffe librarian he referred to some items in the Beard collection as "a little on the junky side," indicating that he did not grasp sufficiently the kind of archive she hoped to build.[11] He ultimately disappointed her; the collection did not materialize. With some bitterness, she wrote in 1951, "Having lured many women to believe that Radcliffe was the best place in the U.S. for a great collection of books and documents respecting women's roles in American and other history, I have regretted that Radcliffe, as far as I knew, was in no great sense apparently warranting that belief."[12]

In March, 1950, ecstatic about conversations and correspondence with Smith College President Benjamin Wright concerning a women's archive, she wrote: "The idea is not dead! It marches forward to victory, I firmly believe."[13] But by October of the same year she was disappointed with Wright's reaction and said to Margaret Grierson, "I don't wonder that that rough blow almost paralyzed you. . . . We know now that there is no use to waste time on any college president; that we must 'go to the women' themselves."[14] And so she went to the women.

NOTES

1. May 19, 1941. Smith College Library.

2. "Memo to Research Associates," from Beard, August 1, 1941. Data came from Dr. Dora Edinger.

3. Letter from Beard to Marjorie White, July 15, 1942. Smith College Library.

4. "Measurements for Inclusion" memo, August 29, 1941. Provided by Edinger.

5. Excerpts from the *Britannica* report appear on pp. 216–224.

6. Beard to Anne Martin Grey, February 27, 1947. Provided by Stephen Fox.

7. Correspondence from Helen L. Carlock of the *Encyclopaedia Britannica* to author in response to inquiry about the Beard project.

8. Letter from W. K. Jordan to Beard, December 11, 1943. Beard Papers, DePauw University.

9. Letter from Beard to Jordan, July 2, 1944. Beard Papers, DePauw University.

10. Letter from Beard to Jordan, January 13, 1945. Beard Papers, DePauw University.

11. Jordan memo to Radcliffe librarian, June 26, 1944. Beard Papers, DePauw University.

12. Letter from Beard to Margaret Grierson, October, 1951. Smith College Library.

13. Letter from Beard to Margaret Grierson, March, 1950. Smith College Library.

14. Letter from Beard to Margaret Grierson, October, 1950. Smith College Library.

Chapter VI

The Second World War had ended the year before *Woman as Force in History* was published. Her best-known book, it reiterated all she had said about women as an undeniable, irrefutable power in civilization, and then went a step further in a detailed assault on William Blackstone and his legal theories, which greatly supported the image of the "oppressed woman."

In that same year, at the age of seventy, Mary Beard told the public:"I'm not a 'woman of achievement' or a 'career woman' or a Ph.D. . . . I'm a woman who works. Works at what? Works at self-education, and I've been brash enough to write my feelings."[1] She was quite serious about not having a career, or a Ph.D., or associating with the academic world. Four years later she would write to a friend, "Career women, like career men, are capitalistic entrepreneurs or retainers of the bourgeoisie."[2] The very notion of careers for women, she said at another time, "trivializes their operations." Mercy Otis Warren, who wrote her trenchant criticism of the Revolution, was not a career woman. Hannah Adams published her "remarkable study of Religions" not with a career in mind. "On the very platform where the feminists were talking woman's historic subjection to men and shrieking against his unqualified tyranny, such practicing women-physicians as the Hunt sisters of Boston were engaging in healing without licenses, and openly; successful businesswomen also sat on the platforms, without the support of 'equal civil liberties' by law."[3]

Still on the same subject two weeks later, she railed against the belief that "women never had an education before they got in U.S.A. schools." Career, thus, meant to her legitimizing by the established experts, whoever they were at the time, but since she denied their legitimacy, at least as far as women were concerned, she repudiated their system of credentials.

It was not merely that she believed it possible for a woman to get educated outside the university; she thought it likely that *only* outside the university could a woman be truly educated. College stifled the imagination of all its inhabitants, but of women even more. What she angrily labeled "intransigent feminism," that which viewed men as dominant and oppressive, often thrived in the academic world. More than the neglect that women tended to suffer in the college community, Beard detested and fought the trap of imitation. Whatever men had—the positions, the appointments, the courses, the status, the careers—women demanded the identical, the extension to them of the male world.

Yet, there were many bright young women in colleges; there were skilled and sympathetic librarians and archivists in college libraries. There were knowledgeable and influential faculty women; there were some powerful, and approachable, college presidents (although, after approaching two, she was somewhat disillusioned). So she turned her attention to the college community in an effort to persuade those within the academic world of the value of her historical analysis.

First, she made contact with innumerable college librarians and solicited information as to the size and range of their selections pertaining to women; upon receiving a response, she would offer suggestions relative to archives that were not well-known and other kinds of sources. In at least one instance, with Margaret Storrs Grierson, archivist at Smith College, an intimate, lasting friendship and close working relationship developed. Margaret Grierson was instrumental in setting up an excellent archival collection.

Second, she established a correspondence with several college presidents, especially those in women's colleges, and offered suggestions concerning library aquisitions, curriculum and faculty. To the president of Smith College, for instance, she had written, "I am noisy, I know. . . . [but] I am confident [there is] a great need of our day for enriching higher education with the ingredient of historic women's shares in setting up, destroying, rebuilding, culture patterns as associates of men. To the rapidly growing chorus of voices calling for an honest-to-

God equal education at last, I add my voice, driven to this vocal exercise by my own demon nurtured on many years of studying history by independent research and on intimacy with men's and women's innocence relative to women in history."[4]

To Sarah Blanding, president of Vassar, she suggested that "you consider what I believe to be a vital necessity for advancing the education of women in colleges and universities from which more enlightenment would seep down through the lower ranges of teaching. . . . I do venture to make the suggestion that you launch at Vassar the project of studying women in long history."[5]

But, most of all, she was interested in the students and in offering her notion of what constituted an equal education. It was not a separate education for women that she desired, but a new approach to learning about women; that new approach would be as valuable to men as to women, she believed. As early as 1944, she was speaking to Margaret Grierson about this approach and how it would be most feasible to introduce it in a woman's college "until such time as it can get into all higher education."[6] Indeed, in that same letter she expressed hope that such a course might be developed. However, she admitted at another time, that, even if Smith were to agree to sponsor such a course, she knew "no one who could give an entire course at Smith on women in history."[7] It would probably be necessary to have a variety of lecturers discuss different aspects "even in American history." Beard also encouraged the faculty and administration at Syracuse University to introduce an experimental course. The sex of the student body made little difference. Women should locate themselves in their historic past and learn to think about their meaning in history, just as they are taught to learn about the meaning of men in history. She believed women should have this opportunity, whether they study in women's colleges or coeducational ones. "In fact, in a woman's college, if the idea of segregation is allowed to run riot," she warned, "education there will have lost its force as a training in mental vigor."[8]

For all her enthusiasm, she knew that there were problems to overcome. Even the women's colleges were not interested in women's history. Speaking of a Bryn Mawr administrator in the 1940s, she wrote to Margaret Grierson that "her conception of women's education as one not requiring the study of women in history still reigns. . . . Ah—the job you have undertaken."[9] The problem was not a new one, though. In the early 1930s, not long after *On Understanding Women* had been published, President Henry Noble MacCracken had invited her to discuss the book before the Vassar faculty. MacCracken, who was the only man present, "had in mind the introduction of a course on the theme of some aspect. But to my amazement, among the great number of women teachers present, only one was not almost violently hostile." Anyone would have been taken aback by the response, but especially Beard, and especially when the "women teachers cried as if one voice: 'The time has come to forget women! Now we are winning equality with men. We are becoming human beings.' With no little heat I replied: 'you can easily forget women. You know nothing to remember.' " The many times she recounted that painful experience indicates the deep effect it had on her.[10]

Even when sympathetic colleges did sponsor courses in the history of women, they rarely satisfied her. Worse than ignoring the history of women was projecting a false and dangerous image of women's past. The more women accepted the dogma of their subjugation "as an interpretation of their history, the more men accepted it," she said in a speech to Radcliffe College, "until in the silence of college circles and in the clamor of the market place for talk and writing it became a fixed idea as the truth about women in history."[11] She was vigorous in her opposition to courses with such a point of view. She wrote in 1943 about a course built "on feminist dogma," given for some time at Goucher College: "I have the syllabus somewhere. . . . I regard it as horrible because such a fragmentary view of the human experience. Do everything you can to prevent that kind of education from getting a foothold—hence a stranglehold—at Smith. The course at Syracuse might have taken some such direction if it had not been instigated by women with more elastic minds." Feminism should be seen and "appraised as a phase of history; not as the total break with history."[12]

However strong and unbending her position on these kinds of courses, her compassion remained. When a fifteen-week course was being set up at New Jersey College for Women, in New Brunswick, she wrote to her friend at Smith College about it: "Silly outline. Pure and simple feminism," was her description. But "this opinion is only for you," she cautioned. "We must not attack the teacher. She is up against dire poverty from unemployment. . . . I was very careful not to use her name or mention this course of hers. I just indicated a point of view. She is a converted Catholic from the Nazi horror in Hungary."[13]

Many feminists stressed the position that women had been helpless, passive, unengaged members of the human race until the nineteenth century, when they rose to throw off the chains of the enemy, Man. According to Beard, they were not only promoting a line that was false and not supportable by historical examination, but were politically irresponsible and dangerous. That dogma *"rules our woman's world and makes women feel subject to men still."*[14] The belief in their inferiority contributed toward making women behave as if they were inferior thus contributing toward actually making them inferior. The "suffragists at their wailing wall"[15] helped to make women feel powerless, when, if they had stopped and looked at their past, they would have realized the strength and power they had throughout all of human history.

She knew that the reeducation of women would be a long, slow, often futile task, but it never seemed to have occurred to her to stop, or even slow down, because of those obstacles. On the contrary. "We've got breakers to swim against," she wrote in 1948.[16] The extraordinary ignorance challenged her. "On two occasions I have dined with college professors of the Hopkins—only four in number. But, they demonstrate the customary attitude of academics respecting women. They spur me to work on, for there is no use in merely bemoaning their naiveté and its attendant bigotry. We've got to feed out so much work that they will be drowned in its flood."[17]

The sly, mischievous irritation she felt with men was replaced by a more profound sorrow and pain when the ignorance or misinformation came from women. A mural exhibited at the Chicago Fair prompted her to write in 1943 that she did "not like it one bit," because of its "strictly nineteenth century feminist presentation of the case for women." It had caused her to "groan over its provinciality and ignorance of the great story of women in long history. . . . The easy acceptance by American women of the assumptions painted into the mural make me yearn to have training given to women in their history at college. My obsession."[18]

Obsession is an accurate word for her to have used, for nothing less than that kind of overriding commitment could have sustained her for years. She was essentially alone in her efforts to project a new, different image of women, and she battled the anti-women forces as well as the militant feminists.

Her entire life was a crusade for women's minds. "Women boost the best sellers, and are the major consumers of books which even *damn* their sex: for example, Phillip Wylie with his curses, and Lundberg and Farnham, with their vile, *The Modern Women: The Lost Sex*. Women must get a better education if they are really educable."[19] Wylie and Lundberg-Farnham were, for Mary Beard, the embodiment of what she detested the most, and they came in for bitter criticism in her correspondence. The Lundberg-Farnham book she referred to as the "Patent Medicine Book" because it was warranted to "cure every taut nerve."[20] "What amazes me," she wrote to Grierson, "is . . . the number of women who say they have read my last book and who then express their inviolate convictions in the old-style feminism, which seems to indicate that they haven't read one word. . . . Our women are not very, if at all, literate, I fear, in this twentieth century. But I pray they may become so."[21] If women were not convinced that they had their own history and their own valuable documents to substantiate and form that history, and if they refused to study and absorb, "they can never be more than mental children. Our own women, so far, are so injured by their historical innocence that they seem to me to be less than mentally curious children. . . . just parrots learning to speak what men teach them to say."[22]

Although she unburdened to Margaret Grierson many of these discouraging thoughts, her passion to convince women of their active past remained unabated for decades.

In 1934, under the sponsorship of the American Association of University Women, she published what constitutes a fifty-page syllabus for a woman's studies course, entitled "A Changing Political Economy as It Affects Women." It outlines, in a cosmic way, what she called a "truly equal education," not simply an extension of male education to females. "Man's education of himself and of his women understudies has become so rigid, so scholastic . . . that to parallel it with the same woman's education of herself . . . would count for very little. . . . But if equal education could now be undertaken, not merely with a view to discovering how far this is both a man's and a woman's world, both sexes might better comprehend how their destinies are bound together and why."

Mary Beard's syllabus examines militant feminism in precisely the manner she thinks it should be examined; that is, as only one aspect of a larger ideology, and in its relationship to the development of a capitalist political economy. The last section, the one dealing with the possibilities in a post-Depression world, projects a community of interests, which can only be achieved by a total reexamination of social forces and social institutions as they affect men and women, and which is possible only through the true understanding of the historic role of women throughout history. She called for a creative enterprise, an "up-to-date nation-planning."

The syllabus seems not to have been used, but she continued her efforts to convince women of the power of their past. She reminded Margaret Grierson, in 1943, as Grierson was about to attend the Second Anniversary of the Friends of the Library, to seize the opportunity to "illuminate the void in women's minds respecting their human identities in a great way." Seven years later, in 1950, she was still at it. "Since the December meeting of the American Historical Association in Chicago promises to be an unusually lively one, I have written to three professors who will be active and articulate there—to go into the neglect to bring women into the teaching and writing of history. I know these professors well. I hope the miracle will happen. I make my call for 'advancing' education in this way."[24]

What her obsession for educating everyone, everywhere, meant to Beard is suggested by her conversation with Lindsay Rogers, a longtime friend and colleague from Charles' Columbia days, who confessed he knew little about women in history, but seemed attentive and impressed with what she had to say to him during a visit paid to her and her husband in New Milford, in 1943. "I marvel that I never harangued him on the subject of women in history for he must have been the only fellow who ever escaped."[25]

In 1949, still poking around with new ideas, she played with the notion of an "academy of women, to be the studious and influential center of this revision of collegiate schooling and a center of adult meaning for education."[26] She set up a meeting with Margaret Sanger; Margaret Grierson; Maureen Leland, of the Smith faculty; Dorothy Brush, who originally worked on the manuscript of *The Force of Women in Japanese History*; and four other women "to rally for an idea for a woman's research institute."[27]

The previous year she had written to Margaret Grierson of an idea for a seminar, which she then referred to as a "Great Laboratory at Smith College." She was particularly interested in having the active participation of biologists and psychologists, who would deal, among other issues, with the reality that Maria Theresa could have numbers of children and Isabella of Spain a large brood and yet still run their states. The laboratory at Smith would be an "ideal way to teach women who they are" in preparation for "a larger conquest in all kinds of colleges, including coeducational." The earlier effort to establish such an inter-disciplinary course at Syracuse was interrupted by the outbreak of World War II and the accompanying loss of personnel and money.

The laboratory scheme would answer a particularly poignant need of young women in the late 1940s. "So many college girls" wrote to her about how confused they felt, while their male friends seemed to have such self-confidence. If they could develop a sense of "group fellowship for the study of their kind," she felt it would help. They had to do it alone, but she could help by setting up a structure. If the men on the faculty became involved, so much the better, for then everyone would be challenged to defend, to broaden, to revise his or her outlook. She dipped back into history for helpful precedents, so that the laboratory method resembled the ancient Greek system of the dialogue between men and women, a conception which Jefferson tried to incorporate at the University of Virginia. "One could call this Laboratory Plan at Smith—classical in the finest sense—taken from the men and women of Greece who together built up a conceptual thought. . . . the whole barbaric West went to school by reading the Greeks. . . . Every one of the great French women of the salon age was a student of Greek literature. In some of their writings one finds how much was known by them about Greek women."[28]

In this one small spin-off from an entire conception of education in the largest sense, one can see her mind at work, using the tools and knowl-edge of the past to build a community of women in the present, incor-porating both men and women, to set the tone for a real equality. As always, she was enthused by the project. At the age of seventy-three, she said to her close associates that they would "take the fortresses on the way to the citadel" until the time came "for hurling the torch. . . . If the Seminar could come into existence . . . that could be the torch."[29]

She hardly had read about the appointment of Benjamin Wright to the presidency of Smith College in 1950 when she sent off a long, detailed letter with suggestions for incorporating her view of women into the spirit of the college. She had toyed with the idea of an interdisciplinary course about women for several years, especially since "no one is yet equipped to integrate the history of women with the history of men in relation to all branches of knowledge." She suggested that the course be open to students from Mount Holyoke and Amherst. In that way, meetings "could partake of the graces and meanings identified with the French salons where men and women mingled in the great discussions of life, as Italian and Greek and Roman men and women had done earlier. From that challengingly amiable intellectual companionship," she went on, never letting an opportunity slip by, "the greatest conceptual thoughts of the past developed. A college should now be that kind of discussion center, vastly heightened by access to the world's historic documents and literature and inciting to the spirit of intellectual companionship for perhaps new mental forces."[30]

But nothing came of her contact with the Smith College president, and her "pipe dream" of a laboratory and women's archive at Smith did not then materialize, nor did the project at Radcliffe or the World Center scheme, and if one were to look at the *Encyclopaedia Britannica* under "Academy, Greek," one would assume that women were never a part of that ancient world that Mary Ritter Beard loved so dearly.

NOTES

1. *Louisville Courier-Journal*, March 22, 1946. Beard Papers, DePauw University.

2. Letter from Beard to Margaret Grierson, December 10, 1950. Smith College Library. In a letter to Dorothy Brush, August 25, 1951, she explains why she did not accept an honorary degree from Smith College. "I had jeered at the whole business so much that I could have seemed ridiculous in letting myself appear to believe I deserved one." To Frieda Kirchway she wrote, September 17, 1936, "Don't think of me as 'Dr. Mary . . .' I remain merely Mary. I have never taken a doctor's degree. The papers wish it on me but it is no doing of mine."

3. Letter from Beard to Margaret Grierson, August 13, 1950. Smith College Library.

4. Letter from Beard to President of Smith College, March 23, 1950. Smith College Library.

5. Letter from Beard to Vassar President Blanding, November 21, 1950. Smith College Library.

6. Letter from Beard to Grierson, January 22, 1944. Smith College Library.

7. Letter from Beard to Grierson, June, 1944 (?). Smith College Library.

8. Letter from Beard to Grierson, July 13, 1944. Smith College Library.

9. Letter from Beard to Grierson, October 20, 1945. Smith College Library.

10. Letter to President Jordan, Janury 20, 1944, and repeated to President Blanding, November 21, 1950.

11. Speech on "The Historical Approach to Learning About Woman," delivered at Radcliffe College, May 22, 1944.

12. Letter from Beard to Grierson, November 9, 1943. Smith College Library.

13. Letter from Beard to Grierson, May 20, 1949. Smith College Library.

14. Letter from Beard to Grierson, November 14, 1950. Original emphasis.

15. Letter from Beard to Grierson, September 28, 1947. Smith College Library.

16. Letter from Beard to Grierson, March 26, 1948. Smith College Library.

17. Letter from Beard to Grierson and Maureen Leland, December 13, 1948. Smith College Library.

18. Letter from Beard to Grierson, May 12, 1943. Smith College Library.

19. Letter from Beard to Grierson, May 28, 1947. Smith College Library.

20. Letter from Beard to Grierson, November 11, 1947. Smith College Library.

21. Letter from Beard to Grierson, February 27, 1948. Smith College Library.

22. Letter from Beard to Grierson, March 26, 1948. Smith College Library.

23. Letter from Beard to Grierson, November 9, 1943. Smith College Library.

24. Letter from Beard to Grierson and Maureen Leland, November 20, 1950. Smith College Library.

25. Letter from Beard to Grierson, November 9, 1943. Smith College Library.

26. Letter from Beard to Grierson, June 29, 1949. Smith College Library.

27. Letter from Beard to Dorothy Brush. Smith College Library.

28. Letter from Beard to Grierson, July 29, 1948. Smith College Library.

29. Letter from Beard to Grierson, November 4, 1949. Smith College Library.

30. Letter from Beard to President Wright, March 23, 1950. Smith College Library.

Chapter VII

What, finally, is the significance of Mary Beard's life and work? This chapter is an attempt to assess her impact in terms of the central thesis that dominated her ambition, her writings, and the conduct of her life.

Looking first at her thesis—her unshaken belief in the active and important historical role of women throughout the ages—how sound is it? Even casual reading of contemporary feminist literature demonstrates unmistakably that the view of women, past and present, as oppressed, subordinate, and powerless remains the prevalent conception.[1]

Is Mary Beard's work so without foundation that succeeding generations of feminists can properly neglect it? I think not. But there are many reasons why even sophisticated and learned feminists have not appreciated her ideas.

The thrust of her life's work was not and still is not easy for feminists to utilize in their political and ideological struggles. If women have been as powerful as Mary Beard said, then why the outcries by most feminists about inequality and discrimination? Beard's position seems, on the surface at least, to lend itself more comfortably to anti-feminist thinking, although such an inference is not what she intended or what is inherent in her work.

It is undeniable, though, that in her overstatement, however correct in essence, she leaves out the opposite reality of subjugation. Mary Beard knew better than most the oppression and insult to which women were subjected. She did not believe that the world was a just place for women. Her work was not better balanced because there is the inevitable one-sidedness that comes with compensation for long neglect. It is hard to overcome the tendency to lean too far the other way when one is redressing balances. Perhaps it is not even desirable. Perhaps Mary Beard wished to arouse controversy by deliberate overstatement. She acknowledged the distortion at least twice. In the first paragraph of a thirty-five-page article, entitled "Women in Long History," apparently submitted to *Collier's Encyclopedia* but never published, she observed:

> Owing to the widely-accepted interpretation of history . . . as . . . unqualified masculine tyranny over woman, making her as a sex subject to man, emphasis is laid in this review . . . on those aspects of woman's history which controvert or qualify that simplification of history.[2]

In the preface to *On Understanding Women* she noted that "there is sure to be an over-emphasis in places but my apology is that, when contentions have long been weighted too much on one side, it is necessary to bear down heavily on the other."[3]

The more serious reason for her overstatement, I believe, flows from her repudiation of equality as a desirable goal for women. What women must do, she felt, was mobilize for change—change initially for women, but ultimately for all people. It is because women are excluded from the traditional networks of power that they have the opportunity to make creative alterations in social institutions and social relations. To aim for equality is to forfeit that chance. Her years in the women's movement had demonstrated the power of the ostensibly powerless to bring about change. In 1914 she published an article that analyzed the legislative influence of unenfranchised women and illustrated the ways any powerless group can organize to achieve its goals.[4] It is in this context that Mary Beard objected so strenuously to college education for young women. Bright, ambitious women, caught up in the careerism and conformity that are fostered in the university, lose their innovative potential in the scramble for a place in the Congressional office, the physics laboratory, or the elitist academic institution. They jeopardize the power that comes from independence.

The strength to resist such professional enticements comes through an understanding of the history of women's work through the ages, in different times and different places. Women through time, as a congregate, as a mass, constitute a force that is limited only by the ignorance of those who do not recognize its power. If women only knew how much they had contributed to the world's wealth, arts, beauty, science, and technology, that knowledge would provide them with a tool of much greater value than the simple cry for equality. Whatever retards that growth of self-consciousness, self-confidence, and self-knowledge is to be rejected. It is with this view in mind that one must assess Beard's struggle against what she felt was the irresponsible and misleading leadership of the "intransigent feminists." Many of her ideas, despite their appearance of absolute certainty, come out of a mind still at work, still testing and grappling with speculations.

Other problems persist in what appear to be contradictions in her work. Beard used three major descriptive categories to explain women's historic roles. She said, first, that women have been indistinguishable from men: as warlike, as industrious, as cruel, as ambitious, as wise. She also said that women have brought to humanity vital, life-giving force: as creators of life itself, as nurturers, as sustainers of life through the invention of agriculture, as launchers of civilization through the creation of art and beauty. Third, women have been different from men, but neither better nor worse: women have been the spinners and men the weavers, women have developed the skills of domesticity, men of industry and commerce. These three different conceptions of women's pasts are woven throughout the same book, sometimes even within the same chapter, as if Beard were not aware of the contradiction. In fact, there is none. A contradiction exists only to those who demand the simple explanation, who insist on knowing "the" right answer. Mary Beard knew there were many answers, and that the story was not only complex but incomplete. As a trained researcher she well knew how much diligent work was yet to be done. More important, she also knew that, just as there was no single description of "man's role," there never would be a single description of "woman's role." Only those who define "woman" as deviant from the norm of "man" require "an" explanation for the way women have acted.

What is lacking is a theoretical structure which encompasses a view of women's historic role as located simultaneously in the center of social relations and at the edge of them. Beard understood, as few others ever have, that history is without meaning if the centrality of women in society is denied. She also knew that the perception of that central position changed over time. More important, she knew that the reality of women's participation in social events also changed. She was not altogether successful, however, in creating a theoretical model to explain what she was able to describe with such rich texture and detail. Still, it is only very recently, and with no more success, that these questions have even been addressed by feminists.

In these introductory remarks, I have not examined in any detail the substance of her books and articles. Much of this volume is made up of selections from her writings, and her work speaks for itself. I have preferred to highlight aspects of her life that would otherwise be unknown. Still, some observations about her work are appropriate.

Many of Mary Beard's most provocative and challenging ideas remain untested. In *Woman as Force in History* she boldly accused the leaders of the nineteenth-century feminist movement of grievously misreading William Blackstone's *Commentaries on the Laws of England* and thereby creating a fiction about woman's subjugation. Beard argued that Blackstone wrote for a legally trained audience, which would well understand the metaphorical rather than literal use of language; that he referred only to married women; and, most significantly, that when he described married women as civilly dead "in law," he referred to Common Law, a semantic distinction which was implicit, but assumed. Other laws of England and America, particularly Equity Law, granted women, depending on their class, many rights denied to them under Common Law. In any case, said Beard, most people, men and women, lived their lives without legal involvement, and therefore to examine women's place in society by use of legal codes was to distort the reality of life. The mid-nineteenth century feminists, in an effort to buttress their just grievances, saddled their descendants with a distorted and essentially untrue description of women's historic reality.

Is Beard correct in this judgment? We do not know. She offered a giant research strategy, not a closed system. Current research in the area of American colonial law as it applied to women suggests that Beard's analysis may be valid.[5]

Mary Beard also argued that until the development of industrial capitalism, in general, women suffered or benefited from social prerogative because of their class position, not their gender. Ruling class women, in precapitalist periods, ruled, as did ruling class men. Lower class women suffered, but as slaves or as peasants, not primarily as women. With the rise of liberal, bourgeois democracy and the supremacy of broadly based, male-dominated institutions of power, women, as women, were excluded from power and demeaned as a group. Is her interpretation valid? Again, the evidence to substantiate or alter her ideas is incomplete, the empirical work necessary to test her hypotheses not yet accomplished.

Mary Ritter Beard's vision of a world where "enduring humanity" would prevail was so fundamentally radical that it left far behind all the women's organizations of her day, whatever their political or ideological persuasion. There was nothing in her radical critique to win over the middle-class women, who represented most of the constituency in the woman's movement. At the same time, her ideas did not appeal to socialist, anarchist or communist women, because those women did not see feminism as a central issue, as Beard did; they identified themselves primarily with conventional radical organizations and dissociated themselves from the feminist movement.

Mary Beard was a young woman when radical feminists like Elizabeth Cady Stanton were active. Beard's mature years coincided with the disintegration of that politically radical-feminist alliance. The women's movement, from conservative to militant, went in one direction, placing women's priorities, however defined, as primary and exclusive. Those who demanded the end of class exploitation, with women's issues trailing, went in another direction. Beard alone stayed in the center, demanding both radical change in social relations and feminism; she made accommodations to neither side.

Mary Beard did not make it easy. Restricted in part by an inherited Calvinist world view, she made few concessions to human frailty. Women who are willing "to cringe before nasty husbands are weak creatures by choice," she wrote to a friend.[6] From her perspective, sexuality was identified with the hated Freudianism that humiliated women. As a result she did not deal with this entire area of human existence, and matters of female infanticide, rape or sexual violence of any kind were not incorporated by her in the reality of women's lives.

In many ways she remained tied to a nineteenth century conception of woman as mother and to the belief that the oppression of women resides essentially within the minds of women. Ironically, Beard's notion that the struggle to eradicate oppression is a struggle for women's minds places her today in the vanguard of radical feminism. She recognized that ultimately the success of the revolution, any revolution, depends on changed consciousness.

Mary Beard must share at least part of the responsibility for her own neglect. Her books are difficult to read. Her style is often heavy and pedantic. What appears to be endless repetition is not endless repetition, as Berenice Carroll has demonstrated,[7] but the writing is graceless and often obscures her ideas. Her letters to friends are filled with warm, enthusiastic reflections as well as hard, tough observations, but her public writing, especially in her books, is cool and impersonal, often dreary. She was a serious person, but not a humorless one, and yet her published writings are usually without humor. Some of the excerpts from the unpublished report on the *Encyclopaedia Britannica* which appear in this volume suggest a style of ironic humor that she frequently used.

Her work, valuable and important as it is, suffered from intellectual isolation. The criticisms upon which one sharpens one's work were missing. Her books were greeted with flattering platitudes, hostile assaults, or they were ignored. Most of the reviews of her major books criticized the too-ambitious task she had set for herself and the cosmic scope of the historical epochs she studied. Reviewers were overwhelmed by what they saw as excessive weight of evidence. Yet few of them discussed her major thesis or appraised her effort to place women in the center of historical examination. The critics were angry, hostile, patronizing, tepid, warm, friendly, but few saw her intent. They acknowledged bits and pieces of her work but did not grasp the essence.[8] The world that might have benefited from her contribution lost by that neglect, but the work also suffered.

Her incomplete view of women in history—the imbalance that minimizes, almost denies, the oppression—profoundly weakens her work. However much we may appreciate the political motivation for that distortion, the distortion remains, and it reduces the power of her writings. The entire dimension of sexual oppression of women is absent from her work. Such a neglect is easily explained when we understand the influences that shaped her thinking, but the neglect further flaws her books. If she had been caught up in the dialogue of a university seminar, if her work had been subjected to criticism from colleagues, she might have examined and resolved some of the stylistic and substantive shortcomings. She knew better, she was better, but nobody engaged her in serious debate, so there was no pressure to change. High up on the list of grievances women have is the deadly effect of not being taken seriously.

If Mary Ritter Beard's work defies easy categorization, her life is no easier to classify. On one level hers was an exciting and successful life. She published books and articles, co-authored famous volumes of United States history that are classics, engaged in major public activities of her choice, delivered nationwide radio addresses, traveled widely, had a long and happy marriage, and enjoyed the parental gratification of seeing her children select careers startlingly close to that of their parents. Both William Beard and Miriam Beard Vagts, who is married to a historian, are themselves historians and writers. Mary Beard's personal life was tranquil and rich; at the same time she was a recognized public figure. She was not as well-known or as influential as her husband, but then his life and distinguished career are hardly reasonable yardsticks by which anyone else's success can be judged.

Still, one is touched by her gnawing sense of failure. The collaborative work was heralded as path-breaking, for its new interpretations and for its use of new kinds of materials, but it was Charles Beard, then and now, who received most of the recognition.[9] The books were viewed as his "with her assistance." The books he wrote alone were widely reviewed and discussed. The books she wrote alone did not give her the same acclaim.

It is hard to believe that Mary Beard enjoyed the organizational work that took up so much of her energy. She said she was not good at it, but she probably was, if only because she was indifferent to the usual rewards. It was not balanced enough, orderly enough; there was too much trivia, too much wasted time.

When she left feminist politics to seek her goals differently, she tried to reach the larger community of women in a variety of ways: speeches, radio addresses, articles in popular journals, women's courses in college, a massive international women's archive, a critique of the *Encyclopaedia Britannica*, as well as the many long and serious books. Each effort was blocked, each struggle frustrated. It was only the passion that motivated her, the single-minded, almost mystical devotion to her private cause that kept her from cynicism and despair. She did not accomplish what she set out to do.

Was her life, then, a failure? Surely not. She devoted years to an idea whose time had not yet come. If her dreams remained unfulfilled, it was not for lack of intelligence, commitment, desire, or devotion. She lived within the limitations imposed by her outer world.

Her force was, indeed, substantial and far-reaching, although not immediate and often not tangible. Historians and social critics may deny the impact of women in general and Mary Beard in particular, but the world nevertheless is altered. In this sense, Beard's life and work embody her thesis: women are neglected in the writing of history, but the effect of their existence is a reality of history.

The insulting assumptions that minimized her role in the collaborative works could not minimize the impact of those works or the contribution she made to them. A recent study that tabulated the sparse references to women in the leading twenty-seven college textbooks in United States history found that Charles and Mary Beard's *Basic History of the United States* ranked highest, although twenty-five of those twenty-seven books were published after 1960; theirs appeared in 1944.[10]

She brought to her writings a new vision of the re-creation of the past, because including the experience of women inevitably broadened the entire base of history. Her emphasis on women did not narrow her scope, but widened it to encompass the wholeness of life. Indeed, it is through a genuine understanding of women's pasts that it is possible to know the ways in which, said Beard, it is "a man's world and a woman's world" and to recognize how "their destinies are bound together and why."

She recognized the importance in history, as she had in politics, of class and community in a way that most Progressive reformers did not. Her early involvement in trade union activity and her popularly written book on the labor movement underscore the class analysis she brought to her feminist politics and feminist writings.

She demonstrated in her life that there was no necessary incompatibility between a close marriage and a very separate sense of self. Whatever her public appearance, she retained a fiercely independent spirit. She conquered the "internal tyrants" of whom Emma Goldman spoke,[11] the internalized conventions that bind. The outer tyrants, those that could humiliate, reject, ignore, and deny, she could not control, but she could struggle against them, and she did. She gave witness that the silent years were not dead years. Hers was a feminist life.

Some of her legacy is direct. The women's archival collections at Smith College and the Schlesinger Library at Radcliffe College exist partly as a result of Mary Ritter Beard's efforts. Much of her legacy is indirect, including the few but persistent Women's Studies programs throughout the university system, the numerous high school and college courses in the history of women, the required reading lists in colleges that reflect a renewed recognition of the roles of women, the feminist journals, and the small but significant interest in the woman's movement today of the special needs of working-class women. The Radcliffe Institute embodies the spirit of Mary Beard.

In her early activist years Mary Ritter Beard associated with the radical wing of the woman's movement in England and in the United States. When she left the political arena to devote herself to intellectual tasks, her work became even more radical. Without support from the woman's movement, without a body of ideas upon which to build, without models of any kind to follow—alone—she audaciously placed woman at the center of history and society, and then she insisted that the world look again from her perspective. She once wrote of how the tyrannical efforts by the Puritan fathers were successful "until Anne Hutchinson laughed out loud."[12] Mary Ritter Beard, too, laughed out loud, and the echo of her voice is with us still. She died having made a small—a very small—ripple on the face of the earth. Although several of her closest associates understood the value of her ideas, very few others heard her. Yet, if great change is ever to come, it will be because women like Mary Ritter Beard persisted and endured.

NOTES

1. There are, of course, exceptions. Gerda Lerner and Adrienne Rich are two outstanding feminist writers very much in the Beardian tradition.

2. Typed manuscript, with handwritten notation that article was submitted to *Collier's Encyclopedia* but not published. Smith College Library.

3. *On Understanding Women*, New York: Grosset & Dunlap, 1931, Prefatory Note. Excerpts appear on pp. 139–146.

4. "The Legislative Influence of Unenfranchised Women," *The Annals of the American Academy of Political and Social Science*, November, 1914. Excerpts appear on pp. 89–94.

5. Joan Hoff Wilson, who is completing a study of colonial law and American women, indicates that her investigations thus far tend to confirm Beard's thesis.

6. Letter from Mary Beard to Anne Martin Grey, February 27, 1947. Bancroft Library. My thanks to Stephen Fox for referring this letter to me.

7. Berenice Carroll, "Mary Beard's *Woman as Force in History. A Critique,*" in *Liberating Women's History: Theoretical and Critical Essays*, Urbana: The University of Illinois Press, 1976, pp. 26–41, reprinted from the *Massachusetts Review*, 1972.

8. For example, Lyn Ll. Irvine, in the *New Statesman*, December 12, 1931, complains of the breadth of Beard's *On Understanding Woman* and concludes that "She who says everything proves nothing." Samuel Putnam, in the *New York Sun*, November 19, 1931, reviewed her book by listing her inconsistencies, giving his corrections, and telling her what she had omitted. J. H. Hexter, in *The New York Times*, March 17, 1946, sneered at *Woman as Force in History*, called it "rather simple," and concluded with "But she cannot fool us." John Chamberlain, in *Books of the Times*, January 17, 1934, described *America Through Women's Eyes* as female "chauvinism." Easily the most serious review she received was in *Progressive Education*, March, 1932, by Helen Drusilla Lockwood, who almost alone of the reviewers caught the exact essence of Beard's thesis.

9. A perusal of the reviews of their books, both those authored jointly and separately, confirms this statement. (See almost any essay in Beale, *Charles A. Beard: An Appraisal,* to illustrate the different treatment accorded Charles and Mary Beard in reviews of the co-authored books. For example, in the foreword, Justice Hugo L. Black wrote: "Many years ago I read *The Rise of American Civilization*, written by Dr. Beard and his wife." The first reference to "the great *Rise of American Civilization*," in the essay by Harold J. Laski refers to "Charles Beard, with his wife," (p. 13); further references by Laski to these volumes are to Charles Beard alone. Max Lerner, in his essay, wrote "When Beard came to write the several volumes of *The Rise of American Civilization*, he stuck," (p. 41).

10. Dolores Barracano Schmidt and Earl Robert Schmidt, "The Invisible Woman: The Historian as Professional Magician," in *Liberating Women's History*, p. 44.

11. Emma Goldman, "The Tragedy of Woman's Emancipation," reprinted in *Red Emma Speaks: Selected Writings & Speeches by Emma Goldman*, ed., Alix Kates Shulman, New York: Vintage Books, 1972, p. 139.

12. My thanks to Stephen Fox for providing me with this quotation.

Part Two.

Mary Ritter Beard:
Selections from Her Writings and Speeches

I.

POLITICAL ACTIVISM—
THE EARLY YEARS

Mary Ritter was born into a conservative, Republican, middle-class world in Indianapolis, Indiana, in 1876. Her father, Eli Foster Ritter, was an attorney by occupation and a zealous Temperance advocate and stalwart of the Methodist Church by commitment. About her mother, Narcissa Lockwood Ritter, little is known, but enough to suggest that she might have been the model years later for Mary Beard's formidable but "invisible" female life-force.

Mary, along with her three brothers and a sister, attended DePauw University, one of the earliest Methodist educational institutions in the West. After she graduated from college, she married her college-mate, Charles Austin Beard. The young couple settled in Manchester, England, where they threw themselves into radical labor and feminist activities. Everything they experienced in this important two-year period must have been challenging and stirring for the young Midwesterners, only recently removed from their comfortable world. No doubt Mary Beard's later concern for working-class women and her radical analysis of politics and history were shaped during these years. While in England, Mary Beard worked with Emmeline Pankhurst, the suffragist leader.

The Beards returned to the United States in 1902, in the midst of Progressive reform activity. They both entered Columbia University as graduate students, but Mary Beard soon left her studies in Sociology. By then the mother of two children, she became active in the struggles for woman suffrage and trade union reform. She worked first with the National Women's Trade Union League. By 1910 she was vice-chairman of the Manhattan branch of the Woman Suffrage Party, and for a while she edited *The Woman Voter*, the publication of The Woman Suffrage Party of New York. She resigned from that position to move to the Wage Earner's League, an affiliate of the suffrage organization, designed for workingwomen. By 1913 her energies were concentrated on women's suffrage activity. She was one of five women selected by the radical Alice Paul to form the Congressional Committee of the National American Women Suffrage Association (NAWSA). When this Committee split from NAWSA to form the militant Congressional Union, the name later to change to the Woman's Party, Mary Beard moved with it. As she had in England, she allied herself with the most militant wing of the suffrage movement.

The writings in this section come from these early years. The first two articles appeared in *The Woman Voter* in 1912. In them she describes how the needs of working-class women must be carefully distinguished both from those of middle-class women and from working-class men. These two short pieces reflect a class awareness which was not characteristic of most reformers of that period. The third selection, which was probably never published, uses the nationwide tour of Emmeline Pankhurst as a vehicle for looking at American attitudes toward feminists and feminism. In the fourth selection Beard examines the influence on legislation of voteless women to illustrate her thesis of the collective force of the powerless. The fifth and sixth selections deal directly with the militant politics of the Congressional Union, the struggle to achieve the federal amendment for woman suffrage, and Mary Beard's active defense of both.

The seventh and last selection is from *Woman's Work in Municipalities*, published in 1915. Although Beard remained with the Woman's Party for years, she was slowly moving away from the role of political activist to one of social analyst. In this book, published years before the suffrage amendment was won, one can see the political reformer using her experience and knowledge to begin to develop a theory of feminism.

1. Mothercraft[1]

NOTE: The Woman Voter, *the journal in which this article was published, was the official organ of The Woman Suffrage Party of New York. In January, 1912, when this piece appeared, Mary Beard was editor of the magazine. She had already served a term as vice-chairman of the Manhattan branch of the organization. Within six months she resigned from her editorial position to work directly with and for working-class women in the Wage Earner's League, an affiliate of The Woman Suffrage Party.*

In this first selection, Beard demonstrates her concern with issues relevant to women as workers and as mothers. She examines the newly developed Institutes of Mothercraft, adult education schools supposedly designed to teach women how to be better mothers by stressing the individual responsibility each mother has in the physical and moral development of her children. Beard's vigorous criticism of the political implications of these institutes reflects two of her special insights. First, she exposes the real meaning of middle-class reform measures for working-class women. "It is easy and cheap," she says, "for well-to-do persons to advise the poor" on proper methods of child nurture. But the "overwhelming majority of women are poor and engaged in a bitter struggle for the barest necessities of life." In this context, "pious precepts" become a "hollow mockery."

Second, she uncovers the social and political roots of attitudes that are often ascribed to the individual. To rear children properly requires "decent housing, leisure to be with the children, wholesome food, living wages" and much else, including "the abolition of child labor." These are not "individual problems . . . at all." The poor mother who struggles on "an inadequate income," who tries to "be clean in a dirty tenement house," who seeks to "secure pure milk from the . . . unclean shops about her" knows the "real problem of Mothercraft." The Mothercraft Institutes leave untouched these basic questions. They emphasize the individual parental role without recognizing the overriding political and social conditons that shape it. "Everything that counts . . . is political."

Every revolution has its counter-revolution. Every social movement in these days of wide-spread newspaper publicity meets its active adversary. Women, therefore, who are working hard for political enfranchisement are wondering whether new opponents are to be met in the promoters of the Institutes of Mothercraft now springing up all over this country. New

1. "Mothercraft," *The Woman Voter*, Vol. 1-2, January, 1912, pp. 12–13.

York boasts a school of this character which was formally opened on December 8th.

The ostensible purpose of the movement is to teach women to be better mothers to their own children: to care more intelligently for the embryo as well as for the moral development of growing boys and girls; to dignify maternity and work for finer results from a eugenic standpoint. So far, so good. Surely no one will decry the attempt to give prospective and actual mothers practical lessons in their own and their children's well-being. . . .

However, as suffragists and mothers (most of us), we do quarrel with many of the premises laid down at the opening ceremony of the New York School of Mothercraft. One speaker, for example, a visitor from Cleveland, laid all the blame for juvenile delinquency, crime, vice and immorality in general on mothers—individual mothers. She maintained that precepts learned at mothers' knees are more powerful than all else in moulding character and that Mothercraft is a thing apart from politics and legislation. In other words, the struggle for existence has no effect on conduct: every evil deed can be traced to an ignorant or selfish mother; every great contribution to society is the result of maternal stimulus. . . . Child nurture and child culture, the speaker insisted, are matters of individual parental control. Wives moreover must get back to the good old regime of complete sacrifice to their husbands' careers that fewer divorces may occur and happier family life be restored. Apparently it is still easier to preach than to practice as the speaker was several hundreds of miles away from her home on a lecture tour including Boston and New York.

Other speakers of the evening dwelt on the necessity of women's assuming the rôle of mothers sweetly and cheerfully and with a full sense of the grave responsibility entrusted to them.

The only social note struck during the evening came from an officer of the Board of Health, who dwelt upon the work of baby-saving in New York, by means of municipal milk-stations. He evidently was under no delusions as to the relation between politics and child nurture, for he gave a graphic account of his struggle for a decent appropriation for baby-saving. He did not, however, come out for Votes for Women as a possible helper in that struggle. Perhaps he thought it untimely. To some of us it seemed vital.

So it is that a big ideal like Mothercraft becomes the petty by-play of a small, comfortable group of middle-class persons. . . . Poverty stands in the way of its realization for the vast majority of our sisters and through no individual fault of their own. Mothercraft is a *social* ideal in the promotion of which the *community* action is an essential. Hygienic practices demand decent housing, leisure to be with children, wholesome food, living wages and many other things which include the abolition of child labor, whether among young nurse girls or factory girls. These things are not individual problems in these days at all. Everybody recognizes the part that individual effort plays in the development of human character and it is easy and cheap for well-to-do persons to advise the poor or ignore them altogether.

The fact remains, however, that the overwhelming majority of the women of this country are poor and engaged in a bitter struggle for the barest necessities of life. Only the poor mother who struggles day by day to make an inadequate income meet the most meagre demands, who has tried to be clean in a dirty tenement house amid filthy streets, who has tried to secure pure milk from the hot and unclean shops about her, or has tried to nurse her own baby in addition to doing heavy household tasks and supplementing the family income by scrubbing—only the poor mother who comes up against the brute facts of life knows the real problem of Mothercraft. In poor families the children are forced for recreation out of the home on to the streets with all their physical dangers and their allurements—moving picture shows, saloons, dance halls—and against the steady pressure of these social forces pious precepts learned at mothers' knees count for little. To ignore these great social facts— political facts, if you please—and over-emphasize the old moral responsibility of the "domestic" mother is a hollow mockery and betrays a hopeless ignorance of industrial and urban conditions in the Twentieth Century.

Mothercraft, domestic science, eugenics, child welfare and child psychology and all the long list of half delusions in new guises but skim the surface at present leaving untouched the basic things—wages, unemployment, industrial accidents, wife desertions, tenement work, hours, congestion, drink—in fact, everything that counts in the common life of the great mass of the people. *Everything that counts in the common life is political.* If dilettanti reformers really understood this, they would understand the scope and power of the suffrage movement. It is because of the persistent pressure of these real facts of every-day experience for the majority of women that equal suffrage is inevitable and will override all attempts of old-fashioned individual moralists to brush it aside.

2. Votes for Workingwomen[1]

NOTE: *In this article Mary Beard demonstrates how to use the knowledge and tools of the historian to examine issues and offer solutions to social problems. "Votes for Workingwomen" appeared in an issue of* The Woman Voter *that was entirely devoted to concerns of wage earners. In this piece Beard tries to show suffragists how to win over unsympathetic working-class men to the cause of woman suffrage. She develops her position with the use of historical evidence. Just as the middle class needed political power to confront kings and barons, just as working-class men needed political power to protect themselves from property owners, so do workingwomen need political power, in the form of the vote, to protect their particular interests. Many workingmen do not realize that they are as resistant to the call for woman suffrage as their opponents were at one time resistant to their workingmen's demands.*

The very men whose "wives, daughters, sisters and sweethearts are working in . . . factories, laundries, canneries and shops . . . will tell workingwomen that a woman's place is in the home," despite the reality that men's wages are insufficient to permit women to remain at home.

Beard argues that workingwomen's needs are somewhat different from those of their brothers. Women need a public voice to deal with such concerns as "the white slave traffic, mothers' pensions, unemployment, education, child labor, war, the tariff . . . pure food and water, city planning, parks and playgrounds . . . transportation and the policing of cities."

Beard's reference in the article to workingmen as the "natural protectors" of workingwomen suggests a premise about male and female roles that she did not ordinarily hold. It is possible that she accepted this view at this time in her life but in none of her other writings does she use either the phrase or the concept of men as "natural protectors" of women.

There was a time, not long ago, when workingmen could not vote, and were regarded by the government as unworthy of notice, except when

1. "Votes for Workingwomen," *The Woman Voter*, Vol. 3, September, 1912, pp. 3–5.

they broke the law. Only property owners and direct tax payers voted. The workingmen did not like this for they thought they were human beings like the men who did vote and, besides, it went hard with them when all the laws were made for and by property owners. Once in a while the men who did all the voting passed a law to help their brothers but this did not happen often and the service didn't go very far.

Now men who own no land, no big tools, no machinery and no property have to live by selling their own labor and they have to live under whatever conditions their employers say unless they too can make laws and help elect the right men to enforce them. So some of the workingmen of New York decided that they wanted to vote.

This scandalized the property owners who had done all the voting up to that time. They thought they had managed things all right and they grew very angry because "rough and ignorant" workingmen wanted to have a say about the laws under which they lived.

You see the property owners and direct taxpayers thought they knew what was good for workingmen better than the workingmen knew themselves. . . . Of course all workingmen did not care about voting. Some of them laughed at the idea and said: "Oh, why should we bother about it? We don't know how to, anyway." The agitators had right on their side, nevertheless, and in 1826 white workingmen won the right to vote in New York. Labor has not been the corrupting influence in politics since that date. It is the one thing we need more of.

Now, very few men in New York, even workingmen, know this story; partly because the right to vote came before they were born; partly because many of them have but recently come from foreign lands and know little of American history; and partly because the history of the suffrage has not yet been written. Even some of our big politicians do not know this story and they say that God gave all men the right to vote just because they were men. As a matter of fact each group of men—first the middle class and then the workers—has had to organize and demand more *"votes for men"* with such vigor that those who did all the voting up to that time were afraid to refuse. Close by us in Rhode Island the workingmen had actually to fight before they got the vote.[2]

---

2. Reference is to The Dorr Rebellion. In Rhode Island, when those in power refused to liberalize the franchise, violence erupted. As a result a new constitution was ratified in 1843, incorporating almost universal manhood suffrage.

Unfortunately these very workingmen who have had, for so short a time, the right to vote are just as contemptuous of workingwomen as their bosses were in the old days contemptuous of workingmen. By voting and recently by forming independent political labor parties workingmen are gradually winning a position of respect in the community. They are making their need felt and, just because they are afraid of losing their power if they don't, politicians are now talking about workmen's compensation, industrial insurance, safety appliances, the right of workers to organize and other labor questions.

Still, few of the workingmen realize how many and what kind of laws and social organization they need. They know very little about government yet. They don't understand that they could force the government to concern itself with the food, clothing and shelter, hours and the steady employment of the people as much as it concerns itself with battleships, forests, canals and protection for manufacturers.

It is just because workingmen don't know their own power and have so little imagination that they are so scornful of the idea of their women folks voting. The very men whose wives, daughters, sisters and sweethearts are working in the factories, laundries, canneries and shops of this city and state will tell workingwomen that a woman's place is in the home, when these men themselves haven't enough wages to make it possible for their women folk to stay at home and live. Why, even their children have to work in factories and tenement shops that the fathers and mothers may have bread. And then there are all the unmarried girls who are the bread winners for old fathers and invalid brothers and brothers who must go to school. There are the widows with their little children and sons to educate and the countless women who have to earn for themselves every cent they have in the world.

What would all these women do in the home to-day? Starve. Every workingman knows it at heart, if he stops to think. But some workingmen think that their women folk don't know enough to vote and so one finds ignorant little boys of fourteen feeling superior to the mothers who bore them, who toil for them and who lie awake at night planning for their future.

There is so much for the workers—men and women—to do together! In a world where young working girls look on marriage as a terror because of the low family incomes and with high resolve refuse to consider matrimony which involves the rearing of children in vile tenements; where young women burdened with the family support shudder at the thought of invalidity or old age; where thousands of mothers after the day's work spend their nights on their knees scrubbing the office buildings of the metropolis; where poverty, tuberculosis, venereal and other diseases, vice and crime stare the workers constantly in the face, it is grievous indeed that the women who suffer most from these conditions of life and labor are so indifferent to political remedies. Still more grievous is it to hear workingmen, their natural protectors, refuse to listen to appeals for votes for working women.

It is just as bad to be a political pauper as any other kind but this is what workingwomen and other disfranchised women are. That is, they have no power to help themselves. They must wait until some one else becomes interested in their problems. What would have happened if the middle class had waited until kings and barons were ready to look out for it? What would be their hope to-day if workingmen had to wait until the bosses were ready to provide them with all the decencies of life? Workingmen do wait for their bosses to-day to put through labor legislation; *but they don't have to wait*. They have the political power which would enable them at any moment they saw fit to send representatives to make laws about housing, hours, safety appliances, fire prevention, child labor, education, health and a thousand other things to make life more worth living for them.

Just last winter when measures for fire prevention were proposed, however, after the Triangle disaster,[3] it was the women who were interested in the protection of their sisters who had to assume the responsibility for getting workingmen to attend committee meetings and make their voices felt in the legislature. Yet these workingmen who so reluctantly took action roared with laughter at the idea of votes for women even though they relied on the wisdom, perseverance and tact of the women to see the measures through the legislature.

Workingwomen need to see workingmen as they are—their faults along with their virtues. *Workingwomen need to vote*, in the first place, because their brothers regard them as inferiors and the vote will win more

3. In 1911 a fire in the Triangle Shirt Waist factory took the lives of 147 workers, most of them girls and young women.

respect from them. In the second place, they need to vote because the vote will give them more independence and self-respect. In the third place, they need the vote for what it can do for them. They must make political issues as their brothers are doing. The white slave traffic, mothers' pensions, unemployment, education, child labor, war, the tariff and all else that affects the cost of living, pure food and water, city planning, parks and playgrounds, employers' liability, transportation and the policing of cities are but a few of the matters which vitally affect working-women and will never be dealt with to their advantage until they make themselves felt as human beings with minds and hearts; with a right to equal opportunities with other human beings; and a right to life, liberty and the pursuit of happiness.

When their little girls will sell their bodies for a few cents worth of recreation because it is so hard to get; when the life of the street becomes more remunerative and attractive than an honest life of toil; when their babies have no chance to be well-born; when marriage can no longer be afforded, it is high time that workingwomen woke up to the situation and demanded a voice in public affairs.

3. Have Americans Lost Their Democracy?[1]

NOTE: *This article was rejected by* Pearson's Magazine *in 1913 because, as the letter of rejection said, "we have all the material of this general kind for which we have space." The article was probably never published.*

With an uncharacteristic tone of anger, Beard compares the vastly different receptions of two European rebels touring the United States to solicit support for their individual causes. In 1851 Louis Kossuth, national hero of the unsuccessful Hungarian rising against Austria, was brought to the United States as guest of the nation. Although he did not get the money he sought, his tour was triumphant. "Even the women of the land . . . showed their loyalty to men" by their enthusiastic welcome, says Beard.

In 1913 the English suffragist, Emmeline Pankhurst, the second rebel, toured the United States. "Do the cannons boom? Do the hosts outpour to hear her eloquence. . . . Do the City Fathers tender her a banquet?" Indeed not, and largely because the deeds of women are not esteemed. "We refuse to accept female heroes." In addition, "when men take to war and women to industry and books," it is military deeds that are valued. In other times, when "men take to industry and to books," it is industrial and scientific progress, not violent struggle, that is valued. Kossuth's visit coincided with worldwide revolutionary struggle. Pankhurst came at the end of a prolonged period of peace.

Very different strategies also distinguish the two rebels. As a revolutinary leader, Kossuth "destroyed life rather than property" in his dedication to the principle of free government. The English suffragists, persisting in what Beard describes as feminine values, "persistently refused to take life," devoting their energies instead to assaulting property. In later writings, Beard qualified her definition of masculine and feminine attributes to forge a more complicated explanation of human behavior.

While living in England from 1900 to 1902, Mary Beard met and worked with Emmeline Pankhurst. In fact, Beard played an instrumental role in arranging for the Pankhurst tour that is the subject of the article. Their close working relationship and Beard's personal involvement in the tour no doubt explain the pervasive tone of rancor and indignation.

---

1. Typescript of this article is in the Woman's Party papers, Manuscript Division, Library of Congress.

Americans have either very short memories or no historical knowledge. Were they possessed of one or the other, a quick recognition of the contrast in their reception of two European rebels would come to their minds.

Louis Kossuth, the former of these rebels, came to our shores in 1851. On his arrival, salutes were fired from the fortification in the New York harbor; the municipal council turned out en masse to welcome him; public and private buildings flaunted gay decorations in his honor; a vast procession of clerical, educational, industrial, military and civic bodies escorted him through the streets to his hotel; the freedom of the city was extended to him; and speeches filled with effusive praise of so illustrious a guest were deliverd by men prominent in public life. Louis Kossuth, moreover, came not of his own volition. An American war ship, the Mississippi, had been sent all the way to Turkey to fetch him from gaol, although he was being treated kindly by the Sultan who liked him.

It was no less a person than William H. Seward who urged the Senate of which he was a member to welcome Kossuth in a manner befitting the pretensions of the United States as a liberty-loving nation. . . .

Senator Seward . . . [explained that] Kossuth was fighting, as he had fought from his earliest days, for voluntary, representative government and that such a principle should still move the hearts of American people.

Even the women of the land joined in welcoming the foreign defender of that principle and their souls throbbed again with the cries: "No taxation without representation" and "Government by the consent of the governed." Thus they showed their loyalty to men.

Enthusiastic ovations greeted Kossuth not only in New York, for he went as far west as Ohio and Kentucky carrying his revolutionary fire and appealing for support for the rights of man. He was invited to speak before state legislatures, in leading churches and before civic bodies of all kinds. The national capital lionized him. He addressed the Senate and was tendered a Congressional banquet. Wherever he appeared there was the greatest enthusiasm on the part of men and women who vied with one another to prove to him the ardor of their affections. . . .

Kossuth's most unique speech was delivered before the Ladies of Pittsburgh. In that address, he dwelt not as much upon the fervor that he felt for political liberty for men. It was a very practical appeal to the women of the United States to perform their usual and reputable function of raising money that the political liberty of Hungarian men might be promoted. He was to be but a temporary visitor as every one knew, his one desire being to secure funds for a renewal of hostilities and to return to the scene of strife. . . . Kossuth destroyed life rather than property but because he believed steadfastly and desperately in voluntary government through consent of the governed and was willing to suffer for that principle and to kill for it if need be, he fired the imagination of the American public in a way that seems incredible to us today. Yet this was only sixty years ago.

We did not object to the established fact that in the eyes of the Austrian government he was a murderer—a criminal. He was not guilty of moral turpitude in our eyes. We gloried in him. We gave him gifts and urged him on. We couldn't say enough or do enough—we men and we women.

Emmeline Pankhurst, the other rebel, comes to our shores in the year 1913. Do the cannons boom? Do the hosts outpour to hear her eloquence or catch the inspiration of her appeal to the instincts of liberty supposedly so strong in every man? Do the City Fathers tender her a banquet and present her with a little wax figure representing a militant knocking the hat off the head of Asquith as a merry jest? No, we have learned dignity in our new country and, with it, conservatism.

The principle of the political rights of man for which our ancestors fought, aided and abetted by Frenchmen and by our own women, and for which Kossuth fought, aided and abetted by American men and women, is a cherished memory for us and for Hungarians. The principle for which Emmeline Pankhurst fights—the political rights of women—is meaningless. At the time that Kossuth came, he seemed to many the leader of a lost cause. At the time that Pankhurst comes, she, too, seems to many the leader of a lost cause. That made no difference in public opinion in the case of the former.

The trouble may not be after all that our memories or our historical knowledge are weak. Can it be, merely, that this is a man's world still and that the deeds women do are not of public worth? In military stages of society, when men take to war and women to industry and books and culture, it is deeds of military valor that count. The priest with his books is laughed at as an old woman, for what women do is silly. In peaceful stages of society, when men take to industry and to books and to culture, it is talk and learning that count. Now talk has driven some of our English sisters to war for their liberty but it is books that count these days for men still count most and men have almost ceased from warfare in western countries.

Louis Kossuth cried: "Give me liberty or give me death." We sent for him, cheered and rewarded him.

Emmeline Pankhurst cries: "Give me liberty or give me death." She too means that literally but she does not propose to fall by the sword, when liberty comes not, in a man's way. She just refuses to eat—a woman's way. Do we cheer her and reward her when she comes among us? Not exactly. We only admit her when masses of suffragists, among whom are many women voters, protest against the order for her exclusion as a common criminal. Having thus grudgingly admitted her, we limit the time of her stay and regulate her freedom of speech during that stay, although it is well known that she is a brilliantly intellectual woman who understands that militancy is not a thing for which we should contend at all times and in all places. We refuse to accept female heroes.

There is so much similarity between the lives of these two rebels—Kossuth and Pankhurst. . . . The difference between the two conflicts has been that the English women have persistently refused to take life, devoting their energies to that less precious but second precious thing—property—in the hope of achieving by rebellion what they had despaired of receiving without. That their appreciation of the relative value of life and property is feminine cannot be denied. What is feminine is hysterical, frenzied, or just idiotic—in a man's world.

4. The Legislative Influence of Unenfranchised Women[1]

NOTE: *In this article Mary Beard examines how those without traditional power can nevertheless exert influence and express their collective will. She illustrates her point by examining how unenfranchised women have affected legislation. The kind of evidence that is available to buttress such a position is necessarily imprecise and inexact. Beard must draw upon a variety of "popular conclusions about women's influence" and sift them through her own experience. Some of her conclusions rest upon statements by legislators attesting to the influence of women they have been forced to recognize. She also utilizes information about the importance of unfamiliar individual women, such as Mrs. Albion Fellowes Bacon of Indiana, which comes from Beard's personal involvement in community activities and would ordinarily be unknown to traditional academic writers. In this way Beard enlarges the subject she studies by combining the training of the historian with the experience of the engaged participant. She reflects upon the importance of the cooperation of men and women to achieve a common goal, a theme which recurs in her work. She observes and demonstrates the growing impact on legislation of organized club women throughout the nation, thus anticipating the thesis of her first book,* Woman's Work in Municipalities, *which was published the following year.*

"The long journey from woman's old spheres" is under way, she says, as women, accustomed to indirect influence, increasingly come "to prefer direct action on their own account."

The forces which actually mold and determine legislative policies in modern society are among the deepest mysteries of political science. Generally speaking, men have had the suffrage for nearly a century in the United States, and yet we still talk, and with reason, of "invisible government," "government by public opinion," "government by common counsel," wondering how much numerical majorities at the polls really count for after all. That the "invisible government" is forceful enough and keen enough to defeat again and again solemn judgments made at the polls is patent to all. Our talk about "bossism"

---

1. "The Legislative Influence of Unenfranchised Women," *The Annals of the American Academy of Political and Social Science*, Vol. 56, November, 1914, pp. 54–61.

and "big business in politics" is not mere gossip. Investigation after investigation has revealed the reality of the economic influences in modern legislation. Even the late Senator Platt, always reticent in the presence of inquisitors, admitted that the large sums which he received from the life insurance companies "might" have had some influence on legislation at Albany. Anti-lobby legislation is another piece of testimony to the effect that the "popular will" registered at the polls is not always the "will" registered at the state capitol. The growth of direct government is an evidence of voters' suspicion that other influences than those of the ballot box operate on their "representatives."

If it is true that powerful economic interests, organized and always alert, have often written their will into law, through popular representatives and in spite of popular will, what can we say of the weight of beneficent influences, and particularly the influence of voteless women? If we cannot estimate accurately the weight of popular will expressed at the polls on legislation, or the weight of determined economic interests, how can we hope, with any degree of success, to gauge the intermittent efforts of women to advance or retard the progress of legislation in many fields? In the absence of data of a scientific character, we can only fall back upon certain more or less popular conclusions about women's influence, some of which have arisen from vague opinion or uncertain feelings, only slightly tinged with information.

These conclusions rest in fact upon such readily available data as the following: the testimony of politicians and legislators as to the extent of women's influence which they have been compelled to recognize; individual examples of moral persuasion or statesmanlike wire-pulling on the part of women; organized efforts of women for the accomplishment of definite programs; lobbies in legislative chambers maintained by women; and coöperation with men in organized legislative effort.

Only the most striking instances can be given of the testimony of legislators as to the influence exercised upon them by women. The first example, and probably the most forceful one, that comes to mind is in connection with the extension of the privilege of voting to women. "When women want it they will get it" is admitted even by the most hardened anti. Men on platform committees, men at the primaries, men at the polls, men in their legislative halls and in judiciary committees would gladly escape the importunities of the persistent hordes of women who descend upon them to question them as they go into meeting places or polling booths about their intentions and question them again as they come forth about their acts with regard to the enfranchisement of women. Where women in large organized groups protest vigorously against the extension of the suffrage, their influence is undoubtedly felt in the legislatures and at the polls, and the cry of defense by the legislator and the voter becomes: "Women do not want to vote." . . . Without their constant hammering at every man whom they can reach, women know, and men know and admit, that the franchise would never be extended to women.

The clearest evidence of this fact lies in the pressure now being exerted for the Bristow-Mondell federal amendment to bring enfranchisement more speedily to all the women of the country. Driven by the women who are now included among their voting constituents, and sometimes boldly admitting it, senators and representatives from suffrage states are asking, seriously at last, for this legislation. Driven by fear of the possibility of women soon forming part of their voting constituents, men from suffrage campaign states are espousing the same amendment or hesitating to oppose it hoping for its postponement; while in the South, where neither woman suffrage nor campaign states, in the strict sense of the term, exist, congressmen are beginning to find themselves in a dilemma owing to the growing support of the amendment among the women of their districts and the additional and more potent fact that the women voters of the North are questioning the attitude of the Democratic party toward the amendment—thus making suffrage a serious issue in view of the present and possible electoral vote to be determined by voting women in 1916. In national politics, then, the influence of women on legislation dealing with their own enfranchisement is plainly seen. It is this which led the Virginia member of the judiciary committee in the House of Representatives to exclaim in committee last spring: "I shall no longer be responsible for holding up this discussion in the House."

Further testimony to the part borne by women in their own enfranchisement is given by Colonel Roosevelt[2] in his recent statement to leading women of the Progressive party in New York:

2. Reference is to Theodore Roosevelt. As Republican Vice-President, he succeeded to the Presidency after the assassination of William McKinley in 1901. He ran for President and won on his own in 1908. In 1912 he ran again on the newly formed Progressive party ticket and lost to Woodrow Wilson. The platform of the Progressive party included a plank supporting woman suffrage.

"I believe that the surest way of bringing about a realization of one feature of the Progressive party program, that of securing the vote for women, is the constant development of what are already the social and industrial activities of women within the Progressive party."

The strongest argument in its favor, thus set forth by the men who incorporated the suffrage feature into the Progressive platform, is the influence of women on other legislation.

Representative government is, to some extent at least, a government by petition, legislators responding to personal appeals from individuals and organizations when they are powerful enough to arouse interest or alarm. National as well as state legislation has been effected in this way by women. . . .

Of course women are not the only senders of appeals to congressmen. They are wise enough to know that, in most cases, congressmen are more affected by men whose votes elect or defeat them. Women therefore prod busy men into letter-writing and the transmission of telegrams. They seek out influential men and see that their messages are sent. . . .

In addition to the indirect influence of petitions, there are instances, that are interesting though rare, of the direct accomplishment of legislation by individual voteless women. Mrs. Albion Fellowes Bacon, of Indiana, practically single-handed, secured the first tenement house laws of value for Evansville and Indianapolis. She did this before the National Housing Association, of which she is now a director, was formed. The recent improvements in the Indiana housing legislation are due apparently to her continued leadership and to the public opinion which she has helped to create. In her case it was personal initiative and moral persuasion.

Another example of personal influence on legislation exerted by women is that of Frances Perkins of New York in her fight for the Fifty-Four Hour bill for the women workers of her state. Unlike Mrs. Bacon, Miss Perkins represented a society—the Consumers League—which asked for this measure, and she was supported in her demand by the Women's Trade Union League and other organizations. The measure would have been defeated, however, as is widely known and acknowledged in New York, had it not been for the personal sagacity and watchfulness of Miss Perkins who captured a senator of dominating power and prevented his escape in a taxi to the station in time to restore him to his seat in the chamber—his vote on the floor bringing with him the votes he controlled. More than one refugee has been escorted back to his duties by women sentinels when legislation on which they were determined has been up for a vote. In such cases the woman's influence lies not in physical force, for she has never been seen to lay hands upon the recalcitrant legislator, but in the occasional subservience of the mind of man to the actual presence of a moral force.

Organized efforts, however, are ordinarily more effective than individual prowess, and women as well as men have learned this fact. Whoever will take the trouble to examine the files of *The American Club Woman*, the organ of the women's clubs of the United States, which records the doings of women's clubs all over the country, cannot fail to be impressed with the drift of women's activities in the direction of legislative action. Societies formed to study Browning or Shakespeare soon begin to be concerned about local improvements of one kind or another. They become interested, for example, in the inadequate recreational facilities of their town or city, and when they begin to act in the matter they usually find it necessary to secure positive legislation or at least appropriations, and thus they are led into bringing their influence to bear either upon the state legislature or the local council. . . .

It is safe to say, therefore, that in the progress of modern social legislation of all kinds—the extension of educational functions, pure food laws, mothers' pensions, development of recreational facilities, labor laws, particularly for women and children, and measures directed against prostitution—not a single important statute has been enacted without the active support of women, organized and unorganized. This much we may say without attempting to apportion to women the exact weight of their influence.

Important as has been that influence, there can be no doubt that in cases of serious labor legislation affecting large employing interests, women's weight has been almost negligible in many instances. Indeed, one of the New York legislators, in a very friendly and confidential talk with the representatives of the Women's Trade Union League, told them that the 35,000 voteless women whom they represented naturally could not carry the same weight as thirty-five voting men. It was just such frank statements as this that turned Florence Kelley and many leading social workers, who sought legislation in their various fields, into ardent suffragists.

Other social workers, anxious to accomplish immediate results and unwilling to wait for universal suffrage, have discovered that one of the best ways to increase women's influence in legislation is to join associations which include men as well as women, even if they have to do all of the work. How far this is consciously done one cannot say, but it remains a fact that much of women's effective legislative work is done in connection with those organizations which draw no sex lines. The weight of women in such societies is evidenced by the number of important executive positions which they hold in local, state, and national organizations for the promotion of public health, education, recreation, housing reform, and the improvement of labor conditions.

In child labor organizations, hospital organizations seeking larger appropriations for social service, anti-tuberculosis work, labor legislation committees, the prevailing testimony, even from women, is to the effect that "we consider our greatest strength in the fact that our work is done by the cooperation of men and women."

With such evidence as we now have before us, we may say truly that women's influence on legislation has grown, is growing, and will grow. This is not very definite in itself, but it marks a long journey from woman's old spheres, the three Ks. And it is interesting to note that those women most actively using indirect influence are coming to prefer direct action on their own account.

5. The Congressional Union[1]

NOTE: *There was so little interest in the federal amendment for woman suffrage that, after 1896, Congressional committees ceased even reporting on it. After 1897 there were no debates on the Senate floor; the House had never debated the issue. Instead, the National American Women Suffrage Association directed its attention to woman suffrage referenda within individual states and offered little support at the federal level. Mrs. William Kent, chairman in 1912 of NAWSA's Congressional Committee, which was responsible for action on the federal amendment, "was given $10 for expenses connected with [Congressional] hearing and refunded change at the end of her term!"*[2]

But the Congressional Committee was soon revitalized by young, energetic Alice Paul, recently returned from three years with the militant wing of the British suffrage movement, where she not only was repeatedly jailed but had also, as had other militants, gone on hunger strikes. She succeeded Mrs. Kent as head of the Congressional Committee. Under Alice Paul's leadership, the Congressional Committee moved away from the national organization and in 1913 took the name Congressional Union (CU). Mary Beard, who had been one of the five members selected for the earlier Congressional Committee, joined with Paul in establishing the Congressional Union.

The CU demanded a full-scale campaign for the immediate passage of the federal suffrage amendment. NAWSA continued its earlier strategy of support for both state and federal suffrage action. In a short time the profound differences between the two groups became clear, for the Congressional Union insisted that all suffrage activity be focused on Congress and the President. By 1914 the two organizations went very separate ways.

Efforts to reconcile the two groups proved futile, as different, and quite antagonistic, strategies evolved. The Congressional Union developed a position, patterned after the political line of the British suffrage movement,

---

1. "The Congressional Union," *The Woman Voter*, Vol. 7–8, January, 1916, pp. 14–15.

2. Eleanor Flexner, *Century of Struggle: The Woman's Rights Movement in the United States*, New York: Atheneum, 1971, p. 263.

that held the "party in power" responsible for failure to pass a woman suffrage bill. Translated to the American political scene in 1914, it meant that the CU held the Democratic party and its head, Woodrow Wilson, responsible for the success or failure of woman suffrage.

Starting in 1914, the Congressional Union and its successor, the Woman's Party, campaigned against all Democratic candidates for Congress, regardless of their individual attitudes toward woman suffrage. It is in this context that Beard concludes this article with the call for "Suffrage First." The CU sent organizers into the nine Western states where full woman suffrage had been won to swing the women's vote against all candidates on the Democratic ticket. When twenty-three of the forty-three Western Democrats were defeated, the CU claimed credit.

And the purpose of such strategy? As Alice Paul said at a political rally in Rhode Island during the summer of 1914: "party leaders . . . will know that we have . . . realized [the] power that we possess, and they will know that by 1916 we will have it organized. The mere announcement of the fact that the Suffragists of the East have gone West with this appeal will be enough to make every man in Congress sit up and take notice."3

The goal of the organization was to bring the woman suffrage amendment, whether or not Wilson approved and whether or not it would pass, to the floor of Congress. The strategy succeeded; the bill lost, but only by one vote in the Senate and twenty-eight in the House.

In 1915 the Congressional Union began its high-powered drive in all forty-eight states. Elaborate demonstrations were organized nationwide to coordinate with a full-scale petition drive that culminated with a march to the Capitol on May 9 and a presentation of the collected signatures to Wilson. During this time, the more conservative, more tepid work of the NAWSA was overshadowed by the militant, dramatic, unyielding strategy of the CU. The Eastern suffrage referendum campaigns conducted in 1915 by NAWSA in New York, New Jersey, Massachusetts, and Pennsylvania all lost.

All though this period, Mary Beard worked consistently, from a position of responsible leadership, with the militant Congressional Union and, later, with the Woman's Party–speaking frequently throughout the country, writing in behalf of the Congressional Union, as in the article below, and doing any kind of political work needed by the organization. For example, she was chosen by the Woman's Party, at an open air rally in front of the Hotel McAlpin in New York City in 1917, to call upon Republican Senator William Musgrave Calder, recently elected to the

3. Speech delivered at Newport, Rhode Island, August 29, 1914, reprinted in *The Suffragist*, September 12, 1914, and quoted in Flexner, *Century of Struggle*, p. 268.

*United States Senate from New York, to urge him to work for and vote for
the national suffrage amendment.*

*By late 1917, when the CU adopted even more militant tactics—
picketing the White House, hunger strikes, bonfires—Beard had drifted
from the organization. However, it is not at all clear that the shift in CU
tactics was in any way responsible for her decision.* Woman's Work in
Municipalities, *which appeared in 1915, two years before the CU shift to
extreme tactics, already marks the move away from political activism.*

*The article reprinted here discusses, explains, and defends the position
of the Congressional Union.*

The Congressional Union claims a distinct and vital place in the suffrage
movement for two reasons: (1) because it works solely for the Federal
amendment, and (2) because it works politically.

The Congressional Union works only for the Federal amendment
because it considers that a quicker, more economical and more certain
way of securing an extension of suffrage in the United States. It does not
believe that state and national work go hand in hand necessarily. Each
successive failure to win in a campaign state increases the obstacles in the
way of a Federal amendment. State work does not, therefore, inevitably
promote a Federal amendment. . . .

An organization that is working for the Federal and state amendments
at the same time will find that one or the other holds its major interest and
gets the bulk of its money. It is easily surmised where that major interest
will lie. One phase of the work will lag behind, and if the referendum
loses one time, its second trial must absorb still more of the attention and
energy and money of its supporters.

The Congressional Union, therefore, refuses to attempt to work for
the two things. It chooses the Federal way exclusively at this moment
because it believes that there is an extraordinary political situation which
justifies that course. It chooses the Federal way, too, because it wishes to
save women's time, money and nervous strength. The Federal way has
other advantages: a progressive education, for suffragists, in politics and
government; a broadening of the mental horizon from local to National
issues; a concerted and intelligent move on the part of women throughout
the country; and an opponent who is a responsible representative voting in
the open.

If the political diagnosis of the Congressional Union is correct, the
Federal way will prove quicker than the state by state method. Its

advocates do not deplore any possible haste now in winning the vote, for they feel that the women of Chicago, in possession of the ballot, are being educated as much by its use as are the women of New York who can only ask for it. So the Congressional Union concentrates on Congress. If the Federal amendment fails, suffragists can fall back upon State referenda. The converse is not true.

The Congressional Union, moreover, works to secure favorable action in Congress by political pressure. That also represents to it excellent chances of victory coupled with economy and dignity of effort. President Cleveland was elected by 1,049 votes; President Wilson by a little over two million votes. There are some four million possible women's votes in this crisis we are facing. Disfranchised women do not have to argue, plead or cajole if enfranchised women will but vote under the slogan: "SUFFRAGE FIRST!" Some of them may not. It is not essential that they all do. It is essential that many do and enough will. . . .

The Congressional Union believes the Federal amendment can be ratified by enough states. It has taken that matter into consideration as a vital part of its emphasis upon the Federal way. It is not a band of dreamers or youthful fanatics.

All sorts of objections are raised against the policies of the Congressional Union, naturally. Enthusiasts of the state referendum place their hope of victory in education and its "ultimate" triumph over selfish economic and political interests. They may be content with a progressive vote. Education is their real aim, and not suffrage first. . . .

Enthusiasts of the Federal way place their hope of victory in immediate political necessities which strengthen all the older and more abstract appeals by women. They are willing to get the vote through representatives of the "people" and let the vote itself educate.

The tactics of the Congressional Union have been sometimes called an English importation, not applicable to American conditions and to American government. It is even disputed as to whether we have party government at all in this country. This seems almost incredible in face of the facts. . . .

The political tactics of the Congressional Union are abundantly justified by the analyses of the way Congress works made by United States Senators and Congressmen themselves. . . .

The Congressional Union is responsible for recognition now in Washington of the grave political significance of this situation. It has insisted on placing responsibility where it belongs. The Congressional Union has not become thereby a partisan organization. It has merely become an efficient organization. It is strictly non-partisan, in fact, because it asks enfranchised women to put suffrage above party.

In the National political campaign that has already indeed begun, it will not be individuals who will be discussed, but the deeds of the Party as a whole. Why, then, should suffragists alone discuss individuals when they are not the point? The point is: SUFFRAGE FIRST.

6. Statement to the House Committee on Woman Suffrage[1]

NOTE: *Dr. Anna Shaw introduced Mary Ritter Beard to the House Committee on Woman Suffrage, where she addressed the thirteen men of the committee, including its chairman, Edward William Pou, Democratic Congressman from North Carolina. Her statement had two objectives: first, to convince the committee members to bring the federal suffrage bill out of committee to the floor of the House for debate; and, second, to urge the committee members, especially the seven Democrats, to support the legislation.*

Beard was an active member of the Congressional Union. She shared that organization's political position that the "Party in power" was to be held responsible for the fate of the woman suffrage amendment. Thus, her pointed remarks to the seven Democrats on the committee carry a threat that unless they and other Democrats can force their party to support the amendment, all Democrats, whatever their persuasion, will be actively opposed by the Congressional Union. The threats were not without substance, because Democrats had been defeated by the active opposition of this militant woman's group.

Since women have listened for generations to "homilies on our duties," she says with her customary irony, "you gentlemen can afford to listen . . . to discussions about yours." There follows an aggressive, hard-hitting, political statement that reveals the knowledge and skills of a veteran lobbyist. She begins by demonstrating that the Democratic party may not maintain its majority if it does not soon espouse votes for women, so flimsy is its lead. The Progressive party and the Socialist party, both of which support the federal amendment, might draw enough votes from the Democrats to topple their lead, she warns.

The "only dependable bulwark" of the Democratic party, the South, maintain its lead "illegally," she says, in an obvious criticism of the disenfranchisement of the Black electorate. Beard here demonstrates how much more advanced her political views are than those of traditional

---

1. In Sophia Smith Collection, Smith College Library.

Progressives, for whom the suppression of civil rights of Black Americans was of little consequence.

Again, she demands suffrage for women, so they may use it "in the interests of women and children," as men use their vote "in the interest of men and business."

The thrust of her address is to indicate that the "cause of suffrage is the obvious one for you to seize upon, even in desperation, and as a matter purely of political expediency, if you can not accept it from higher motives."

Gentlemen of the committee, I always represent my husband when I speak on suffrage. Just as some of the men of 1776 claimed to believe that they could not maintain their rights in their integrity or discharge their full duties as citizens while sovereignty lay absolutely in the crown of Great Britain, so we women to-day declare that the only way in which the masses of women can be sure of performing their duties to the race properly is by the possession of the same political power that you possess, in order that they may use it in the interests of women and children, as you have used yours in the interest of men and business. Like President Wilson, we want to be our own masters and enjoy the new freedom. We know our duties, and we know these social and economic conditions under which they must be performed. We know our duties, and we will perform them. That is enough to say about our responsibilities. . . . We have come today to talk to you about your duties, and I trust you will see nothing discourteous in the shifting of the attention from us to you. We are actuated in this change of attitude not by a spirit of vindictiveness, but purely by the spirit of fair play. We have listened for untold generations to homilies on our duties. You gentlemen can afford to listen for an hour more to discussions about yours.

Your first responsibility, which I ask you to consider, is that to your party—to the Democratic Party—for it is our task to convince the majority of this committee today rather than the Republican minority. You are loyal members of the Democratic Party, and you want to maintain that party in power. I intend to show you that you can not maintain it in power unless you espouse votes for women as a party measure.

You may ask, "Why may we not do that without taking such a step?" My reply is: First, because the election returns for President Wilson in 1912 revealed the fact that you are in power in Washington with so flimsy a majority that if at the very next presidential election the votes of but one-eighth of the women in the suffrage States are changed from your support, a party that stands for equal suffrage will supplant you in the Nation. The Progressive Party stood second in the race in 1912, and may or may not prove as strong a factor again; but the rehabilitation of the Republican Party will surely draw from the strength given you by voters who gave you their ballots as a protest against Theodore Roosevelt. Furthermore, you will have to count on the possibility of the growth of the Progressive Party. There is also the rising Socialist vote, and the Socialist Party believes in woman suffrage. Socialists are far more likely to draw from your ranks than you are to drain theirs. The second reason why your duty to your party requires you to support the suffrage cause is revealed by a study of the electoral vote of the country. That study is proving intensely interesting to the American women and to all true Democrats.

The facts I have stated show that women voters have been given a shadow rather than the substance of political power by men who meant to play fair. In legislative parlance, we may say that nationally our enfranchised women have been presented with a "gold brick." As an illustration, let us look into certain figures. Let us compare the weight of the individual voter in the suffrage States with the weight of the voter in the Southern States, which are the only dependable bulwark of the Democratic Party. The total vote for President in 1912 in California was 663,065; in Mississippi, 64,319. Mississippi cast about one-tenth the number of votes cast by California, yet Mississippi has 10 electoral votes while California has only 13. The total vote in Oregon for President in 1912—another suffrage State—was 137,040; in Florida the vote was 50,047, yet Florida has 6 electoral votes while Oregon has only 5.

The total vote of Washington in 1912, was 317,925; and of Virginia, 136,976; yet Virginia has 12 electoral votes, and Washington only 7. The total of votes in the five states—Arizona, Utah, Wyoming, Idaho, and Kansas—in 1912 was 647,551. These States have an electoral vote of 24. The total number of votes of the States of South Carolina, North Carolina, Georgia, Alabama, Louisiana, and Florida at the same election was 662,926, about the same number as cast by the States of Arizona, Utah, etc., yet they have 63 electoral votes as against only 24 electoral votes of the Western States I have named. But you say that electoral votes are based on population. So they are; but the South has that unduly large electoral vote illegally. You know what constitutes that illegality. The men of the East also have an undue electoral vote as compared with the people of the suffrage States; but they hold it unethically. Women are disfranchised there, and they are trying to make good that discrepancy by working to enfranchise the women. That is one reason why they are becoming suffrage campaign States.

A little mathematical calculation will readily show that 1 voter in one section of the country counts for as much as some 25 voters in other sections. Knowing this fact, the Democratic Party reposes in a tranquil assurance of power which is only apparent to the most superficial observer. The same calculations will show that when the western women got the right to vote for President and Representatives, they did not get the right to have that vote counted at its full value. These women are not going to be content with government by a party which regards their sex as mental and moral incompetents. In face of this situation what has the Democratic Party to say about the sincerity of its belief in majority rule? If you argue that you do believe in the people in spite of all, we ask in what people?

Whatever your answer as members of the Democratic Party may be, the fact remains that your strength lies in some 13 States, where your men, who can, will not vote. Those 13 States, however, which are the seat of your power, do not represent enough strength to maintain you in the White House and in Congress. Unless you can win Northern support again your chances at the nest election are hopeless. Now, there is not one suffrage State or one suffrage campaign State of which you are at all certain. That counts out 20 States as opposed to your sure 13 States. Nor are you sure of Ohio, Wisconsin, or Michigan, which have been suffrage campaign States and which are keeping up the agitation for the enfranchisement of women. That makes 23 States in which woman suffrage is the livest issue of the day as opposed to your 13 Democratic strongholds. Therefore, the Democratic Party is confronted with this situation: That is, a North and West and East deeply and persistently interested in suffrage, but not really committed to your party; a South committed to you, but not equally aroused on the suffrage question. The South is not able to maintain your national supremacy in spite of its great electoral advantages. Your only hope, therefore, for the next election is to espouse a cause that is popular in all the other sections of the country. The cause of suffrage is the obvious one for you to seize upon, even in desperation, and as a matter purely of political expediency, if you can not accept it from higher motives.

It is not enough, however, for you to accept suffrage in 1916. You will have to make known then your previous achievements as a test of competency to remain in office as the choice of the people of the whole Nation. If in the meantime, therefore, you have worked for the Federal amendment to enfranchise women, you might justly go before the people in 1916 as a Democratic Party prepared to defend the proposition that this should become what it has pretended to be—a Government of the people, by the people, for the people. So much for your duty to the political party with which you are affiliated.

Your second duty, as I see it, is to the House of which you are Members. Now, the prestige of that House in the popular esteem is seriously endangered. On more than one occasion recently public confidence in the superior representative feature of your chamber has been disturbed by your failure to act with the Senate in the interest of the masses. As we look to the immediate future, we observe a new type of Senator entering the portals of the Capitol, one chosen by a wider constituency than any of your Members represent; a man forced to win his election by the direct approval of large groups of people. The senator who now comes to Washington has had to stump his State. He has had to stand for popular measures and obtain the confidence of very many classes in his State. The interests can not make him their spokesman hereafter as easily as they have done in the past. He has become the voter's man. In that respect you and he are not unlike, but he now represents more voters than you, and we may therefore reasonably expect the voters to regard him as the broader type of representative unless you realize the impending rivalry for the confidence of the people.[2] If, instead of becoming the provincial representatives, you awake in time to feel the pulse of public opinion, too, we may indeed look forward to a Democratic régime which will surpass any which our Nation has ever experienced. The test is before you, and nothing will prove to the country your recognition of your true position as representatives of the voters as conclusively as your attitude toward women and the suffrage. The Senate has appointed its committee

2. Reference is to the struggle over passage of what became the Seventeenth Amendment, for the direct election of U.S. Senators. By 1902 the House of Representatives had five times passed resolutions supporting such a constitutional amendment, but each time it was defeated in the Senate. In the period before the ratification of the amendment, which occurred in 1913, many states provided what was, in effect, a direct election of Senators by obliging state legislatures to choose the Senatorial candidate designated by the voters. In fact, by the time the amendment was ratified, most states with large Progressive constituencies were already installing Senators chosen by the general electorate.

to look after this matter. Will you do as much? The approval of the people is no idle dream. . . .

. . . There remains one more important consideration: Your responsibility as individual Democrats, believing in majority rule, government by consent of the governed, by the will of the people at the polls. Obligation to your own sincerity implies some self-analysis. You must see your rightful place in the present political situation. Now, this, your committee, is composed of 13 men. Seven men constitute the deciding vote on our appeal for the establishment of the woman-suffrage committee. These seven belong to the majority, the Democratic Party. One of those seven Democrats comes from a suffrage State, Illinois, where women now have some share in directing the future of the party, and another member comes from a suffrage campaign State, New York, where the Democracy of the State has declared itself in favor of submitting this question to the voters. He will scarcely feel that the national Democratic Party can ignore so important a declaration of the New York State section of his party. I shall, therefore, limit my examination to five gentlemen whose point of view will, in all probability, decide the women's destiny in the House of Representatives, at least for the moment. These five gentlemen all represent one section of the country, and my analysis of them is made in the hope that they will secure a national point of view and help us obliterate sectional feeling.

Who are you, gentlemen, who hesitate to promote, if you do not actually obstruct, our progress with this amendment? In looking over various public records I find that the honored chairman of this committee holds his strategic position as a result of the will expressed at the polls of 7,623 men. Opposite his name should be written: "No opposition." Another of the 5 men comes here through the vote of 13,906 men. Another is sent by the very small group of 6,474 men, and the remaining 2 of the 5 gentlemen represent, respectively, 18,000 and 16,000 men. The total vote behind all 5 of these gentlemen is 63,570. These 63,570 voters, therefore, have the decision of this momentous question. Are they entitled to speak for the Nation? We find that 1 man from the House of Representatives, from the State of Colorado, represents as many votes as all the 5 men who thus control our destiny. Another man from the same State represents nearly as many votes, having been elected by 54,504 Democratic men and women. Sixty-three thousand five hundred and seventy voters have the power of decision as to whether our right to be free in this country shall be discussed honestly in the House of Representatives. They send 5 men to express their will. One hundred and seventeen thousand five hundred and four voters believe in woman suffrage. They send 2 men to express their will. These 5 men happen to be a majority of this Committee on Rules; the 2 men sent by the 117,570 [sic] voters have no say at all, unless the 5 grant them the privilege. Is this democracy? Is this satisfactory congressional procedure?

If you are content with this situation from the standpoint that women only double the vote, and therefore do not really count, let us try some other figures on your form of democratic government. Remember, first, the 63,570 men who have the power of decision over our claim today. Then place against them such votes as that for Congressman Stone, of Illinois, for instance, who was sent by the votes of 20,956; Hobson, of Alabama, with his 10,065 votes; Bailey, of Pennsylvania, with 13,626; and Stevens, of New Hampshire, with 21,794 votes, and the vote of all other suffrage friends from new suffrage States. More votes were cast in Ohio for suffrage, where suffrage did not carry, than were cast in several Southern States for President Wilson. The same thing can be said of Wisconsin and Michigan. The point of it all is this, that the Committee on Rules itself has undergone changes throughout the history of the House.

You know the fight that you Democratic men put up against the combination by the Committee on Rules under the leadership of Speaker Cannon,[3] and you yourselves led that fight against the domination of the Committee on Rules over the House. You are in this same position today of political power. Can you consistently, then, oppose now the things for which you fought so bitterly a short time ago? I have here a list of the committees you appointed. This is called "Congressional committees." We know the committees which you have appointed all through your history—how rapidly you have done it when the changed economic conditions demanded it. I have also here your fight on Speaker Cannon because of his domination of the Committee on Rules, because the Rules Committee was dominating the House. I have also here the report of the

3. "Uncle Joe" Cannon, as Speaker of the House and chairman of the Rules Committee, firmly controlled appointments to committees and debates on legislation. By 1910, progressive Republicans, under the leadership of George W. Norris, opened a debate that went on for thirty hours and ended with Cannon's removal from the Rules Committee, which was thereafter elected by the House. But, since Cannon remained as Speaker and conservative Republicans continued to control major committees, very little change at that time occurred.

Committee on the Judiciary for the special session, showing what work it did, what action it took, how many sittings it held, and all that sort of thing, which proves conclusively that the committee has not time for the consideration of this thing. Furthermore, granting that we could get one of our suffrage men in the House, and others voting with him, to call for a report of the Committee on the Judiciary, you know you value far less a vote that has been dragged out that way, and you know the difficulties in going behind the committee action in that way. I have lobbied in the New York Assembly, and I know those conditions myself as well as all other women who have lobbied.

Gentlemen, we come not as suppliants. We make our request knowing that we have behind us an aggressive section of the Democratic Party; that the party that stood second in 1912 is with us; that we have strong political friends all up and down the country; that we have free women who propose to work for the unfree.

Gentlemen, in the face of all this, we stand pat. It is your move.

7. *Woman's Work in Municipalities*[1]

NOTE: Woman's Work in Municipalities, *published in 1915, was the first book Mary Ritter Beard published alone. (She and Charles Beard jointly wrote* American Citizenship, *which had appeared the previous year.) While Mary Beard continued to work actively with the Woman's Party for woman suffrage, one can see the future course of her life's work taking shape. This volume reflects the transition from a life devoted to narrowly focused political activism to a new view of feminism as a central principle in examining social and historical issues. The activist Mary Beard expresses hope that the book will induce more women to participate in social movements and convince men that women have always made important contributions to public welfare. The feminist theoretician Mary Beard wishes to offer a "new evaluation of woman's work in civilization . . . feeling, seeing, judging, directing, equally with men, all the great social forces."*

"The awakening of women to the low social status of their sex is the most encouraging fact of the century," she writes in perhaps the most important statement in her book.

It is an extraordinary study, overflowing with startling new ideas and still unexplored ways of looking at the familiar. It comes out of her years in the woman suffrage movement and the trade union movement. For the first time, the varied activities of club women all across the nation and the experiences of women in assorted organizations are pulled together, observed, and analyzed. The pattern that emerges is recorded clearly and simply. The selections below only hint at the richness of the material in the complete book.

For example, the anti-noise movement must not be confined to the middle class, she warns, for "jaded nerves are to be found in large numbers among the factory men and women and boys and girls whose daily bread is won amid the incessant din of wheels and engines."

She points out that it is ludicrous to lecture overworked, burdened

---

1. *Woman's Work in Municipalities*, New York and London: D. Appleton & Co., 1915. Selections are from the following pages: vi–vii; 3-5; 10-11; 22-23; 34; 43; 45-47; 56; 61; 94-95; 97; 100-101; 112; 115; 117; 124; 130-132; 134; 201-202; 220-222; 227; 256-257; 259-260; 265-266; 286; 318; 330-331.

mothers on the virtues of nursing their babies. "No philanthropy will solve the requirements of infant welfare when poverty . . . [is] the root of the problem. Thus, "babies' milk . . . becomes essentially a social-economic problem."

To those who are willing to permit prostitution on the ground that "our own daughters" are thereby protected, she says, "All women are [our] daughters." Recognizing that prostitution is more closely connected to poverty than to morality, she sees industrial training, housing reform, improved labor conditions, recreation facilities, minimum wages, and mothers' pensions as more reasonable responses than high-minded moralizing.

In an insight that is still pertinent today, she notices that, in relation to crimes against women and girls, "there is no class line. . . . No group or class of women has escaped the ravages." As a result, a "feeling of solidarity [has] evolved" among women. But that sense of sisterhood has, unfortunately, not yet developed in the fight against poverty, because the "sting" of poverty remains "a class experience."

The book is primarily a "story of woman's achievements and visions . . . an assembling of hitherto disconnected threads and an attempt at the classification of civic efforts." It describes women's efforts to establish kindergartens for the education of the young, adult education schools for new immigrants, and schools for teaching industrial training. It describes women's work in founding libraries. It examines the process by which women have been drawn into movements for a comprehensive public health program. It describes women's efforts to establish municipal recreational facilities to stimulate "community spirit and an increase in the real joy of living."

Housing reform, spearheaded by women, requires surveys to accumulate needed data, and women are better equipped at that because "of the greater readiness of women to admit women into the secrets of the home. . . . Women can best understand women's and children's needs." The new field of social service, essentially staffed by women, in turn leads to the need for other personnel trained in sociology, economics, health, education, community hygiene, and city planning. So many crimes are offenses against women and children, Beard says, that it makes sense for women to take an interest in criminal law and correction, and to demand police matrons, women physicians in courts, and perhaps, ultimately, women on the police force.

Certain themes recur in the detailed description of women's work in municipalities. There is, first, the perspective of class. There is, second, the recognition of the social nature of individual needs. Questions of *recreation, prostitution, education, housing, social service, infant mortality, are all social problems that need collective, community solutions. Third, she points out that the women reformers engaged in community activity gradually became aware of how little could be accomplished alone and how necessary organization was to accomplish any genuine social reform. And as social action takes that organized form, it becomes even clearer to the women involved that they need the vote to protect and extend their reform activities. In the process of working through indirect political means, middle-class reform women are often converted into ardent suffragists as they realize that "municipal housekeeping" is handled through elected officials.*

Beard returns at the end of the book to her persistent assertion of woman's distinct interest in society. When women ultimately occupy, as they will, positions in municipal life in proportion to their numbers, "they will [not] be better or wiser, but . . . there will always be certain things where children are concerned which they will know more about and care more about than men."

FROM THE PREFACE

If this new evaluation of woman's work in civilization seems to err on the side of women, we shall be satisfied if it helps to bring about a re-evaluation which shall include women not in an incidental way but as people of flesh and blood and brain—feeling, seeing, judging and directing, equally with men, all the great social forces which mold character and determine general comfort, well-being and happiness.

Whichever evaluation is ultimately accepted, the following data are offered not for the purpose of imparting an inflated sense of woman's importance. Indeed, in spite of what she has done, woman must still feel humble in the presence of the work outlined for the future and of the human problems that appeal to her for solution. Instead, therefore, of seeking to inspire an exaggerated ego by means of this story of woman's achievements and visions, it is told in the hope that, by the assembling of hitherto disconnected threads and an attempt at the classification of civic efforts, more women may be induced to participate in the social movements that are changing the modes of living and working and playing, and that those who have watched their own threads too closely, may perhaps lift their eyes long enough to look at the whole social fabric which they are helping to weave.

Finally the story is told in the hope that more men may realize that women have contributions of value to make to public welfare in all its forms and phases, and come to regard the entrance of women into public life with confidence and cordiality, accepting in their coöperation, if not in their leadership, a situation full of promise and good cheer.

FROM CHAPTER I: EDUCATION

If the teaching by women in the schools has been narrow, ineffective, and unsuited to the realities of American life, the responsibility lies in part upon the colleges and normal schools that train them, and these institutions, in administration and curricula, have been largely dominated by men. By concentration of attention upon unapplied and inapplicable natural science, narrative history, English literature, and empty "methods," women actually have been deprived of the educational opportunity for discovering what the world is really like. It will be only when more women alive to the necessities of modern social life, industry, and government gain some power in the training colleges and schools that curricula will be devised to supply the needs of women teachers for the great tasks that, in present day society, fall upon them.

* * *

Although we talk of equal educational opportunities for men and women, as a matter of fact in many states, particularly in the East and South, there is nothing approaching equal facilities. There are many "opportunities" for education in most states, it is true, but until the *best* opportunities are open to women, there is nothing like equality. In states where adequate facilities are not open, we find women awaking to the obligation to see that they are soon provided through public or private funds.

* * *

Moreover, when the charge of inefficiency is brought against women teachers, it must be remembered that the administration of the schools very largely has been in the hands of men, and the women have been merely routine agents of the authorities. The type of person always content to carry out some other person's orders is not likely to have either force or initiative. Women seem to have both. Women are no longer content to be mere agents of school authorities. They are seeking and obtaining high administrative positions, and demonstrating by their efficiency and capacity for sustained and unselfish labors their fitness for such work.

* * *

The kindergarten idea appealed from the beginning to women and private experimentation along that line was one of their most successful endeavors. Boards of education have in instance after instance been persuaded to incorporate into the public school system the plan of kindergartens demonstrated to be practical and of social utility by women in their private capacities. Annie Laws, in the *Kindergarten Review*, states that she "can trace the social spirit of the kindergartner as an important factor in stimulating, and in some cases, even initiating, many of the social movements of today, among them playgrounds, social centers, vacation schools, public libraries, mothers' clubs and school and home gardens." The New York Kindergarten Association of today, like many others, is composed of men and women but largely supported by the latter, financially, as well as by active service.

* * *

Special schools for foreigners have generally been started by women, we feel safe in claiming, after a review of all the evidence at hand. The Civic Club of Allegheny County, Pennsylvania, composed of men and women, inaugurated the work among foreigners in Pittsburgh and Allegheny, but the women seem to have given most of the time necessary to make it a success.

* * *

So many organizations claim credit for the first vacation school that we shall make no effort to locate it. We do know that the Social Science Club of Newton, Massachusetts, a woman's club, has maintained a vacation school for seventeen years. In Chicago the Civic Federation opened one vacation school in 1896, the first in Chicago. The next was opened by the University Settlement. In 1898 the women's clubs took up the work and opened five schools. . . .

While women's clubs have long been interested in the vacation school, most credit for it is due to the hundreds of women teachers who have given of their services to make it helpful to the child and to the community. These teachers have often, and nearly always in the beginning, given their services without compensation and where they have been paid a salary they have generally taught for less money than they would have received for regular winter classes.

With these summer school teachers, women librarians cooperate as do visiting nurses and other social workers. The children are taken by their teachers on municipal excursions, often too, to visit places of public interest and gain some idea of municipal enterprise and government.

All-year-round schools are projects now in the air which are a natural combination of regular and vacation schools.

* * *

Women are also actively connected with the National Society for the Promotion of Industrial Education. Under Miss Cleo Murtland, assistant secretary of the Society, a study of the dress and waist industry was made by the New York committee of the Society, and that study together with a study of the cloak, suit and skirt industry, made under the direction of Charles Winslow of the United States Department of Labor, have resulted in a practical program for factory schools which has been approved both by the unions and the manufacturers.

An illustration of the necessity of the woman's point of view being brought into the discussion and organization of vocational training and guidance is afforded by the criticism made by Alice Barrows Fernandez, of the Vocational Education Survey, in reviewing the report of Dr. Schneider, of the School Inquiry, on "Trade Schools."

"It is unfortunate that Dr. Schneider's report, which is so valuable in regard to boys' vocational training, is no different from other reports on the subject of training for girls. One and all devote themselves to what is to be done for boys, and then in an aside mention the girls. Out of every four persons at work in this city one is a woman, and out of every four women here one is earning her livelihood. You can't dismiss 400,000 women in a parenthesis. This will happen as long as there are not more women on the Board of Education, more women who are workers engaged in gainful employment.''

* * *

No survey of women's work for education would be complete without some mention of their part in promoting the circulation of good books. The educational work which women have done through libraries is both great and obvious, although the public that profits by them may not fully realize the number of traveling libraries and stationary and circulating libraries that women have directly established.

The first large concerted movement on the part of the club women was for the extension of education through books and scarcely a woman's club in the country fails to report an initial activity in that direction. In little log cabins on the frontiers as well as in splendid buildings in the cities books have been housed and distributed among readers by the earnest efforts of women whose culture early ceased to be individual; that is, they were anxious to pass on to the multitudes such culture as they themselves possessed.

With their interest in reading and encouraging the reading habit in others, women have helped to develop a wonderful social service for the library. As truly as any other group of social workers, librarians are educators and physicians of mind and body.

* * *

FROM CHAPTER II: PUBLIC HEALTH

It has been through conferences, conventions and publications that women have gained an appreciation of the manifold activities that must be included in any comprehensive public health program, but they have been led up to the point of effective participation in health conferences through their own practical experiences.

In the first place, the self-preservative interest or the mere instinct for a proper environment has forced women into public health activities; in the second place, they have done their health work well considering their own indirect influences, the opposition of interests, and popular indifference; in the third place, they have sought to avoid duplication of effort by establishing clearing houses for information and guidance for themselves and for the public; in the fourth place, they have moved step by step into the municipal government itself, pushing in their activities through demonstrations of their value to the community and often going with their creations into municipal office; and lastly and most important of all, as the climax of their wisdom and endeavor, they now begin to realize that the government itself in towns and cities should absorb most of their activities, coördinate them and be itself the agent for public health for the sake of greater economy of time, money, effort and efficiency, and also for the sake of eliminating all flavor of charity. In brief, it may be claimed that women have broadened into the democratic and governmental point of view toward health problems at the same time that they have been perfecting the machinery by which democracy may lay its foundation of health, happiness and power in governmental functions.

This does not mean that even in fundamental matters of physical well-being the accomplishment of the means to that end have been simple in any case. There has had to be a strong organization of the women in a given community who were interested in its health problems. These women have had to study the most intricate mechanical problems like municipal engineering. They have had to understand city taxation and budget making. They have had to educate those less interested to something approaching their own enthusiasm. Moreover they have had to work for the most part without political influence, which has meant that they have had to overcome the reluctance of public officials to take women seriously; they have had to understand and combat the political influence of contractors and business men of all kinds; they have had to enter political contests in order to place in office the kind of officials who had the wider vision; and they have had to watch without ceasing those very officials whom they have helped to elect to see that they carried out their campaign pledges. Sometimes it has happened that women have campaigned for a non-partisan ticket pledged to put through certain municipal health reforms and the ticket has been defeated at the polls. Under such circumstances they have had to renew their courage, maintain their organization, raise more funds and keep up the fight. Women who have experienced these political reverses have often become ardent suffragists, because they realized that the direct way to work for sanitary municipal housekeeping is through elected officials, and, having been unable to influence the votes of men, they have acquired the desire and determination to cast the necessary ballots themselves.

All these educational methods which women have used for their own development and for the instruction of voters, the political machinations with which they have had to deal, the necessity they have been under of "nagging" without mercy until they achieved their desired results, the sympathy and encouragement on the part of men, the coöperation of progressive officials, their ways of raising money, their means of perfecting organization, and their publicity enterprises will be illustrated in the pages that follow. Some of their failures to obtain the municipalization of certain proposals will also be recorded.

In spite of all the handicaps under which they have had to labor, women have steadily forged ahead in medical knowledge and skill. It was the munificent gift of a woman to Johns Hopkins on the condition that it admit women as medical students that forced open the doors of that institution to them. Now Dr. Louise Pearce of that university has been appointed assistant to Dr. Simon Flexner at the Rockefeller Institute for Medical Research in New York. Women moreover hold high executive positions in the leading medical societies of the country today. Only within the last few years, however, have women been accepted anywhere as internes in hospitals and yet some municipalities, Jersey City for instance, have women physicians on the staffs of their city hospitals. Failing to get experience in other hospitals as internes, women have often established their own and they serve as superintendents, internes, consulting physicians in many such institutions.

* * *

In this social battle to arrest and prevent disease, the campaign against infant mortality assumes an ever larger proportion, and as we should naturally expect, women are also in the front ranks here. More or less quietly for a long period women have studied and worked on the problem of infant mortality.

* * *

It is futile to insist that a mother who is physically able shall nurse her baby if she is so poor that she must work under conditions that weaken her and thus reduce the grade and quality of her milk or that preclude leisure in which to nourish the infant. The question of poverty, that skeleton in every social closet, looms up here with an insistency that nothing will banish. No kind of philanthropy will solve the requirements of infant welfare when poverty or labor conditions are the root of the problem.

Babies' milk thus becomes essentially a social-economic problem. It is so recognized by many women and is becoming more and more recognized as such by those who work along baby-saving lines. No one sees this fact more clearly perhaps than Miss Lathrop who joins in the ever-growing cry for a "war on poverty." Mothers' pensions, and every attempt to increase the wage of the husband or of the wife before the child-bearing experience has entered into her life, that she may lay by a sum for that function, reaches infant mortality more fundamentally and directly than do milk stations.

* * *

That many women are not unmindful of the fact that the anti-noise movement must not be purely a middle-class movement is indicated by their activity against prolonged hours of work amid the whir of factory machinery. Noiseless machinery has not yet been a possibility, whatever the future may hold in store for us in that respect; but any attempt to limit one's interest in health to a particular group is short-sighted, to say the least. Jaded nerves are to be found in large numbers among the factory men and women and boys and girls, whose daily bread is won amid the incessant din of wheels and engines during a long work day.

FROM CHAPTER III: THE SOCIAL EVIL

The awakening of women to the low social status of their sex is the most encouraging fact of the century. With the revelations which have come both from women and from men physicians, nurses, and scientists of the causes, spread, and effects of venereal diseases, the conscience and intelligence of women have fairly leaped in response to the demand made upon them for recognition of the situation and for remedies and prevention.

Their work here as elsewhere has been varied; for the problem of prevention is complex, many causes more or less combining to produce the undesirable vice conditions.

* * *

The mother who must work out of the home long hours, or the father who toils on a night-shift or for ten, twelve or fourteen hours a day has no time or strength to devote to children, however great the inclination.

Parents who have themselves grown up in a congested area, who have been overworked and underfed and surrounded from infancy with a vicious environment cannot be reached always with a religious or moral appeal and, even if they are, they cannot always persuade their children to forsake the attractions of the street and the saloon and the resort for a quiet evening of prayer at home with the father and mother. Many women accept the judgment and observation of Dr. Abraham Flexner that the social evil swallows up in greater proportion than any other "the un-skilled daughters of the unskilled classes," and they would therefore substitute for, or supplement, the instilling of moral precept, by industrial training, housing reform, regulations of hours and conditions of labor, control of recreational facilities, the minimum wage, mothers' pensions and many other reforms.

* * *

This wider social program is now on the horizon of all those women who supplement individualistic morality by social morality and attempt to understand the causes which operate on men and women in masses. Where the women have this larger vision, they are demanding to know the facts—the plain, unvarnished facts. They will not be put off by a "There, there, now," or "The time is not propitious." We see women everywhere backing movements for commissions to study the social evil in all its aspects, individual and social, and where such commissions are established we frequently find women serving on them or coöperating in the investigation.

* * *

In a struggle against entrenched and highly profitable evils, women may seem to be at great disadvantage. In this case there is also a body of men—small, perhaps, but of a sort that cannot be pooh-poohed—who have been carrying on an equally effective campaign of publicity and education. Women, in fact, have some advantages over men in such a contest against the powers of evil. They have as yet no party traditions to hamper them; no direct business relations to be jeopardized; and, above all, they have a larger amount of daytime leisure in which to do detail reform work and to convert small groups of people.

The federal judges and attorneys generally take into account the circumstances in the case and only in clear cases where white slavery is accomplished by force have the full penalties been imposed. The transportation of regular prostitutes was not punished, in one instance the judge saying that thus "our own daughters," are better protected. Women with a social conscience take the position that all women are their daughters and that no daughter is safe until the traffic is suppressed. Moreover they seek to protect their sons wherever they are and they call upon the national government to help them do it.

*   *   *

You may talk to women of the futility of figuring social sex sins, but they seem to be congenitally incapable of believing you. I heard a man talk to an audience in behalf of this measure, and when he touched upon that old, old text—*it always has been; it always will be*—there came a curious resemblance in every woman's face within my vision; for every face had hardened, stiffened, was marked with the family likeness of rebellion. The lecturer was addressing himself to deaf ears, to eyes determined not to see.

*   *   *

Recognizing that ignorance in matters of sex is one of the leading causes of prostitution, women working on the problem of the social evil have decided that the conspiracy of silence shall be broken all along the line and that we shall have all the light we can get.

*   *   *

The ideals of society must be so changed that young men may not be weakened and corrupted by the passive acceptance of false standards of morals. One of the most important factors for the attainment of this end is the same education of boys and girls in the matters of sex, from which all secrecy, except that which is necessary from true modesty and refinement, shall have disappeared.

We as parents must recognize and help establish the truth of the law that the same virtue is needed in both sexes for the happy development of that family life on which the security of the race and the progress of civilization depend.

*   *   *

FROM CHAPTER IV: RECREATION

The old maxim, "All work and no play makes Jack a dull boy," has been amplified in the past twenty-five years in many ways. All work and no play may make Jack a sick boy or a delinquent. If Jack plays not at all, neither can he work. What is true of Jack is true of all the members of Jack's family and of all his relatives and neighbors. What is true of Jack is equally true of Jill. In order therefore to prevent dullness, illness, crime and delinquency, recreation has been provided in cities in homeopathic doses, at least, for Jack and Jill and their relatives and neighbors.

The interest in, and advocacy of, municipal recreational facilities for the people of the urban districts grew out of the knowledge that, unless wholesome recreation is provided, unwholesome recreation will be sought and found. There is no alternative.

* * *

It has also been made clear that municipal prevention of arrests, illness, unemployment, inefficiency, is cheaper than municipal care of delinquents and criminals, of the sick, of those illy equipped to earn a livelihood, and of the vicious whose supervision entails such administrative expense and anxiety. Even motives of economy therefore may lead to this form of municiapl enterprise.

Because the keynote to all modern social activity is prevention and because prevention is cheaper than cure always, recreation today is of public concern. That the public's interest and belief in municipal recreation has been guided into faith in its educational advantages is due in no small degree to the patient work of women in behalf of amusement facilities. In their recreational work, women have also sought to make recreation serve the purposes of family unity, community spirit, and an increase in the real joy of living. . . .

The history of their work for playgrounds shows that like almost all modern social endeavor, there has been, first, private demonstration of a public utility, then city control, then state-wide legislation to bring backward communities into line with forward urban movement. Women have everywhere been largely instrumental in initiating the playground work, they have followed it in many cases by service on appointed commissions and as paid city playground employees, and in other cases they have held positions on state recreation commissions.

Interesting and important as has been the work of individual women in this great battle for adequate recreation in cities, it is of course the associations of women that have been most powerful and determined.

FROM CHAPTER VI: HOUSING

Housing reform, in its larger aspects . . . is a persistent struggle to control the situation permanently by legislation, efficient inspection, garden cities, and model small houses in place of tenements. Added to this is the necessity of assimilation work with foreigners, of education in personal and public hygiene in schools and homes, and control of profit-making interests for the sake of homes for the people.

*   *   *

The more thoughtful women interested in housing reform soon came to realize that mere sentimental talk about housing evils is futile, and that effective improvements must be based on actually known conditions, their causes and effects.

Surveys have therefore taken precedence generally of propaganda for legislation or enforcement of laws; and many of the very best of the housing surveys in the country have been made by women. Here again it is because of the greater readiness of women to admit women into the secrets of the home that investigations carried on by them are apt to be more successful. Women can best understand women's and children's needs in the way of shelter, for one thing, and how far the labor of one woman can accomplish housekeeping results. Theirs having been the tasks of doing the family wash, guarding the babies at sleep and at play, cooking and serving meals, removing dust and rubbish, they are in a better position than men to know what conveniences facilitate that work and what deprivations retard or prevent its accomplishment.

FROM CHAPTER VII: SOCIAL SERVICE

Social service is not an exact science and it does not mean the same thing to all people. Charity or philanthropy was more definite and has always been more or less of an official concern in municipalities. In times of crises, floods, panics, fires, earthquakes, extreme cold or excessive heat, cities and towns have supplemented the help rendered by individuals in alleviating hunger, homelessness, illness and want. The municipality thus often makes charitable doles to the victims of the elements, regarding the service as necessary, but temporary; remedial, not preventive.

The social investigations which have been made in recent years, together with the revelations made by charitable organizations, have driven home the fact that while intermittent fire and water and industrial crises and heat and cold undoubtedly add to human helplessness or distress, there is a steady and constant helplessness and distress based on underfeeding, homelessness or bad housing, unemployment, lack of vocational training, low wages, ignorance, occupational diseases and accidents, sexual irregularity, and other causes for which spasmodic almsgiving, however tenderly and efficiently applied, is no remedy whatever. Added to this definite knowledge is the knowledge, based on the experience of charity workers, of the opprobrium which is cast upon charity of the personal type, at least, by industrious wage-earners, the products of whose toil, instead of being used to provide them with the creature comforts, are, in many cases, consumed by those who toil not, neither do they spin, but who are active in distributing alms to producers.

Partly to satisfy their own intelligence and partly to overcome the resentment among working people at the idea of charity, the social worker has come into being and social service has developed into a philosophy, an education, and to a certain extent into a science. Step by step it has been pushed into municipal departments—notably, the health and educational departments. Where associated charities have been well developed and the city has the idea of social service in its charitable work, the tendency is to use the word "welfare" and to designate this function as "public welfare."

It is the same development which has characterized all other public work—the growth from remedy to prevention—and the growth is stable for the reason that it represents economy in place of the former waste of money and effort and because popular education is leading to the demand for prevention and justice rather than charity.

In this expansion of municipal functions there can be little dispute as to the influence of women. Their hearts touched in the beginning by human misery and their sentiments aroused, they have been led into manifold activities in attempts at amelioration, which have taught them the breeding places of disease, as well as of vice, crime, poverty and misery. Having learned that effectively to "swat the fly" they must swat its nest, women have also learned that to swat disease they must swat poor housing, evil labor conditions, ignorance, and vicious interests.

Sometimes the mere self-preservative instincts have forced women out to work among their neighbors; for in cities one's neighbors may murder in innumerable ways besides with the pistol or dirk.

Middle- and upper-class women, having more leisure than middle- and upper-class men, have had greater opportunity for social observation and the cultivation of social sympathies, for the latter accompanies the former instead of preceding it, as all active emotions are the reflexes of experience. It is these women therefore who have seen, felt, experimented, learned, agitated, constructed, advised, and pressed upon the municiapl authorities the need of public prevention of the ills from which the people suffer. In their municipal demands they have often had the support of women of the working class and of working men, among others, whose own preservation is bound up with legislation and administration to an ever-increasing degree.

Just in the proportion that social service develops into public action, and away from private philanthropy and personal interference, is the help of working people secured. With the increase of the demands of working people for the means with which to prevent their own destruction and the undermining of the rest of society, will come, many predict, the absorption of social service into organized public service just as the absorption of the settlement is gradually being accomplished by the school center.

Whatever may be the outcome of the present tendencies in social service, it is certain that women are actively engaged in every branch of it: in organized charity, in all the specialized branches of kindred work, such as care for the several types of dependents and delinquents, in organizing women workers in the industries, in making social surveys and special investigation, and in creating the literature of social service.

*   *   *

In educational progress; in the promotion of public health, which necessarily includes individual health; in prison reform; in the study of eugenics; in the improvement of country life, and in all social, civic, and economic problems men need and welcome the help of women. Neither can accomplish much *alone*; together they must strive and overcome, together they must win or lose. Together they must attack ''the conditions which injuriously affect child life'' until all children shall have opportunity for development into useful citizens. This being true no one can deny that Social Service is woman's work.

*   *   *

The development of organized charity and social service with their investigations and legislative and institutional activities has produced the need for workers trained for research and the preparation of data—trained in sociology, economics, and industry; in health, education and hygiene. . . .

As private philanthropy advances to social service and then to public action, women all over the country are asking, ''Shall the control which we have hitherto been exercising be turned over to the men voters alone?'' They are, in increasing numbers, answering this question in the negative.

Club women and women teachers and doctors last summer (1914) declared emphatically that social activities must continue to be the joint work of men and women and that political equality is a prime essential in the evolution of social service.

*   *   *

FROM CHAPTER VIII: CRIME CONTROL AND CORRECTIONS

There are abundant reasons why women take so much interest in the whole problem of criminal law and correction. A great many crimes are definite offenses against women and children; their comparative defenselessness makes them suffer more than men from brutality, neglect, and vices; and there are certain technical legal requirements of the law that constitute, in the matter of punishment, sex discriminations which arouse rebellion on their part.

Perhaps other reasons predominate, however. The interest in public correction is but a simple and inevitable extension of the function of private correction which has been generally allotted to women in the home and in the school. Even over husbands they have been urged by church and moralists of all kinds to exercise reformatory influences and their acknowledged sphere of "protection" and "prevention of delinquency" is evident in the popular explanation of every great man by the fact that "he had a good mother."

Again, middle-class women have more leisure than men under modern conditions of industry, and an army of women choose to spend their leisure mothering the poor and the friendless or in the prevention of poverty and dependence. Furthermore women spend more of the world's wealth than men spend, and hundreds of well-to-do women are becoming, with their advancing education and travel and observation, satiated with material possessions, and are spending their wealth for social possessions—public health, public ornamentation, public recreation, protection of girls and boys, infant welfare, and the like. Even the "sheltered" woman has grown to realize that all children as well as her own need homes, protection, education, sympathy and justice; that even self-preservation and self-respect for herself, her husband and her children are endangered by proximity to vice, crime, neglect, disease, and immorality.

Moreover, there is no class line in crime or vice and the need of their correction. No group or class of women has escaped the ravages of these evils, and thus a feeling of solidarity is evolved in the fight against the social evil and various forms of delinquency, which is not as yet developed in the fight against poverty, the sting of which is a class experience.

* * *

More difficult than the opening of probation work to women has been the no less obvious task of installing a sufficient number of police matrons. An examination of the records shows that these important officers have been established through the efforts of women in all large western cities and also extensively through the East. The Women's Prison Association of New York is seeking to secure police matrons in all the stations instead of having women dragged about to different stations to find them. This association was instrumental in getting patrol wagons, moreover, so that women might not be taken through the streets by policemen.

*   *   *

The employment of women physicians in courts for women is a necessity strongly urged by women's probation and other associations. In some courts they are already serving in that capacity.

*   *   *

From these various official positions occupied by women, it was only a step to secure the appointment of women on the regular police force to aid in the protection of the young. This step was first taken in Los Angeles, California when Mrs. Alice Stebbins Wells was placed upon the police staff.

*   *   *

Women and policemen are each a problem to the other of the deepest concern. The uncorroborated testimony of a plain-clothes policeman against the girl or woman whom he arrests on the street is often accepted in the court whereas corroborative testimony is required in the case of a man arrested for sexual irregularity. Voteless women strikers have been grossly mistreated by the police in industrial centers and the graft exposures have revealed the all too frequent alliance of the police with the vice interests to the injury of the city's womanhood.

Women's entering wedge into the police department, the police-woman, we venture to predict, will not be withdrawn, but rather will attacks be made until, through a constructive program, all human life is better safeguarded in the communities of this country, and the idea of social service permeates the police departments, as it does other municipal departments.

*   *   *

FROM CHAPTER XI: CIVIC IMPROVEMENT

From this cursory and necessarily imperfect review of women's work in civic improvement, it is evident that whoever labors for the city or town or village beautiful in the United States may find intelligent and hearty support on the part of women's associations, even though they are, in many places, merely organized for literary or "cultural" purposes. Thousands of men may loaf around clubs without ever showing the slightest concern about the great battle for decent living conditions that is now going on in our cities; but it is a rare woman's club that long remains indifferent to such momentous matters. Nor, as we have seen, is this movement for civic betterment confined to the greater cities. In thousands of out-of-the-way places which hardly appear on the map, unknown women with large visions are bent on improving their minds for no mere selfish advancement, but for the purpose of equipping themselves to serve their little communities. They form local associations. These local associations are federated into state and national associations. The best thought and experience of one community soon become the common possession of all. Thus we see in the making, before our very eyes, a conscious national womanhood. Here is a power that will soon disturb others than the village politicians.

* * *

When a municipality has arrived at the stage when it really wants the best return for its money it always has employed [women]. . . . It does not get sentimental and expect or want any perfection. It has entirely discarded the "ministering angel—thou" attitude. It assumes that under a true democracy a part of the people who pay its taxes may have a not unreasonable wish to take an active part in its administration, and when it can get such people—fairly faithful, often amply efficient and willing—it takes them where they stand.

* * *

The hour must come when women will occupy in proportion all these higher municipal posts. They will be found ready as soon as the men are found who are ready to give them their opportunity. It is not contended that they will be better or wiser, but that they will take a more intelligent and lasting interest and that there will always be certain things where children are concerned which they will know more and care more about than men.

II.

FEMINISM AS A WORLD
VIEW—THEORY

Her political-activist period behind her, Mary Ritter Beard moved into what became the focus of her mature years. The core of everything she wrote and everything she did was her conviction that women were undeniably a power in civilization, and that history and politics were incomplete without that recognition. The rest of her long life was devoted to trying to persuade women of their own vital historic past and of the power that was within their reach to change the present. She began a crusade for women's minds that took many forms.

I have divided the sections which reflect her feminist world view into "Theory" and "Practice," although the integration of her ideas and actions often makes such a division difficult.

In the first of nine pieces in this segment of theoretical contributions, Beard surveys the thought of American women of letters to investigate the relationship between women's place in society and their critical evaluation of that society. *On Understanding Women*, the second selection, was published in 1931, and ushers in the decade of her most creative work. In this volume, Beard presents, for the first time in an extended argument, her thesis on the force of women in history, a force which has been used both for social good and social harm. The third, fourth, and fifth selections examine different aspects of women and education. The third suggests that a college education is probably more damaging than useful for the genuine education of women. The fourth challenges the premises and goals of the feminist movement of her time, arguing that feminists should use their energies to create a better society, not settle for an equal share in this inhuman one. The fifth selection comes from an address in 1937 to the alumnae of Mount Holyoke College. In it, Beard urges women to sustain and extend their tradition of enlightened humanism in the struggle against international militarism and violence. The sixth selection, which appeared in 1940, places nineteenth century feminism in the historical context of Enlightenment ideas and capitalist political economy.

Selections from *Woman as Force in History: A Study in Traditions and Realities*, constitute the seventh piece. Her most well-known book, it denies categorically the notion that women have always been oppressed, asserting, with the support of much historical evidence, that women have been a powerful force in human history.

The eighth and ninth selections are two nationwide radio broadcasts that Mary Beard delivered, one in 1939, and one in 1950. Both are popular, concise statements of her theme of woman as force, a thesis that is summed up in the title of one address, ''What Nobody Seems to Know About Women.''

1. American Women and the Printing Press[1]

NOTE: *In this probing article, Mary Beard ponders what it is that holds women today "so loyally to the realms of the practical" rather than to the philosophical or critical. Why is it, she wonders, that the greatest thinkers in the modern epoch continue to be men? It is not for lack of publishing opportunity, for the "field is free and open to the sexes alike." If publishers prefer male authors in the areas of science or philosophy, it is largely because women "seem not as yet to have that combination of learning and wisdom that makes them authoritative in such fields." Nor is it because women have been excluded historically from the world of writing. Modern times "may witness the first female engineer, motor truck chauffeur . . . or federal prohibition officer," but literary women "run back through all the ages since the art of writing was invented." Why, then, are American women not in the front ranks of intellectual excellence? They have certainly had great opportunities and "unique adventures" in the world of politics, power, warfare, and pioneering. American women have not been deprived of education, for before the establishment of public schools, says Beard, they got much the same exposure to ideas as men did. Nor is it the lack of time "since the sex which has the greater leisure . . . writes the less."*

Perhaps, she suggests with piercing insight, just the reverse is true; that it is "work and responsibility [that] are the underlying impulses to literary expression." It is not accidental that in times of "tremendous social upheaval," such as during the Civil War in the nineteenth century or the expansion of capitalist enterprise in the twentieth, women examine social issues with greatest intensity. Women who are caught up in great social battles write seriously, says Beard, because at those times they have something serious to write about. They are "women singing of freedom," women such as Anne Bradstreet, Phillis Wheatley, Edith Wharton, Dorothy Parker, and Emma Lazarus. In general, then, "American women think [in terms of] the masses [and] about [great social] movements." Beard follows this thought to conclude that women may be too much absorbed in "making democracy vocal" to have sufficient time for "wide-ranging sweeps of philosophical and critical fancy."

1. "American Women and the Printing Press," *The Annals of the American Academy of Political and Social Science*, Vols. 143–145, May, 1929, pp. 195–206.

> *She is apparently not satisfied with this hypothesis and, as if she were thinking aloud, she offers another explanation for why so few women are outstanding thinkers in today's world. "Great thinkers and writers have never been spectators," she argues, suggesting that women in modern America are. "If the heights of reasoning" are to be achieved by American women, "they will be reached only through the avenue of experience" which has thus far been denied them.*
>
> *There is an elusive quality about this article. There is a disquieting ambiguity that will often recur because Mary Beard never satisfactorily reconciles contradictory aspects of the history of women. The major theme in her mature writing is the powerful and real force of women in all phases of social life, now and in the past. At the same time she also knows the truth of the opposite: that women have been denied a central place in society. In this article, she moves back and forth from the first premise to the second, without ever making space in her theoretical structure to encompass and explain both tendencies. When she discusses how women, occupied by great social battles, use their literary talents to write of freedom, the underlying assumption is that women are an effective and vital force in the center of society. When she suggests, at the end of the article, that women witness but do not participate in the major events of their time and are thereby deprived of experiences to nourish critical writings, the underlying assumption is that women are on the margin of society. What Beard never was able to confront is that both assumptions, while contradictory, are simultaneously true and must be understood as part of a dialectical process.*

This is not an essay in literary criticism. It is not an attempt to compare an Edith Wharton, let us say, with a Gertrude Atherton of her own sex, with a male compatriot, or with European scribes. It is not an effort to appraise the observations, emotions, and dramatic power of a Katherine Mayo or a Gertrude Williams in the light of Indian portraiture by an E. M. Forster. Nor is it an analysis of imagery, stylistic devices, or vocabularies. . . .

This is an experiment in the evaluation of the writing by American women as a whole—as a pattern of modern mentality, interests, and force. The greatest writers of the past have been venerated as thinkers and seers. Especially is the great poet praised for his ability to pierce veils which lesser mortals fail to penetrate. Therefore, it is the inspiration and theme of which words are the medium of expression, rather than the forms which the words assume, which will be treated here. In short, it is the American woman as a thinker revealing herself on the printed page whom we shall try to examine. If she is to achieve prime and lasting distinction in Letters, she must be more than a song bird, lovely as some of those creatures may be; more than a gossip relating lively tales, absorbing as such can be; more than a collector of data and a compiler of thoughts others have had.

The colleges of the United States are crowded with aspiring youth and extension classes are filled with ambitious adults who hope to do great things with their pens. But when they have learned all the technique of organization, unity, harmony, and charm of phraseology, there will remain one essential of power that can hardly be taught—something to say.

*   *   *

The market is greedy for material. The field is free and open to the sexes alike. There was never a time when an excellent manuscript was so little in peril of being refused. Publishers were never so eager for artistry, for freshness of view, for originality, for scholarship, for the findings of experience, for wisdom, for speculation of every sort. . . .

If, therefore, in the elaborate series of social, literary and scientific works, prepared by "experts," to which publishers are turning with increased interest, the writers are mainly or exclusively men, it is not because of prejudice by the editors and publishers, but because women seem not as yet to have that combination of learning and wisdom which makes them authoritative in such fields. They may write gracefully, but they are apt to think too gracefully as well. Even on the subject of the Family, it is difficult to draw in a woman commentator of equal distinction with a Havelock Ellis, and Robert Briffault has done the big work on Mothers. . . .

And yet the precedents for feminine self-expression run back through all the ages since the art of writing was invented. The literary woman of today is no exotic phenomenon. She is no more the first writer of her sex than the contemporary man of letters is the pioneer among men. The era may witness the first female engineer, motor truck chauffeur, radio broadcaster, head of an aviation school, or federal prohibition officer, but it has not produced the first thinking, creative, and writing woman by any means. In the ancient world, long studied in classical texts, Sappho was ranked with Homer by Aristotle, "master of them that knew." And throughout the cycles that have intervened between the days of Greek pride and our own, women have recorded on parchment and paper, by stylus and brush, with pen or with typewriter, their impressions of the Passing Show and their hopes and fears for the morrow. Into the little stream of philosophic thought have flowed scientific treatises, comments on political events, analyses of the roots of literature, dramatic concepts, and many other varieties of mental exercise. . . .

But women of the ancient and medieval societies did not exhaust the experiences of human life and therefore all the reasoning about it. American women have had unique adventures and opportunities. Beside traditional revolutions, civil war, foreign alliances and fighting, they have helped in shaping a republic and have been political equals in a democracy. They have been pioneers of a peculiar sort, agitators, reformers, belligerents introducing new elements of warfare, educators, scientists with novel laboratory equipment, professionals, technicians, travelers, leisured ladies with cash at their disposal, slave owners in their own right, spenders on an unheard of scale, industrial workers, capitalists, politicians and office-holders of high degree. These enterprises make up a wealth of active experience which would appear to be material rich enough for the making of a new mind, if we knew how minds are made.

Nor have American women been deprived of education. Before the epoch of public schools and collegiate training for their sex, they got much the same introduction to philosophy, art, science, and letters as did men, through routes then customary, such as private tutors, travel, and libraries in the home. Great political and social movements they learned through their skins. Discussion took place at firesides, which often surpassed in scope and profundity that now heard in public forums. . . .

The annual production of books, by women, is now what would be registered in previous records only over long, long cycles. Women undoubtedly take generous advantage of the printing press. But not as much as men. Their output rates something close to one book by a woman to seven books by men. Since the sex which has the greater leisure thus writes the less, clearly free time is not the root of literature in an epoch of democracy, if it ever was. Just the reverse is true indeed. Work and responsibility are the underlying impulses to literary expression as figures amply prove.

Who then are the women who have written and who continue to write in the modern era in America? What is their background? How much of their time is devoted to thinking and setting down their thoughts? Are there professional thinkers in the sex?

Apparently ladies of the leisure class take up their pens very little in their free hours. They remain mostly languorists or motorists instead of becoming thinkers, or lively writers of any sort. This is as true by and large of the capitalist lady as it was true of the lady of slavery days. The very study of *The Lady* herself as a social product was made by a teacher, Emily James Putnam. Not until some tremendous social upheaval comes along to jar their status and intensify their feelings do they develop beyond the simplest creatures of soft circumstances. Southern ladies began to find something to say when the American fratricidal war tore them loose from their old moorings and they had to look at the Black Gauntlet in retrospect, relate their sufferings during sieges in Vicksburg and elsewhere, write biographies of confederate heroes, record their adventures and observations as army nurses, testify to the aftermath of abolition and economic devastation, or hold up to the young generation the mirror of historical truth as they themselves had framed it.

Among Northern ladies of the leisure class, Jane Addams is a shining exception. She was lifted from potential complacency by a realization of the significance of the class cleavage, even in her own country, and she had the mental and physical energy to try to bridge the chasm she saw yawning between them. She turned, therefore, from the idleness, which could have been hers, to social work among the tiny children of the city streets, among industrial laborers, and among distraught aliens. . . .

Some of the most vigorous social portraiture has come from The Woman of Letters. Edith Wharton's preoccupation with the rise of divorce in reputable ruling circles, with the manners of the nouveaux riches at home and abroad, with their age of innocence, and general manifestations of internecine class strife, has resulted in masterful canvases of the times that were gilded by the rawest capitalism. And out of her labor has also come one of the most penetrating volumes in the international literature of the soil—*Ethan Frome, a story of mother earth and her claims.* . . .

Then, like a century plant blooming after careful nurture and tireless waiting, come young women singing of the freedom secured by the great sisterhood of agitators. It is a long, long way from Anne Bradstreet, born in 1650 to be the "Tenth Muse lately sprung up in America," who compiled poems with "great variety of wit and learing, full of delight," to Dorothy Parker glorying in "Enough Rope" at the second quarter of the twentieth century. The latter with her free running liberties is almost at the opposite people even from the Victorian Elizabeth Barrett Browning with her close loyalties. . . .

Edna St. Vincent Millay, her forerunner, now grown more sober under the fire of public tragedies, such as the Sacco-Vanzetti trial, demonstrates freedom maturing into responsibility—fortunately with artistry retained.

The poetic route which lies from Bradstreet to Parker has many blazed trails leading along important byways. For instance, Negroes lift their voices both in bondage and in freedom. Phillis Wheatley Peters in 1754, a slave, composes on paper while her people sing on the plantations. New melodies, redolent of servitude, but born of the surging present and problematical future, pour now from the spirits of freed Negro women, as they labor in industry and arts. Jewish elements in the American melting pot also enrich the stream of poetry, as is demonstrated in the *Songs of a Semite*, by Emma Lazarus. Catholics have had many representatives. . . .

What seems to be an outstanding fact is that, with rare exceptions, such as an Elinor Wylie writing poems and novels for the more precious classes, and an Emily Dickinson jotting down philosophy for her own soul's sake, American women think for the masses, about immediate movements, and as a consequence of concepts of democracy. . . .

It may be that American women have been too involved in making democracy vocal, democratic and intelligent about itself to have had time for wide-ranging sweeps of philosophical and critical fancy with views of humanity and life universally considered. It may be that so-called idle curiosity must abide an idler hour for the digestion of experiences so strange as those of the modern age. It is possible that there is no such thing as genuinely idle curiosity, or at any rate that what appears to be idle at the finish did not begin that way—that the original impulse was not detached—and that the subtler involutions of logical thought, in the large, are at bottom really a professional pastime akin to the tortuous mental exercises that went on within medieval cloisters. A third "ponderable" might be the fact that women have long been on the periphery of politics, not very close to its heart. The question at least forces itself to the front as to whether it is an intuitive or a biological variation that holds women so loyally to the realm of the practical merely embroidered in their Letters with gossip, romanticism, movement, and personalities.

In the meantime while an answer is awaited, we may assume that, if the heights of reasoning, as heights have hitherto been defined, are to be ultimately attained by American women, they will be reached only through the avenue of experience. . . .

Great thinkers and writers have never been sheer spectators of the pageantry of life. The Greek philosophers were statesmen and teachers, transmitting first hand knowledge of clashes and events in terms of ethics and social law. German philosophers often show direct traces of nationalistic and economic politics. French philosophers of the first rank drew their rationalistic enthusiasms from the conflict opening between magic and naturalistic discoveries. Ruskin reached synthetic reasoning as an artist posing questions of values to an onrushing industrial culture. In the very heart of the latest society's novel energies, surely women will in turn find more to think and to say that transcends gossip, song, story, and the incident of the hour.

2. On Understanding
Women[1]

NOTE: On Understanding Women *was published in 1931 when Mary Beard was fifty-five years old. As is true of many women, she entered her most creative period in her middle years.*

This is the first book-length statement of Beard's theoretical proposition that that woman is "the elemental force in the rise and development of civilization." As an extension of her "responsibility for the continuance and care of life," woman invented the domestic arts, and in this way is responsible for "launching civilization."

Woman's crucial role in the maintenance of life and the creation of culture is not officially recognized, she says, because when classes emerged and "engage[d] the attention of historians, women . . . dropped out of the pen portraits." But "they remained in the actuality." Women have participated in almost "everything that went on in the world," sharing the "burdens and privileges of their respective classes."

And what will the future bring? If capitalism survives the economic crisis (the Great Depression had just begun), she says, women will continue to demand and will receive increasing shares in their societies. More and more women will be admitted to the professions, businesses, and schools, and "those who sit at the feast will continue to enjoy themselves," ignoring the revolutions that have pointed to "the world of toiling reality below."

She considers other possibilities. "The free and easy political democracy of early capitalism may be turned into a middle-class dictatorship," and "a fascist regime is a menace to the liberties of women," she observed in 1931! The future of women in the Soviet Union she views with uncertainty, observing that it is a society where "the bourgeois form of marriage is in the process of dissolution" and where the emphasis is on "woman as a worker."

In all modern societies she sees the State as usurping functions that traditionally belonged to families. Will this trend threaten the future of monogamy? she asks. She has no certain answers, but suggests that

1. *On Understanding Women*, New York: Grosset & Dunlap, 1931. Selections are from the Summary and Epilogue, pp. 513–523.

perhaps "monogamy will at least be tried on its merits," thriving not for economic motives but "for reasons deeply fixed in human nature and experience." There will probably forever be need for women "in the operation of caring for life" and to live according to "nature's laws."

Beard concludes the book with the observation that, however legitimate the criticisms voiced by the current feminists are, those grievances are not rooted in the inherent relationship of men and women, but rather reflect given conditions at a particular time. At some point the "sex antagonism" of feminism, bearing the "wound of honorable battle" will achieve its goal and cease to exist. In time it will be possible to recognize that "with respect to the . . . enjoyments of life the sexes are one." Then, "the eternal feminism . . . at the center of all things—that is, the care of life" will remain.

There are many ways to understand Beard's questionable reliance upon the notion of the "eternal feminism . . . at the center of all things" and her use of the idea of "nature's laws." Earlier in the book she apologizes for what will surely be overstatement by explaining: "when contentions have long weighted too much on one side, it is necessary to bear down heavily on the other." She was also so determined to provide women with a sense of self-worth, to counteract centuries of inculcated self-doubt, that she sometimes engages in hyperbole. Her determination to prevent women from getting swallowed up in a world dominated by male values also prompted her too often to unfortunate rhetoric. And many of her ideas, despite their appearance of certainty, come out of a mind still at work, trying to grapple with unsettling ideas.

Ultimately, Mary Beard is herself guilty of the accusations she threw at the feminists. Just as the "sex antagonism" of the feminists was rooted in a specific historic past, so too does Mary Beard's "eternal feminism" and "nature's law" have a historic reality and not a metaphysical one.

Looking backward toward the horizon of dawning society, what do we see standing clearly against the sky? Woman—assuming chief responsibility for the continuance and care of life. We are in the presence of a force so vital and so powerful that anthropologists can devise no meter to register it and the legislator no rein strong enough to defeat it. Whether woman possesses sex or is possessed by it may be left to masculine metaphysicians for debate. Its reality however cannot be escaped. To an extent not yet gauged by historians, hunting, wars, states and institutions have been shaped to meet the supreme exigency of continuing life and must be if mankind is to go on living at all. Whether it is the primitive woman bringing a mate to her house, Henry VIII breaking with the Pope, or Napoleon rearranging the alliances of Europe with reference to his dynasty, the final necessity is always present. Otherwise human life and everything built upon it would perish from the earth. Church fathers may curse it, woman brought to death's door in childbirth may wonder with Erasmus at her "folly," and man caught in the institutions of support may rage at his "chains," but while life remains it must be continually recreated, nourished and esteemed. From this elemental force in the rise and development of civilisation there is no escape and more of human history can be written in its terms than any of Clio's disciples have yet imagined. . . .

But sex itself has been only one segment of woman's life, far less important than the collaterals issuing from it in connection with the care of life once created. Thus we see primitive women as the inventors of the domestic arts—cooking, spinning, weaving, garnering, guarding, doctoring, providing comforts and conveniences, and making beginnings in the decorative arts. They are launching civilisation. Other animals have sex and continue life but none surround it with such artificial supports which, examined closely, are found to form the prime substance of culture. Woman, by means of these domestic innovations, lifted her low-browed male companion above the wild beasts that he hunted with stone and club and devoured in the raw. Under all the social forms and transformations that have existed since primitive times, activities connected with food, clothing and shelter, woman's first interest, have continued, setting commerce in train, spurring invention, establishing systems of economy more amazing. . . . Amusing as it may seem, it is primitive woman's interest that is now the prime concern of the civilised men. War for war's sake is no longer openly celebrated by the male, however zealously he cherishes in secret his passion for battle. Modern societies—bourgeois, democratic, fascist and communist—all agree in declaring that their fundamental end is the manufacture and wide distribution of those commodities which the old Romans of the republican era declared tend to effeminacy—the conveniences and luxuries that give ease and satisfaction in the continuance and care of life—primitive woman's burden and one that will abide while mankind endures.

After the great State was founded on primitive societies by the sword, when kings, priests and noble classes were established to engage the attention of historians, women merely dropped out of the pen portraits. They remained in the actuality. They were members of all the castes from the slave stratum at the bottom to the ruling families at the top and, even where restrictions were the tightest, took part in nearly everything that went on in the world. Whether it is Aspasia lecturing to Pericles and friends, Sappho "teaching" Socrates, Roman women participating in senatorial conflicts and battles over the succession to the imperial throne, queens contending for their patrimonies, the daughters of the rich setting fleets and caravans in motion to bring them the luxuries of the East, or the wife of Pythagoras interpreting and spreading a faith, the truth that women have always been in or near the center of things is illustrated. They have shared in the burdens and privileges of their respective classes, have joined in wars, have owned and managed vast estates, have insisted on dominance in disputes among ruling families, have displayed the lusts of men, have served the temples, and have been deified as gods. If the formalities, such as exclusion from public gatherings in Athens and from the senate in Rome, are penetrated and realities are kept in mind, the energies and influence of women are easily discerned. There was no great historical contest in politics in which they did not appear somewhere. There was no religious cult which they did not affect. There were no exercises in intellectualism which they did not practice. If poets from Ovid to Molière made fun of learned women, these women were no funnier than most of the men who crowded the salons, as the court jester was fair enough to indicate, and some of them spoke with authority on poetry, mathematics, science, philosophy and ethics.

For a time after the dissolution of the Roman Empire, if most of the histories ring true, women retired in favor of the sword, but the retirement was certainly temporary if not illusory. They early appeared in the Middle Ages as managers in the families of barbarian conquerors and their princely retainers, as heads of convents and schools, as restorers of the arts, as manipulators in the papal politics of Italy, as theologians and saints, as the symbol of virtue divinely typified in Mary the Mother of God. They labored with men in the fields providing the economic goods on which the upper structure of mediaeval civilisation rested. They worked in the crafts around which were built the gilds and urban liberties. They suffered as witches, died as heretics, and furnished a military leader in Jeanne d'Arc. The whole art of chivalry, whatever may have been its civilising influence, developed around woman. The writers of canon law and its administrators were endlessly harassed by her conduct. Again and again women of the upper classes shone as the literate wives of illiterate lords and knights, thus sharing with the clergy the world of written wisdom. Exclusion from Oxford and Cambridge did not condemn English ladies to total ignorance; what a complete survey would reveal no one knows but the guess may be hazarded that the women of the upper classes, in fact of all classes, were about as well educated as the men of their circles. Even the famous abstract speculator, Abelard, had to have an intellectual companion, Heloise, as a foil; and Francis of Assisi, critic of scholasticism and learning, the girl Clare as counselor and friend. Although the law of property ran inevitably in favor of the fighter, so constantly exigent was defense, it did not run against woman as such nor did it in practice prevent thousands of women from holding and controlling property, from devoting it to the patronage of religion and the arts as well as to the intrigues and uses of their class.

In the modern age there have been changes in form rather than in substance. Women patronised and assisted directly in the development of the new learning—the recovery and enlargement of ancient secular wisdom. It was a woman, Queen Isabella of Spain, who was chiefly responsible for the underwriting that sent Columbus forth on the voyage of discovery destined to open a new epoch in the history of Europe and reveal to it the smallness of its empire; after a Queen had dared, kings were prepared to support other voyages. When secular learning widened out into natural science, women acted as promoters, critics, and creative thinkers and workers. They faced all the hardships involved in the conquest and settlement of the New World, standing steadfastly beside the men under the wintry clouds at Plymouth and beneath the sunny skies of Virginia. The Catholic fathers had scarcely reached the frontiers of Quebec when dauntless nuns appeared to carry forward the task of evangelisation. When natural science was touched with humanism and became an instrument in formulating the concept of Progress, it was mainly by the salons of French women that ideas were patronised, tried out, and set in circulation. In this age, no more than in mediaeval times, did a general exclusion from universities mean ignorance among women; the very notion is based upon an exaggerated view of the rôle of institutions in the origin and diffusion of learning. It is yet to be known whether institutions help rather than hinder thought.

With the rise of machine industry and the multiplication of occupations, the restrictions of all inherited law were found irksome, attacked and broken down, after many a stubborn battle to be sure but with surprising speed considering the herd capacities of the human race. In the rise of political democracy, women were belligerent—Mary Wollstonecraft joining Tom Paine in vindicating the rights of man—a favor reciprocated when the rights of woman were also to be vindicated. Finally, women have been identified with the ideas and movements of social amelioration from the sixteenth century to the latest hour, as thinkers, experimenters, propagandists and administrators.

And now that the long trail has been trod to this point, what of the life ahead of us? What are its possibilities and probabilities? There exists the assumption that what is called the bourgeois, or capitalist, order of things, lately acquired, will endure, if not forever, at least indefinitely. At the present moment it seems to be shaky in France, bewildered in England, disturbed in the United States, questioned in Spain, and distressed in Japan. But its current troubles may pass. If the established economic mill keeps running, then the future before various women is clear. They will acquire through inheritance, transfer, or their own efforts more property with all the rights and privileges thereunto attached. The number of professions and employments open to women will increase. The thousands of workers engaged in supplying luxuries to the plutocracy will grow and the gainful occupations of women will become more gainful. Into the great games of business, advertising, selling and speculating, they will enter with expanding zest, with profit to themselves and economic security. Hundreds of callings, though bearing a dubious relation to the care of life in the large, will give them personal independence. The learning of the schools and the facilities of the laboratories will be placed at their disposal in enlarging measure. The parasitic women of the bourgeois circle will spend, patronise, dabble and entertain and occasionally, very occasionally, play with fire like Marie Antoinette. In other words, those who sit at the feast will continue to enjoy themselves even though the veil that separates them from the world of toiling reality below has been lifted by mass revolts and critics. While this state of affairs lasts, no great thought will be imperative, on the part of women or of men within the prosperous circle, and the repetition of conventional formulas about the Kingdom, the Reich, the Republic, or Democracy, will suffice as in Cicero's day for wisdom and for statecraft.

But other contingencies enter into speculations. The free and easy political democracy of early capitalism may be turned into a middle class dictatorship, as in Italy, managed by men who naturally will look out for themselves in the distribution of economic plums. Supported by arms, dominated by a small self-appointed clique, and bent on the perpetuation of its power, the fascist régime is a menace to the liberties of women. And yet fascism is in the process of evolution. So far it has been able to steer a zig-zag course between capital and labor, closer to the interests of the former than the latter but not completed by any means. In Russia another type of dictatorship is in vogue, autocratic in its form of government but communist in economic theory and to some degree in practice. There the privileges and luxuries of the bourgeois are materially curtailed, if not extirpated, with corresponding effects upon the position of the women formerly belonging to the upper classes or serving them as caterers and retainers. Hence in Russia the bourgeois form of marriage is in process of dissolution, if marriages and families remain. The emphasis in communism, if its ideal is realised, will be on woman as a worker, and the opportunities for a life of leisure, patronage, noblesse oblige, religious service, and idle curiosity will vanish. What that will produce in terms of culture, the future alone can say. After traveling a long and strange road, women of the upper orders in Russia are back where all women began in primitive days, to the prime concern with labor and the care of life, where the vast majority of women in all times and places have stayed through the changing fortunes of politics.

Amid the hopes for bourgeois endurance and the contingences of change, the eternal battle between the Sate and the Family promises to continue. The State, originally built on the family, is confronted as of old with family loyalties inimical to the public service and to the common life and the common good. In a sense it is true, as political and social critics of the family have long contended, that men and women struggling to advance the family in status and satisfactions often act as enemies of the State . . .

The State may try to iron out handicaps of birth and domestic neglect. Even in an individualist nation like the United Sates, the family is invaded from two directions—one political and the other economic. The State insists upon domestic changes favorable to civic stability, and bourgeois marriage dissolves with amazing swiftness owing to the shift in forms of property and the individualisation of women in the arena where goods are produced. . . .

What would be the outcome of State supremacy it may be impossible for any one to forecast though there have been in the past a few brilliant cases of insight into the future. Some speculators see the end of monogamy. But this is an assumption. Monogamy has always been one form of sex relations, surrounded by many others. It is conceivable that the aggression of the State upon the family may mean that monogamy will at last be tried on its merits, certainly with less and possibly with no economic incidence, surviving the storm for reasons deeply fixed in human nature and experience. Though the State may take over more of the education and nurture of children, it will still find that women must be employed in the operation of caring for life. Perhaps by the route of trial and error along new lines, with birth control, humanity will decide that amenities of the home are more conducive to the fundamental mores upon which civilisation depends in final analysis than any abstract loyalties that it can generate through politics and economics alone.

If this analysis of history is approximately sound and if the future like the past is to be crowded with changes and exigencies, then it is difficult to believe that the feminism of the passing generation, already hardened into dogma and tradition, represents the completed form of woman's relations to work, interests and society. In so far as it is a sex antagonism, even though based on legitimate grievances against exclusions or discriminations in employment, it is and has been partial and one-phased, not fundamental. The converse is true with respect to man's hostility to the presence of women at the center of every sort of activity. Women have always been alive to everything that was going on in the world. They always will be. If, as our engineering writers are constantly telling us, society is to be increasingly technical in nature, then competence, not sex, will be the basis of selection and women will have to stand that test with men. Feminism as sex antagonism bearing the wounds of many honorable battles may then drop out of sight. Masculinism as sex monopoly may then yield to concepts of expertness.

The ordinary woman who has functioned in accordance with nature's laws does not hate man or exaggerate his importance; most of the time she is as indifferent to him as he is to her; but with respect to the amenities and enjoyments of life the sexes are one. Love, joy, and beauty are bound up in their relations. As Aristophanes could say twenty-three centuries ago, "there is no pleasure for a man unless the woman shares it," so the modern feminist will soon discover, if she has not already, that there is no pleasure for a woman unless the man shares it. Yet if the feminism of the older generation passes, the eternal feminine will be here at the center of all things—that is, the care of life—and, unless the growth of positive knowledge and the humane applications of science during the past three hundred years are a delusion and a mistake, governments and economic institutions, all the arts of comfort and delight, will revolve around the care of life, renewing themselves at that fountain of eternal youth whence come healing waters for despair and cynicism—the enduring belief that it is good to live, to love, to suffer and to labor.

3. University Discipline for Women— Asset or Handicap?[1]

NOTE: *In 1932, when Ph.D.s were waiting their turn on bread lines, Mary Beard drolly suggests to an academic audience that it might be good for women to be forced out of academia. University discipline, she audaciously states, is probably a handicap for most young people, but an even "graver handicap" for women, who are taught to believe that they must "follow . . . masculine leadership . . . without deviation" and thus do not develop their own critical imaginations. Women on their own, learning through experience in the world rather than relying on men for "ideological management," are better off, she asserts.*

All the hard work and energy it took to force open professional opportunities for women should now be used "to rescue them from the slough of unquestioning equality in a collapsing economic science." Women must not be satisfied with "the crumbs that fall from the great men's tables," she warns, but must create new goals that "contribute toward the total improvement of mankind." It is in this sense that Beard so strongly criticizes "mere feministic enthusiasm for sheer equalitarian effort." Her attack upon the demand for equality, which many saw as conservative, is actually radical in its implications. Women must take the education that they have fought for and "socialize it . . . render it of permanent value by stretching it beyond the privileged and idle services of a class . . . to make it . . . an agent of humanitarian evolution."

The audience to whom she addressed these provocative remarks was indeed "privileged and idle," and therefore her glib remarks of the value of college should be taken more rhetorically than literally.

In a period of financial panic such as the western world is now experiencing, every institution, as well as popular philosophy and line of conduct, faces appraisal as a social utility. Institutions must be supported and their claim upon economic sustenance or their contribution to economic life must in lean years pass the test of public value. If they have none, they may be swept aside. If they have only a modicum, they may be allowed to continue but on a reduced scale. The needs of humanity at large may become paramount over the needs of caste or class. Again and again,

[1]. "University Discipline for Women—Asset or Handicap?" *Journal of the American Association of University Women*, Vol. XXV, No. 3, April, 1932, pp. 129–133.

even in American history, a crisis has summoned to the bar of social judgment privileged purposes and means of attainment. One has only to recall the list of private rights once legal, now defunct, to realize how insecure in the long run, at any rate, are the immunities of the few as against the many.

Criticism of ideals and behavior in a series of cyclical depressions has thus become traditional. Hence it is inevitable that formal higher education in our colleges and universities should now be weighed in the balance and estimated both from a monetary and a cultural point of view. It is of the deepest significance moreover that our modern education, long a fetish, French inspired, German guided, should now in its turn receive a harsh analysis in the post-war deflation and new reckoning. . . .

This law of institutional appraisal affects women perhaps in a peculiar way. Into the learned caste of university-trained citizens they have been the last to enter, and just as they prove their capacity to belong on equal terms, the caste itself loses much of its preciosity. If it be true, as the survey made among its members by the American Woman's Association of New York City seems to indicate, that in this depression the woman with a Ph.D. is faring the best from an economic standpoint, two things must be remembered: first, that in many parts of the country Ph.D.'s are actually selling ice-cream sodas at fountains, chopping and trying to sell wood from the forest for fires, or confronting bread lines in cities; second, that acceptance of this survey's implication on the part of multitudes would produce a flood of the highest trained university specialists, which might do what floods usually do, namely inundate the scene. There is in fact a rush of collegians, male and female, unable to secure positions at the present time, back to the seats of learning in the hope that more education of a formal variety will bring its economic reward, for even culture must be paid for. Is their hope to be realized or is their tragedy simply in the making?

Society at best can assimilate only a given number of educated specialists. Culturally they may possess superior dialectic or informed minds, but unless they can make an essential place for themselves in the common life, unless they can apply their powers of reasoning to social needs and use their discipline for solving public problems, they must expect to meet the same fate as the uneducated in periods of trouble. This is not a time when private patrons can necessarily maintain the army of "intellectuals" devoted to the vagaries of idle curiosity or the minutely specialized themes of academic research. Nor can we be sure that from popular taxation sufficient funds can be indefinitely wrested to support an unlimited army headed in that direction. Women who seem bent in increasing numbers on the acquisition of the Ph.D. must therefore reckon with the hosts. In history the ranks of scholastics have again and again become overcrowded and have had to be weeded out.

Would this be a pity if it should recur? Would it be a feminine misfortune if, at the very hour when female talents for becoming doctors of philosophy or experts in learned pursuits of a lesser degree are beyond dispute, the ground under their feet should become as quicksand? History raises doubts. History demands that women question the easy assumption that this is a man's world and that, in consequence, women must follow men's lead in education loyally and exactly, as their genius permits. This subservience overlooks the intellectualism of women before the era of university degrees, the powerful and dramatic record of women's influence in making history. It is possible that university discipline for women today may even be a definite handicap, as it may be a definite handicap for a large percentage of the young men who submit themselves to it with an expectation of economic return. What is more, it may conceivably be a graver handicap for women than for men.

The fact that women are mainly trained by the male of the species in his own modes and manners or in his notions of her "proper sphere," for one thing, may unduly crush the initiative of the girl student and force her to believe that she must follow the masculine leadership or authority without deviation and at all costs. Women actually tend to out-Herod Herod in their devotion to established thought, to standards often unrelated to their own useful instincts and desires. There is considerable warrant for the thesis that university careers guided by men have deepened the intellectual cowardice of women instead of alleviating it. By accepting man's estimate of his own behavior, economic, political, industrial, and mental, at his own figures without considering the long and important drama of feminine behavior and feminine interests, women may lose ground both intellectually and economically.

The objective of equal pay for equal work, or the mere feministic enthusiasm for sheer equalitarian effort with scholastics, has developed in women an over-respect for established thought. Having thus lost the play of their critical faculties which education should impart, they have failed to grasp the import of a learned caste. That is one of their intellectual hazards through excessive instruction of the present form. On their own initiative, through more worldly experience, they might regain their poise.

If there is intellectual hazard in woman's acceptance of a man-made system of education, there is also economic hazard. Modern seats of learning have somewhat reshaped women's mentality, and thereby affected proportionately their economic plight. They can only compete in a man's world, if they believe it to be that, on his terms. The result is that their imagination is apt to be stifled even in the matter of earning their daily bread; trained women are inclined to sink low in the ranks of the helpless overspecialized and inert brain workers who can thrive only in a society with an elaborate surplus with which to maintain scholastic luxuries. As long as there are foundations provided with sums of money which they can devote to supplementing teaching positions, the learned of both sexes may find employment, unless such foundations are directed by men along the lines of their peculiar enterprises, whether nurtured by the gifts of women or not. If men keep their hands on these subsidiary funds as they do on collegiate institutions, learned women may not even reap the full advantages in research fields that their discipline suggests. In both directions they may become too dependent on men—for sustenance no less than for ideological management. In all this there is a sharp irony, owing to the fact that the whole scheme of university careers for women was mainly devised by non-formally educated women—inspired by theories of sex equality, it is true, but on the whole also by social perspectives. They expected their sex to profit through prolonged study but at the same time to make social contributions of importance through their enlarged knowledge, as they were themselves doing self-taught.

It took great initiative to open the avenues of higher education and better teaching positions to women. It took energy and imagination likewise to launch women on the wide sea of social service. It will take even greater imagination to rescue them from the slough of unquestioning equality in a collapsing economic scene. And the issue arises of ways and means. Can the learned save themselves from the wreck of their own hopes until "hope creates from its own wreck the thing it contemplates," as Shelly expressed the problem of movement, or will the *bankruptcy* of the intellectual follow the *treason* of the intellectual into the historical record again in this our day?

This is the issue I would have collegiate women and older women face. And in so doing I would call their attention again to the fact that, notwithstanding such dicta as Spengler's that men make history, women have made it just as much and possibly more. Modern anthropological and archaeological knowledge, novelties in mental development, reveal the amazing share women had in early cultural history. It now appears that women launched civilization; that they played the grand rôle in the first terrific human crisis by creating clothing, extending the diet, and healing the sick, and at least helped to shelter the shivering, hungry, suffering, and homeless human animal. They may have discovered agriculture—that incalculably useful human enterprise; leading investigators of the past give them the credit in accordance with the best suppositions based on available data. In later periods we find women always at the center of social movements, making states, promoting exploration, cooperating in scientific advances; they have never been solely on the side lines observing passively or waiting for men to put them to needed work. In every crisis women have helped to determine the outcome. Indeed, they have been so positive and active in shaping events and social forms that it seems as if the major decision was often theirs. So down to this our day no story of cultural history is adequate which neglects or minimizes women's power in the world.

If the formal education which they have won the right to enjoy does not turn to ashes in their hands, women must help to socialize it, to render it of permanent value by stretching it beyond the privileged and idle services of a class, to make it of deeper consequence than was the Renaissance, to make it a reflection of the world spirit and an agent of humanitarian evolution. Their cultural rôle cannot end with the acquisition of the highest degree, or a position as head of a seat of learning. If it does, their economic independence will be curtailed. They must examine their latest privilege in the light of common needs and see what it has to contribute toward the total improvement of mankind. Otherwise it is but a laborious and casual way of filling up gaps in employment, a sheer amusement, or a mistaken choice of equipment for the harsh necessities of economic life. Waiting for men to make the first move will avail little unless women continue to prefer the crumbs that fall from the great men's tables.

From the man's world hints begin to come of new planning, of fresh intellectual and economic excursions. What is coming from the woman's?

4. The College and
Alumnae in
Contemporary Life[1]

NOTE: *As Mary Beard moved from political activism to what would now be called feminist consciousness-raising, her interests increasingly centered on persuading women of their own vital history. She reached out to many different kinds of audiences through a variety of means. In the address reprinted below, which opened a symposium at the biennial convention of the American Association of University Women, she directs serious criticism at the militant feminists because it was in the community of educated women that they had their greatest following. She saw herself as engaged in a fierce struggle for the minds of women and the feminists as obstructing her progress. Beard sought to free women from the retrogressive effort of striving for whatever it is that men have. She offered, instead, a vision in which women, strengthened by the knowledge of their power and force, create a more humane society in which both men and women flourish.*

To buttress her argument that women should not settle for an education identical to man's, Beard utilizes the tools of cultural anthropology, which was still an undeveloped social science in 1933, to examine the evolution of mass education in the United States. Democratic education developed in America at a time when "expanding capitalism was opening the path to class mobility," and part of the process was the socialization of women and girls to satisfy the political and educational needs of a bourgeois, competitive society. Feminists unthinkingly accepted the rules of the capitalist game and demanded an equal place in it. Each time women could demonstrate, for example, that they "could compose just as rigid documents for their doctoral theses as the most sterile man," there was rejoicing by the "egalitarians."

There were really important things for women to rebel against, such as the "blind instinct for power" and the "rugged individualism" of capitalist society. Instead, feminists demanded the right to share these

---

1. This address opened a symposium at the biennial convention of the American Association of University Women in 1933. It was reprinted in the *Journal of the American Association of University Women*, Vol. XXVII, No. 1, October, 1933, pp. 11–16.

prerogatives. But the suffering brought about by the Depression, says Beard, forces women to recognize that, for them, there is no escape from "the central problems of life." Woman is indeed "a primordial force," but she continues to waver "between the will to create" and the will "merely to enjoy."

In her earlier writings, Beard chose to accentuate the creative aspect of woman's historic powers, suggesting that woman's force is essentially positive. In this speech, the emphasis is more on woman's power as a neutral force, capable of being used in many ways, for social good or "merely to enjoy." It is this emphasis that she usually developed in later work.

In view of the kinds of objections Beard raised to the militant feminists of her day, it is inaccurate to classify her as a conservative critic, as many of those feminists did. Quite the contrary. Her critique is from a stance so radical as to be politically light years away from the woman's movement of her time. One could better criticize her radical vision by noting that she provided no logical steps for middle-class reform women to use to reach her goal. Beard's early involvement with trade union women enabled her to define the woman's movement from a working-class perspective. What her analysis lacks is a ruling-class perspective. That is, she does not integrate into her feminist theory the kind of analysis that could lead middle-class feminists, who represented most of the woman's movement, inexorably to her radical vision. She saw clearly the limitations of their goals and the strength of her own, but she was not able to demonstrate to them why it was in their interest to reject their individual values and embrace her social values. In defense of Beard's lapse, nobody has yet done any better in resolving this question.

The lens through which any social system or one of its aspects is surveyed would seem to be the first consideration in its discussion, for the nature of the cultural lens employed determines the interpretation of the culture observed. For example, the American Puritan, religionist and economist, still on the carpet for judgment as to the value of his scheme of life and thought, takes on chameleon hues according to the spectacles used by the religious, economic, and political cults or by the skeptics, historians, and feminists who study him. Hence if one wishes to form an unbiased opinion about Puritanism, account must be taken of the reflectors turned upon it. And what is true with respect to thinking about Puritanism is true with respect to thinking about any of our contemporary matters, such as education. . . .

Gazing neither to the right nor the left, the feminist peers through her frame of equality and concentrates on what the man receives in the way of education, satisfied to have a gentleman's discipline if that is what he gets, training for banking or corporation management if men's training runs in those directions, or preparation for preaching if the man preaches. Within the women's colleges are some teachers who refuse to recognize any value in women's study of themselves; they declare that the time has arrived for a sexless consideration of the world. Other teachers seek to draw education into closer correspondence with the rôle of women in the home. . . .

If I may be so bold as to offer one more mirror, cultural anthropology, I shall justify it on the ground that it reckons with all the others. Cultural anthropology integrates education into the total situation, an integration demanded by the very statement of the subject we are here to discuss today: The College and Alumnae in Contemporary Life. Contemporary life comprises the whole of reality—action and thought. It includes the feminist, the anti-feminist, the Daughter of the American Revolution, the scholastic, the benefactor who finances schools, the financed, the domestic scientist, the priest, the iconoclast, the innovator, the Tory, and the radical. It likewise includes the proletarian, the capitalist, the unemployed, the urbanite, and the farmer. . . .

Cultural anthropology helps us to see our action and our throught in relation to all life. Associated with world history, it covers in all times and places the relation between education and the economic system in which it operates.

*　　*　　*

If society becomes predominantly bourgeois, as it did become in the United States within the past seventy-five years, and if it becomes as rich as this American bourgeoisie became, it creates a school system designed to fit young people into its dominant scheme of things.

In the study of this dominant American culture, which got into its full stride after the great social war of the sixties, one encounters such early educational leaders as Horace Mann, Henry Barnard, and Lucy Stone, who rendered the philosophy of democratic schooling popular and explored the possibilities of higher learning with reference to a competitive age. According to their vision, men and women were to be given a chance to rise from the soil, throw off the bondage to kings and priests, learn to be competing units in a competitive system, and discover their natural levels.

Horace Mann, Henry Barnard, the feminists, and the labor agitators who united in the demand for democratic schooling, presented their program and tried to apply it at a period when an expanding capitalism was opening the path to class mobility, when machine production was breaking industry into specialized manipulations calling for peculiar skills and experiments in management, when the battle lines were forming for the conflict which was to end in the destruction of the obstructive planting aristocracy, when lawyers and doctors, writers and advertisers, lecturers and entertainers, buyers and sellers, clerks and secretaries, seemed to have a boundless area and a limitless future for their display of energy. The growing urge for an acquaintance with the learning and art of the past, hitherto suppressed by poverty or Puritanism, was at the same time giving patronage to scholars and musicians, painters and sculptors. The social trend was distinctly bourgeois; that is, middle class, capitalistic, democratic—what we summarize in the term "white collarism" to distinguish it from agricultural economy. And the appropriate educational set-up was brought to perfection in the high noon of prosperity that followed the World War. Schools of business administration were then planted in the colleges beside the existing schools of law, medicine, the liberal arts, technology, and the fine arts. The wonder that was Rome may have been monuments and law. The wonder that was America was democratic education. We did not use the words capitalism and the bourgeoisie in the heyday of prosperity and institutional education.

In this capitalist development and its shadowing education, women were intimately involved, whether as conscious rebels such as Henry Adams described or as natural concomitants of a changed economy. It was women and girls who "manned" the first textile mills which launched machine industry in America and thereby made good the declaration of Alexander Hamilton, first secretary of the treasury and father of our industrial revolution, that the revolution could be achieved because there was this available labor competent to the task. It was women and girls who helped to push capitalism forward by their work in typing and filing and warehousing, by their service as capable secretaries to big businessmen, by their own adventures into trades and professions, and most of all by their purchase of the commodities that flowed from the mills.

To the educational accompaniment of capitalism, women and girls proved an equal adaptability. And every innovation on their part was acclaimed as a triumph for democratic liberty. Every new post won within the seats of learning that brought women nearer the highest post held by a man was a cause for exultation. The more women who crowded into the departments of pedagogy, where method of teaching rather than content of thought was the safe if insane code, the better in the eyes of an egalitarian. There was cause for intense gratification when the first woman Ph.D. won her letters, and continuing gratification that women could compose just as rigid documents for their doctoral theses as the most sterile man. Pleasure was derived from the fact that she could concoct as quaint intelligence and personality tests as the main playboy. The fact-finders, adders, and compilers satisfied the flair for proving efficiency in their fields. And it was supremely thrilling to watch women rushing into offices, trades, and professions! Getting admitted to the learned and literary societies! Doing the high jumps and the shot-putting and the airplaning! Leading in adult education and social work! Bringing child-understanding and humanism to bear on family relations! Holding public office! Getting into Congress! Being talked about for President!

All along the line the effort bent toward equality and liberty was productive, notwithstanding the fact that rich women were inclined to bestow their benefactions more generously on the education of men. The new women, unknown to 1840, whom Henry Adams called "shifting visions," were admittedly successful rebels, even if the only thing they knew to rebel against was maternity. There were other things to rebel against if they had but known it, and the chief of these was the blind instinct of power which the man who paced them possessed. Their conception of education was simple because it trailed men's; what was good enough for men was perfect for women. And the men's was simple because it relied instinctively on power, instead of reckoning rationally on the antithesis of power. Men believed in the perpetuity of rugged individualism, centering on "catch as catch can." Unfortunately for them and for their adherents, by 1929 the catch seemed to have worked out and we began to hear about the Lost Generation. But meanwhile even the teachers had been inarticulate about things they saw ahead. Did they meditate on the future?

With the belated but frank recognition that reactionary capitalism has met its Waterloo, slowly but surely comes the recognition that its shadowing bourgeois education is defaulting. As legislatures reduce appropriations for state colleges and force them to consider the closing of entire departments of learning, as faculty salaries are cut again and again, as teachers are dismissed because there are no funds for their maintenance, as the flood of graduates looking for posts flows hither and yon without finding empty nooks, as schools turn the keys in their doors or keep open on a basis of teacher martyrdom, educators begin to summon emergency conferences and argue "ways out" for education as capitalists argue "ways out" for business enterprise. But no way out is yet in sight for business, teachers, or taught.

Since the college, the alumnae, and contemporary life are a single entity in fact, what is the import of such current intellectual phrases as the "organization, transmission, extension and application of knowledge; awakening, developing, enlarging, disciplining and harmonizing abilities, interests, appreciations, and attitudes; inspiring dedication to the common good?" If we use these phrases must we not inquire, in the midst of a shattered individualism, what precise knowledge is to be organized as well as how it is to be transmitted and applied? If there is to be a dedication to the common good, must we not define the common good in intelligible language? If education is a part of the cultural anthropology, into what new totality is it to be integrated?

It can scarcely be idle speculation to ponder on the possibility that another social revolution in America is a *fait accompli*. One reason why there have been so many explanations for the fall of Rome is that the Romans themselves did not know when it had fallen. The upper structure of the society sank down so gradually into the substratum that there were professors in the University of Bordeaux who did not realize that the Empire had passed when barbarians were in actual possession of the Eternal City. So today professors are apparently sitting quietly in their berths, for the most part, gently musing on the likelihood that Roosevelt is saving the whole bourgeoisie.

Between Communism and Fascism all Europe and indeed the Far East as well now hover. The literature and practice with respect to sex privilege within those systems of economy and power must cease to be academic propositions to us, as our own bourgeoise system slides down the financial hill. We cannot turn the clock back to 1848, when the Women's Declaration of Independence was framed and given to the world; for the civilization of 1848 is not the civilization of 1933. By 1940,

Henry Adams prophesied, the meaning of the new American woman would be revealed. "By whom?" we may well ask now.

Is the meaning of the new woman to reveal the preponderance of the *vis inertiae* of the family interest again? Or is it a conscious purpose to be disclosed which will comprise the state no less than the family? Will the advantages in the way of initiative, courage, experience in new fields, and self-respect, gained under the capitalist individualism, be lost to the coming generations of American women? Or will American women bend the future to their will as a result of this heritage, and demonstrate an energy of brain as of body, aware of the limits to individualism as well as the shortcomings of sheer *vis inertiae?*

The bourgeois mother or wife may concentrate on her biological and emotional needs, devise finely conceived training for parenthood, and test the double life of domesticity and public work to her heart's content as long as the economic foundations of the bourgeois family hold taut. But as these weaken, even the good wife and noble mother must face the larger actuality in which the masses are involved—the actuality of food, clothing, and shelter, the primordial struggle for existence.

The truth is that there has never been any escape for women from the central problems of life, except for a brief moment while the capitalist merry-go-round was whirling. The theory of subjection to the contrary notwithstanding, no system of economics, politics, or education framed by men has ever been able to go its own way for any length of time as an illustration of man's will alone. Man may not intend to help woman. He may devise political systems with his own desires in view. But there is also to be reckoned with the woman's will which continuously asserts itself. Henry Adams saw her will too exclusively as inertia, for she could both build up and destroy civilization. Woman is a primordial force, no doubt. But she wavers always between the will to create and the will merely to enjoy which leads to her doom.

If Croce is right, in the particular the universal is disclosed. Thus what we do today is characteristic of what we have always done. But if modern American women could, in their thinking, move closer to the center of life, understand where they actually get sustenance, how they in fact are eternally either building up or tearing down civilization, then strengthened and glorified by their greater awareness of their historic and potential role in culture, they might answer one of the greatest riddles of the universe—what do women want of life?—And come nearer to getting it.

5. *The Direction of Women's Education*[1]

NOTE: *This address, delivered in 1937 at the centenary celebration of Mount Holyoke College, is a succinct and tightly constructed analysis of the history of women's education and the tradition of enlightened humanism, what Beard calls the "feminine principle of history." Despite the widespread belief that women were uneducated until the nineteenth century, women "always had access to the education and culture of their societies," Beard once again asserts. It was men who "created the body . . . of knowledge, thought, values and methods called education," kept it under their guardianship, and then excluded women. Thus, when feminists claim that they pioneer in demanding equal education for women, what they mean is that they seek equal access to that particular form of male-dominated educational system that developed relatively late in human history. Abigail Adams and Elizabeth Cady Stanton, without a "Harvard, Yale, Princeton or Columbia degree," were highly educated women, although the institutions of formal learning were closed to them. The masters of these institutions try to define education for all of us.*

At the very time when young American women were finally admitted into the academic institutions, those institutions were expounding doctrines that were built upon "amoral and mechanistic, insensate, laissez-faire" propositions. The formal education which was finally granted to women after generations of struggle "condemned every humane tradition of the education which had been woman's heritage from the Enlightenment." The "new learning" was false and one-sided. Fortunately, humanism was to reappear, expounded by such women as Jane Addams, Julia Lathrop, and Florence Kelley, who offered a philosophy "less in conformity with the stockyards." They reintroduced the ethical dimension into learning, but usually by having to go outside the "academic cloister."

The choice remains, Beard dramatically concludes, as to the direction women's education will take: "the barracks, the battlefield, the concentration camp, soldier-breeding, and . . . scholasticism" on the masculine side; and "the home, the arts of peaceful industry, training for life, and . . . cultural values" on the feminine side. In a world so weighted on

---

1. This speech was delivered at the Alumnae Luncheon for the Centenary of Mount Holyoke College, May 7, 1937. It was printed in *The Centenary of Mount Holyoke College*, pp. 44–61.

the side "of militarism and sheer force," it is incumbent upon women to "take their stand for the cause of enlightened humanism" and in behalf of the "enduring values."

In this speech Beard forcefully reaffirms her earlier thesis that woman's historic role has been a positive and creative one. Before criticizing her exaggerated claims, let us remember Mary Beard's passionate commitment to social action, and the state of the world in 1937. In the last piece of this collection, "The Economic Background of the Sex Life of the Unmarried Adult" (see pages 227–239), Beard develops a considerably more balanced view of women's complex role in history. That article was written for a general audience. In this selection she speaks to a well-bred, cultivated group of college-educated women, meeting to celebrate the anniversary of the founding of their elite woman's college. It was a genteel assemblage. Except for a few appropriate remarks in deference to the occasion, Beard's intemperate and explosive words are aimed at rousing these women to action in the face of the terrifying international threat to "enlightened humanism."

This would certainly be a trite comment on this celebration at Mount Holyoke in the year 1937 were it not for the popular belief that Mary Lyon, one hundred years ago, in this new world of America, pioneered in the establishment of equal education for women. Nor is such a belief popular only. It prevails among distinguished specialists in our seats of the highest learning and finds constant expression there in fateful ways.- . . . Gratifying as it is to American pride, this presentation of the case does not correspond with historic events and it carries implications that lead to a profound misconception of education and of women's relation to the subject matter and the process. Consider the substance and the upshot of these implications. There is a distinct thing called education—a unit complete in itself. Men created the body, or unit, of knowledge, thought, values and methods called education. It was long in their exclusive guardianship. America pioneered in giving women equal access to this masculine creation and heritage. The great prize has been won at last. Consequently, it is not incumbent upon women to criticize ungratefully this education so lavishly opened to them now; any one who has received it in any institution of learning on the accredited list is fully competent to instruct them; whatever is handed out to them in the guise of education is to be accepted by them as the true substance and sum of education; when they have received it, they are to regard their minds as trained; and there is nothing more to be done unless perchance they wish to hand it on to others in the form of adult education. In short the history of the business is closed like Goethe's book with seven seals. The victory is good. There is really nothing left but to crown the heroes and heroines with laurels and sing in unison: "Peace on earth; goodwill to men."

But in my opinion this conception of what has happened in America and woman's education does not square with the facts. Indeed in all the ledger of American illusions there seems to me to be none more untenable as history, more provincial in outlook, so inconsistent with the total experience of mankind. In part it must be charged to the desire of Protestants to break with the past as error. In part it must be charged to the exigencies of the woman's rights movement which likewise made the past all a wretched mistake.

Of course no illusion is a sound basis for a value-judgment and as a working hypothesis this particular fancy is a perilous one for women. Hence it is important for us to consider what Mary Lyon actually did a century ago in America. Granted that she was a crusading educator, where lay her goal? Of what culture did she propose to make education for women an agency? What culture did her enterprise reflect? We may say, with confidence I believe, that what Mary Lyon actually did a hundred years ago in America was to promote education, within a seminary, for girls of the lower economic brackets representing a class then deemed the bulwark of this republic on the basis of a Protestant ideology, inspired with a zest for missionary effort including the urge toward charitable work of a Christian temper. Unquestionably this was in the nature of an innovation. Just as unquestionably it mirrored the culture of her day and habitation when, from tiny villages in New England, Protestants, following in the wake of European Catholic missionaries, were setting forth to convert the "heathen" of the world and stimulate them to humane undertakings. In aspiring to train young women for American life, Mary Lyon also aspired to train missionaries.

How well the missionary effort succeeded was demonstrated for me a few years ago when I visited a woman's Christian college in Japan; there I heard Mary Lyon's name spoken with reverence as we speak it here today with reverence; there I saw a remarkably faithful reproduction of the Protestant humanistic education given by Mary Lyon to girls of the humbler social classes, for the students in the Japanese institution were likewise of those classes.

But what Mary Lyon did not do and could not do was to pioneer in equal education for women. And the truth is that no one ever "pioneers in increasing opportunities and participation." The juxtaposition of those words is meaningless. And actually women had always shared in the prevalent education of races, nations, and classes and in fixing as well as enjoying cultural values. . . .

How could any American ever have supposed that any economic, political, social or intellectual scheme could have rooted itself in any land without the consent and co-operation of women? Throughout the ages of human societies, even before the founding of colonies in the New World, women had shared in the substance of education devised for and reflecting their class whatever it was. From time to time women were also spurs to new forms of education deemed by them more suitable than the training à la mode. . . . Certainly no man had written more skilfully on that crucial chapter of English history, the revolutionary movement of the Puritan age, than Lucy Hutchinson in her Memoir of her husband, Colonel Hutchinson. And she was matched in the new world later by Mercy Warren who displayed literary power, insight and critical political judgment in her three-volumed *History of the American Revolution*. While Abigail Adams like Mary Astell yearned to have her sex better educated, Abigail Adams like Mary Astell must be acknowledged as a substantially educated woman of the century in which she lived and asserted rebellious leadership. Her letters during the Revolution and afterwards from England compare well with any letters written from Massachusetts or England by men and women in the twentieth century decorated with college degrees.

The broad view and the long view of education therefore seem to lead alike to the conclusion that America did not exactly pioneer in opening educational opportunities to women. In the age of Catholic unity and in Latin countries, women had enjoyed educational opportunities of many kinds. Where the doors of formal institutions had been barred to women, they had managed to acquire an education in other ways. Though Harvard, Yale and Princeton were closed to American women in the Protestant age, the women of the American Revolution were without a doubt not only indispensable to the triumph of economic independence but were also independent and forceful thinkers.

That illiteracy was not the common lot of white women in America before the day of equal opportunity in formal education is made evident by the early surveys of the Census. The first survey, taken in 1840, shows that slightly over 90 per cent of the white men and women twenty years of age and older could read and write. Although the next Census taken in 1850 reveals a small drop, still 90 per cent of the native white population could read and write. When deficiencies in opportunity are considered, the relative education of women is amazing. In seven states there were more illiterate men than women and out of a total in round numbers of 936,000 illiterate whites the excess of illiterate women over illiterate men was only 183,000 in round numbers. In respect of the Latin tradition to which I have referred, it is interesting to note that among the whites in New Mexico in 1850 the number of illiterate men exceeded the number of illiterate women. It would be improper to make these figures mean too much but they surely dispose of the fiction that women were far behind men in literacy in 1837 when presumably the pioneering in equal education began. In adopting the illusion that they had been nothing with respect to education, in cutting loose from their own vast heritage of knowledge, experience, and thought, in casting off the ennobling memory of themselves, women lost their bearings as women and therefore as human beings all of whom are either men or women. Thus when the doors of institutions of formal learning were unlocked for them, they too lightly accepted as education the body of knowledge and the developing doctrines which the masters of those institutions deemed to be education in its fulness.

This terrific break in woman's tradition may be illustrated by a single example although a large comprehension of its significance can only come from an intimate acquaintance with the archives of women—that is, with the speeches and writings of the hundreds of American women who in the middle period of American history were public personalities. The single illustration I have selected is afforded by the thought of Elizabeth Cady Stanton with reference to American democracy and civilization. Despite her lack of a Harvard, Yale, Princeton or Columbia degree, this mother of many sons accustomed to ask her basic questions about history, nations, government and law, replied to them out of a wide and deep knowledge illuminated by her humanist sympathies. For many years two o'clock in the morning was her regular bedtime and the intervening hours were spent in reading the opinions of the wise and turning these over in the alembic of her own intelligence. What was produced in her own mind was given to the public, from the platform, over a period of twelve years and more, during eight months annually, as she toured the continent under the auspices of the Lyceum bureau.

* * *

The break in that feminine tradition of concern with social principles came with college education for women. In the formal instruction which girls began to receive in the sixties and which led in the eighties to the elevation of Mount Holyoke from a seminary to the status of a college, the controlling influence, aside perhaps from the courses in belles lettres, was the secular, amoral, materialistic, mechanistic doctrine of each against all, sometimes described in a daintier fashion as laissez faire. William Graham Sumner expounded this doctrine to the men at Yale and his disciples expounded it to women blessed with an equal education. . . .

This creed regnant upon American campuses in the era of equal college education in the so-called "humanities" denied the role and force of interests in society, left the power of property out of its reckoning, and offered nature in the raw, freed even from the interests and unions of class, as the foundation of life and labor, of humanity, of civilization and culture. Other points of view, older points of view, became mere "sentimental twaddle" conducive to debilitating "effeminacy." If any young woman on a college campus argued that all economic and political activities spring from social and moral interests, as the founding fathers and mothers of our democratic republic had formerly argued, her voice was drowned out by the thunders of the schoolmen and school administrations in the early days of equal collegiate education.

Hence in the process of oral instruction and textbooks on American campuses through which amoral and mechanistic, insensate, laissez-faire indoctrinated the education of women, one of the strangest pages in their history was shaped. A few details point the amoral. In 1884 Professor Laughlin published an edition of John Stuart Mill's *Political Economy* which became the authoritative text. In this edition he reduced the enlightened individualism of Mill to the level of a sheer animal struggle for existence. He claimed to have simplified Mill but in reality he mutilated Mill by cutting out all his humanism and retaining every defense of greed. . . .

In other words, that formal education to which women had won access and which was said to be such a blessing repudiated and condemned every humane tradition of the education which had been woman's heritage from the Enlightenment. Fortunately, by the time women had been thoroughly imbued with the new learning, that very learning began to be understood as a hollow mockery of life. It was so one-sided as to be untrue. It was so unreal as to be false in letter and in social temper. Just as women had proved that they were able to carry the full college program to which the pioneers had won access, its presuppositions and assurances blew up in their faces. Laissez faire did not operate in practice all round as the professors had prophesied and, where it did, the conjuncture of plutocracy, urban poverty and farm tenancy could not be universally regarded as fulfilling the promise of American life so defined on the campuses. So the reappearance of the humanism of the Enlightenment forced a reconsideration of all education, even for men, and of the social policy of which education is phase.

In this American renaissance and revision, a noted triumvirate of college alumnae living in Chicago—Jane Addams, Julia Lathrop, and Florence Kelley—in the very center of individualistic political economy, history, biology and sociology calling itself science, revived the feminine tradition and accepting the fact that they were women, though equally educated, offered society and its educational institutions a philosophy and learning less in conformity with the stockyards. With Professors Richard T. Ely and John R. Commons, themselves not subdued to the concept of liberty as unrestrained license, these collegiate alumnae took leadership in a vigorous campaign for thought and action better conceived. Within a short span of years they helped to write ethical gains into legislation and transform the outlook of American education for men no less than for women. This they did by going outside the academic cloister, by recognizing other life than that in dormitories, by remaining true to their own experiences and reasoning, by maintaining close contact with the realities of the common life—in short, by insisting upon that realism which is in fact the essence of the scientific spirit.

It was in harmony with this American renaissance and revision that Mary E. Woolley began to direct the education of girls as President of Mount Holyoke at the turn of our own century—a tendency that bridged the chasm cut by laissez faire in the Enlightenment. The new spirit had already begun to clear up the imperative of academic dogmatism and reconstruct the essential contact with the common life. For President Woolley the college was never a mere cloister for refining ancient theories or splitting hairs inordinately split in times past. That was never her idea of a liberal arts course. . . .

Before us all indeed is the urgency of an intelligent choice in the direction of women's education. Before us is the choice between the acceptance of sheer force and the rationalization of its emotions which are in the main the masculine historic inclination, and the humanism of enlightenment with the power of intuitive insight into moral and esthetic values which are in the main the historic feminine inclination. It is the choice once more between the barracks, the battlefield, the concentration camp, soldier-breeding and cloistral scholasticism on the one side; and the home, the arts of peaceful industry, training for life, and the exchange of cultural values on the other side. With good reason do Nietzsche and Bäumler and all their affiliates make women the eternal enemy of the military state.

In the choice which women now make lie the perils of extreme effeminacy no doubt—the preference and quest for ease, comfort and luxury, that is for over-refinement. However, at this hour when the balance is so heavily weighted on the side of militarism and sheer force, the women who know their history and understand their role in the processes of a humane civilization can make only one decision. They must cling deliberately and firmly to their principle of history, take their stand for the cause of enlightened humanism, and make their direction of the education of girls serve the ends of that grand cause.

But let there be no misunderstanding of that education. It means no mere instruction in the arts of keeping house, in child psychology, in sex wiles, in marital relations or the technicalities of scholarship and research, however, important these may be as subsidiaries. It does mean education based squarely on the feminine principle of history, without surrender to men on the march for the kill, and sensitive to the public responsibilities which inexorably flow from that principle.

The preservation and development of this education is, then, no simple tea party for little women and little men. "In much wisdom there is much grief and he that increaseth knowledge increaseth sorrow." So the preservation and development of women's education is a phase of that eternal conflict between the ideal and the real which now splits western civilization to the bottom of its heart. It is a phase of that everlasting struggle for the maintenance and enlargement of those enduring values, the cohesive forces of society, which alone make possible the opportunities in education, economy and culture for all men and women of goodwill.

Woman *is* and *makes* history. *Sub specie aeternitatis.*

6. *Feminism as a Social Phenomenon*[1]

NOTE: *In this concise statement, free of polemics, Mary Beard examines nineteenth century feminism in its relationship to the ideas of the Enlightenment and the development of capitalism. The feminist program and philosophy formulated in the 1840s was built upon the previous century's ideals of progress and equality. At its best, she says, it was embodied in the life and work of Elizabeth Cady Stanton, who not only framed a feminist program of democratic rights but extended those principles to call for the "elimination of poverty [and] slavery in the fields, mines and factories." In time, the feminist program degenerated, as did most social values in the nation; it became "humanistically anemic" as it turned into a crusade for vigorous individualism.*

Women as force for good or evil reappears as the theme. Beard sees feminism, not as the end of the struggle for human rights, but as one link "in the long chain of women's historic affirmation," which could, if women so choose, represent a "new creative philosophy."

Every great creative idea, formulated as a philosophy, has a social setting—in time, in a geographical location, in a political economy, in a matrix of interests and knowledge. It is not a free-swinging phenomenon like a balloon without moorings. It is not produced in a vacuum and, being creative, it does not work in a vacuum. Nurtured on things experienced and things known, it reaches out toward the unknown like a flower on a stalk growing out of the soil. And this was as true of the feminist philosophy and program of action formulated a century ago in America as it had been true of every preceding philosophy and program of action.

The time setting of American feminism in the 1840's was the lingering age of the Enlightenment, with the ideals of which all the intellectual leaders of the new world as of the old world were still imbued.

One of those ideals was the idea of "Progress," first clearly formulated in 1737 by l'Abbé de Saint-Pierre of Paris as an optimistic view of

---

1. "Feminism as a Social Phenomenon," *Woman's Press Magazine*, November, 1940.

humanity's future. At that date it was still heretical to believe that humanity had developed, instead of degenerated, through the ages of the past, from its original perfection in a golden prehistoric age. . . .

The other ideal advanced in the Enlightenment was Rousseau's—the doctrine of Equality as a natural right, as a birthright—embodied in his *Contrat Social* published in 1762. This doctrine emphasized the worth of the individual beyond its estimation in the Renaissance and furnished the philosophy for democracy.

In the closing decade of the eighteenth century, Mary Wollstonecraft of England formulated a philosophy of feminism which had the distinction of combining the enlightened ideal of individual worth and personality with the enlightened ideal of continuous progress in general welfare through the assumption of social obligations. Her *Vindication of the Rights of Women* was widely read in the United States and was a stimulus to American feminist insurgency.

Like Mary Wollstonecraft, the American feminists of the 1840's were sensitive alike to the claims of the individual and to the claims of society. If ruggedly individualistic, they were also ruggedly humanistic and reformist. Their speeches and writings rang with the idea and word "progress," used in an ethical-social relation, as l'Abbé de Saint-Pierre had used it, while they asserted the right of women to equal civil liberties with men. Indeed, throughout her long public career, Elizabeth Cady Stanton, one of the prime organizers of the 1848 convention at Seneca Falls which framed a feminist program for action, combined, with her demand for democratic privileges for women, the demand for progress in the elimination of poverty, slavery in fields, mines and factories, and ignorance. Amid the rise of a self-interested plutocracy and the heightened drive of capitalistic enterprise, she retained the spirit of the Enlightenment, in its two-fold idealism.

Despite its rise in a humanistic era, American feminism veered steadily toward obsession with natural rights and the idea of equality in self-interestedness. It grew vigorously individualistic. It became humanistically anemic. It again illustrated the truth that ideas and movements mirror time, physical circumstances, political economy and culture. . . .

What then is to be celebrated in 1940, by feminists, as a century of progress? Is it the sweep from the humanistic impulses of early feminism and the idealisms of the Enlightenment to the depressive reality of mature individualistic feminism and "Grapes of Wrath"? Is it the symbols of "careering" while the substance crumbles away for the continuity of progress conceived in terms of competitive prowess alone?

Whatever this celebration undertakes to exalt, it is set, like all celebrations, in a time and a place, in political economy and in culture. It will either sing a dirge, while it fancies it is singing a paean to the future or it will re-enact women's historic role of invigorating thought and action with a new consciousness of needs and creative opportunities.

In every great crisis of history, woman has been a Force in the thought and action evolving out of crisis. She has even been instrumental in helping to bring on crises by her greed, avarice and ferocity, equaling man's. She has helped to build up and helped to destroy all the civilizations on the records of the ages. When they have dissolved, through the excesses of warfare and/or the exploitation of the many by the few, women have gone to work to renew society at its sources.

Women of the past did these things for instance:

> Launched civilization in the beginning by creating the arts of life. The best available evidence credits them with discovering agriculture. This changed nomads into settled, civilized human beings. It promoted family life, prolonged infancy, made the fireside a beloved thing
>
> Participated in the cultivation of thought about life and society. Every new level reached by the power of the mind reflected the challenge of men's and women's minds in social communion
>
> Shared importantly in the enlargement of positive knowledge, including scientific findings, and in the dissemination of knowledge
>
> Contributed to all the arts, including Letters
>
> Played a major role in erecting the great Atlantic States of Europe out of feudal chaos
>
> Initiated and joined in war-making, tyranny, pomp, extravagance of all kinds, oppression, and other ruthless demonstrations of power
>
> Initiated and joined in business and professional enterprises throughout the ages
>
> Indicated that Woman was Force

Feminism in America has been another link in the long chain of women's historic affirmations. Despite the modern dogma to the effect that women were a subject sex until the nineteenth century "emancipated" them from history, women in history had demonstrated strong wills and purposes, had made assertions, and had directed or influenced all human destiny, including their own, since human life began.

Presumably, therefore, if women now knew their own history of thought and action and were not merely familiar with hearsay about it, largely man-inspired, they would, in America, re-analyze themselves and their purposes in the light of their traditional Force, and formulate in a changed American setting a new creative philosophy for themselves and for society of which they are necessarily a part.

7. Woman as Force in History: A Study in Traditions and Realities[1]

NOTE: Woman as Force in History *is Mary Ritter Beard's most famous book. It represents the culmination of her years of study and writing on the subject and stands as the mature statement of her thesis on the historic role of women. Many of the ideas and themes she developed in earlier years are pulled together and deepened in this major work. Her analysis of the ideas of William Blackstone and their impact on American feminists occupies a significant portion of what is new and of immense significance in this volume.*

The false and tyrannical idea that women have always been a subject and oppressed sex was manufactured by the American feminist movements in the middle of the nineteenth century, says Beard. The authority cited by feminists to support this proposition was Blackstone, author of Commentaries on the Laws of England, *published in 1765. In his chapter entitled, "Of Husband and Wife," which is frequently referred to by feminists, Blackstone asserts that woman was civilly dead at marriage and that her "very being or legal existence" is "consolidated into that of the husband."*

Mary Beard then effectively shatters the interpretation of that phrase used by feminists one hundred years later. She argues that Blackstone's language was meant to be taken metaphorically, not literally; that he was, in any case, referring only to married women; and, most importantly, that when he used the phrase "in law" he meant precisely and only "in Common Law." According to Beard, those readers trained in law, for whom he was writing, understood all of these qualifications. The Common Law was, Beard says, "only one branch of English law." Other laws of England which could and did modify the Common Law were acts of Parliament and old customs, which were often left undisturbed. Most important, there was Equity, which was administered by a special court and which provided, "in the name of justice, remedies for wrongs for which the Common Law afford no remedies." Many powers denied to women under the Common Law were, says Beard, granted women under Equity. In addition, there were many private agreements of men and women which rarely even were brought to court, but which regulated much of ordinary daily affairs.

---

1. *Woman as Force in History: A Study in Traditions and Realities*, New York: The Macmillan Co., 1946. Paperback editions by Collier Books, 1962, 1971, and 1973. Page citations refer to the original edition.

American feminists, misunderstanding the technical aspects of Blackstone's legal writings, adopted the theory of total legal subjugation as the foundation for the Seneca Falls Declaration of Sentiments and Resolution in 1848, and in so doing "they adopted a fiction about human behavior."

In times past, theologians and moralists insisted that woman was evil and ought to be subjected to man, but it was the feminist manifesto, using Blackstone's dictum as evidence, that argued that woman had, in fact, been subject to man.

Much of the rich detail of the remainder of the book is evidence Beard accumulates to demonstrate the validity of her thesis on Blackstone. The selections reprinted here provide some sampling of that historical material. In the middle ages, she says, sharp class lines determined how one behaved and what rights one had, but sex distinctions, even when they were in law, were so often defied in practice that it is not possible to use any single formula to describe woman's role. Women in the ruling class, she goes on, exercised enormous power. It was not until power passed to parliaments, which were elected by men and composed of men, that women were excluded from the exercise of power.

Beard claims that in precapitalist societies women had most of the privileges and burdens assigned them by their class, and that when women suffered, it was because of their class position, not their sex. It is only with the development of capitalism, she argues, that discrimination on account of sex, regardless of class, becomes pervasive. It is in this time that women are driven out of the professions, out of politics, out of power. The feminist movement, which is born during the period of diminished legal rights, assumes that such restrictions always existed. They then concoct a description of the past that is profoundly untrue.

Mary Beard's challenge to the traditional feminist view of history and politics is important. It has also been largely ignored. To test how valid an interpretation it is requires the kind of empirical work that is only now being undertaken.

FROM THE PREFACE:

This volume, as its subtitle distinctly states, is a *study*. In no part of it is any claim made to an all-embracing fullness or to philosophic completeness.

In the first place, it is a study of the tradition that women were members of a subject sex throughout history. This tradition has exercised an almost tyrannical power over thinking about the relations of men and women, for more than a hundred years.

In the second place, the idea of subjection is tested by reference to historical realities—legal, religious, economic, social, intellectual, military, political, and moral or philosophical.

Since American feminists have long laid emphasis on the alleged subjection of women by law, pointing to Anglo-American Common Law as expounded by Sir William Blackstone, special attention is given to (1) an analysis of his views of that law, (2) an exploration of women's property rights in mediaeval English law, and (3) an examination of the rise and growth of Equity in England and the United States. Stress is laid on Equity for the reason that it almost parallels the development of the Common Law in time and had thoroughly riddled common-law doctrines on married women's property rights long before Blackstone published the first volume of his *Commentaries* in 1765 and more than a hundred years before the feminists of 1848 adopted Blackstone as the prime authority for their belief in the historic subjection of women.

In the third place, inasmuch as for more than a century it has been widely claimed that the idea of equality furnished a perfect guide to women in their search for an escape from "subjection," the origin, nature, and applications of this idea, which had become traditional by 1848, are brought to the inquest.

FROM CHAPTER I: EVERYBODY'S INTEREST: MAN AND WOMAN

Fatefully interlocked with all the visible, vocal, and revolutionary upheavals which, in our own time, have been ripping open and transforming great societies inherited from the nineteenth century and its long past are the relations between men and women. Even underground movements for counter-revolutions, revolutions against revolutions, take vitality from these relations. Thrust into the global violence which marks our age is the dynamism of women who, with men, have set the world on fire and helped to frame plans for its reconstruction.

In the war of propaganda accompanying this war of arms, women have been intransigent combatants. Their old roles of intriguing and spying have been reënacted. Millions of women have been devoting their energies for many years to feeding, clothing, and equipping with munitions the men who fight on land, from the air, on the seas, and beneath the seas. Without the enlistment of women by conscription or their voluntary support, these bitter international contests for military dominance could not have gone forward on such a scale to their fates in the morrow. As in the beginning of organized warfare, back in the aeons of unrecorded history, so in its latest forms the sanction of women is deemed essential to its terrific force.

The competition among the revolutionists for mastery in the human world has been emphatically marked by a competition in conceptions of sex relations.

* * *

The word "man" has been making confusion in many respects for more than a thousand yeras. It was certainly used in the Anglo-Saxon language as early as 825 A.D. to mean specifically the human creature in general; but about the same time it was also used to mean an adult male person; while contemporaneously the word "woman" was in use as meaning an adult female human being. And persons who have occasion to study Anglo-Saxon laws and literature, if they care anything at all about exactness, have to be constantly on guard as to whether "man" means a human creature in general or an adult male. Of course if precision is no consideration, then the translation of the word *man* or *mann* from Anglo-Saxon into English may simply run riot at the will and pleasure of its repeater.

Additional ambiguities have arisen in connection with the word *man*, on account of the tendency to identify it with many other terms in common usage. . . .

So many uncertainties appeared in the administration of the law in England, as citizens, judges, and administrators wrestled with the terms *man* and *men* that Parliament tried in 1850 to clear some of them away by legislation. A law known as Lord Romilly's or Lord Brougham's Act provided that "words importing the masculine gender shall always include women, except where otherwise stated." As a matter of fact, however, conflicts due to uncertainty of meaning did not end, even in

England, respecting the use of the word *man* in statutes and judicial decisions.

Nevertheless, historians, sociologists, literary critics, and other commentators on human affairs have paid little attention to this linguistic problem—a problem of clarity in speech and writing. Yet it involves their judgments on everything human. How does one know whether any writer is using the troublesome words, *man* and *men*, generically or with reference to males only, unless the meaning is made plain by the context or a positive statement? The issue can best be defined in the form of questions perhaps. Are adult males and adult females identical in nature? Are they equals, equivalents, interchangeable parts of humanity, so that these words, *man* and *men*, may be freely used without explanations and at all times? Are the speakers and writers who use these words willing to justify their usages as self-explanatory? If self-explanatory are these words accurately used in all, many, or any cases?

This is no mere quibbling. Naturally men are deeply interested in affirmations about men with their masculine qualities. Unquestionably men are also deeply interested in women. When are they expressing their interests in themselves or in women? Sometimes they take the public into full confidence in this matter. But much of the time they lay themselves open to the accusation that they have failed to think their way through the linguistic, historical, and sociological difficulty.

This problem of clarity in thought, or the lack of it, looms large in hundreds of thousands of printed pages where the words *man* and *men* appear in bewildering profusion, as well as in common and formal speech. The wide and loose circulation of these words is one of the striking features of modern loquacity and even of modern "science." No lawyer accustomed to seeking precision in terms could possibly translate with confidence the words *man, men, person, people, and mankind*, which are strewn through and adorn the articles, books, reviews, essays, and addresses of our times. Freedom of speech allows for large liberties, but speech so free as to be inexact and unintelligible is markedly licentious—and dangerous—when such subjects as human nature, the emotions, education, science, art, democracy, government, society, literary values, history, progress, retrogression, barbarism, and civilization are brought under a discussion intended to be serious and informed.

* * *

How far then do men who write history enforce or deny the thesis maintained by living women that women were a subject sex throughout the long ages of the past? Or do they consider women something even less important than subjects of men—exactly nothing? . . .

For example, "The American History Series". . . consists of five volumes long used as authoritative in American colleges and universities. One of these volumes on *The Middle Period 1817–1858*, was written by Professor John W. Burgess. In all its five hundred pages, only rare references are made to women, obviously, unmistakably, women. One cites a Virginia statute imposing heavy penalties on white women who cohabited with negro Slaves. Mary Brown, who owned a slave that ran away, is mentioned in a passage on the fugitive slave law, and Ellen Crafts, a fugitive slave herself, is cited in connection with the rumor that she was concealed by "some of the most high-toned people" of Boston, presumably including some woman or women. But Harriet Beecher Stowe is not in the index and so was apparently not in the history of the middle period. Nor were other women.

To be sure, any man has a right to confine his attention entirely to the doings of men in political history if he lets his purpose be known in the title of his book or of the series in which it appears. But the series to which this volume by Professor Burgess belongs is called *history*, and on the least possible reckoning women were more than incidental to men's history in the United States from 1817 to 1858, even to their political history. And failure to admit it is an attitude with respect to women.

* * *

With the slow and halting development, in late years, of what is styled "social history," male scholars, and occasionally a female scholar, have gradually manifested more consciousness that women had been *in* history and had done something, whatever it was, in the *making* of history. As to the state of things before this movement for the writing of social history was well launched, Arthur Meier Schlesinger, one of the pioneers in it, appropriately commented in his *New Viewpoints in American History* (1922): "An examination of the standard histories of the United States and of the history textbooks in use in our schools raises the pertinent question whether women have ever made a contribution to American national progress that is worthy of record. If the silence of the historians is taken to mean anything, it would appear that one-half of our population have been negligible factors in our country's history.''

Although the social historians who recognized that women had been in history brought about some shift in the emphasis on man-made history, they gave many signs that they were puzzled in trying to deal with women. Many of them worked on as before, ''bringing in'' women here and there as if they were not really an integral part of all history; but none of them made any serious contributions to the bibliography, documentation, theory, and practice of the subject of women in history. In fact some of the social historians paid so much attention to the struggle of women for the suffrage and for ''equal rights,'' that they helped to confirm or freeze the view that prior to the rise of feminism in the nineteenth century women had been nothing, or next to nothing, in the long course of previous history—indeed, enslaved or partly enslaved to man in a man's world or a ''man's civilization.'' Hence despite the useful labors of the social historians and some monographs on specific phases of ideas and activities in history, the conventional view of women as negligible or nothing or helplessly subject to men in the long past continued largely to direct research, thinking, and writing about American history.

At all events Professor Schlesinger's appeal of 1922 for some consideration of women's contributions to the making of history effected no immediate revolution in the thinking of his gild. How completely it could be ignored was illustrated in 1940, nearly twenty years later, in *The Course of American Democratic Thought: An Intellectual History since 1815*, by Ralph H. Gabriel. This work deals with thought of or about democracy. It covers the period which witnessed the rise and growth of an invincible movement for women's rights, inspired by democratic theories, the tremendous agitation of thought that accompanied the movement, drastic modifications of the common law by legislation and equity, and the struggle that in the fullness of time culminated in the national enfranchisement of women. It treats of an age in which thousands of articles, pamphlets, and books on various aspects of democracy, law, and justice were written by women. Yet in the bibliography attached to Professor Gabriel's text no work by a woman is cited. For him, it would appear, the huge six-volume work on the *History of Woman Suffrage*, containing many ''thoughts'' about democracy, or at least what may be regarded as a phase of it, had no pertinence whatsoever.

FROM CHAPTER IV: THE HAUNTING IDEA: ITS NATURE AND ORIGIN

As for centuries the Ptolemaic conception of the astrophysical universe dominated discussions and "reasonings" in astronomy, so the theory of woman's subjection to man, the obliteration of her personality from consideration, governs innumerable discussions and reasonings in relation to human affairs. Here, there, and almost everywhere, it gives animus, tendency, and opinionative assurance to the man-woman controversies of our day.

There came a time, however, when the Ptolemaic idea of the starry universe was tested by patient observation and study—with the aid of scientific instruments—and declared to be a myth—a false theory. When that decision was made on the basis of more knowledge then Ptolemy possessed, rapid progress in astrophysics occurred and the art of navigating uncharted seas was brought nearer to perfection.

* * *

It is difficult, admittedly, to trace all the mental processes which converged into the idea that women were a subject sex or nothing at all—in any past or the total past—until they began to win "emancipation" in our age of enlightenment. But, if one works backward in history hunting for the origin of this idea, one encounters, near the middle of the nineteenth century, two illuminating facts: (1) the idea was first given its most complete and categorical form by American women who were in rebellion against what they regarded as restraints on their liberty; (2) the authority whom they most commonly cited in support of systematic presentations of the idea was Sir William Blackstone, author of *Commentaries on the Laws of England*—the laws of the mother country adopted in part by her offspring in the new world. The first volume of this work appeared in 1765 and the passage from that volume which was used with unfailing reiteration by insurgent women in America was taken from Blackstone's chapter entitled "Of Husband and Wife."

That passage (7th edition, 1775) ran as follows: "By marriage, the husband and wife are one person in law; that is, the very being or legal existence of the woman is suspended during the marriage, or at least is incorporated and consolidated into that of the husband; under whose wing, protection, and *cover*, she performs every thing;" . . . .

It is also a matter of historical record that for nearly a century or more Blackstone's *Commentaries* was a standard textbook for the training of lawyers, particularly in the United States. . . .

Whenever an American writer after 1783 was moved to instruct women on what he regarded as their rights and duties, he was almost certain to employ the authority of Blackstone, and likely to associate with the *Commentaries* expositions of divine law. . . .

. . . Such was the nature of Blackstone's dictum to the effect that woman was civilly dead after she married, that her personality was merged into that of her husband and lord. To what extent and with what meaning was it true, if true at all? This question leads to Blackstone himself and the circumstances in which he formulated his dictum.

On his father's side Blackstone sprang from a mercantile family. His father kept a small silk shop in London. His mother was the daughter of a landed gentleman. By the assistance of his mother's brother, young Blackstone escaped from the silk shop, acquired an education at a gentlemen's university, Oxford, and entered the practice of law, at which he was a failure. Early in his course, he married the daughter of a landed gentleman and, like many a good bourgeois, settled down at a country seat where he assumed the role of a village "squire."

In politics Blackstone was an old Whig or a new Tory—a foe of reforming radicals, but not a sworn enemy of the English Revolution of 1688. Like many a commoner, Blackstone outdid the gentleman in his effusive praises of the ruling class in State and Church, with which, by fortune and ambition, he had become affiliated; his thinking and writing about law were visibly influenced by his acquired sentiment of class.

But more than this is involved in the identification of Blackstone, namely, the circumstances in which he composed his *Commentaries*. Before he became so warmly attached to the common law of England, he had tried to get a professorship at Oxford University to teach Roman civil law. When he failed in this effort he was mortified. Had he been able to get that appointment, he might have taught from his chair the domestic law of old Rome which made marriage a kind of partnership between husband and wife, each having definite property rights but using their rights for certain mutual purposes.

* * *

The question of Blackstone's intentions in his interpretations of the common law cannot be answered beyond cavil, of course. Motives are seldom unsealed to the most careful student of personalities. But it was widely known in England that Blackstone disliked the equity jurisprudence, which invaded common-law doctrines and introduced into the laws of England principles akin to those of the Roman law in respect of married women's property rights. His love of the strict injunctions of the common law became intense. This was a matter of general knowledge in England. . . . Blackstone was not a scholar exceedingly cautious about his choice of words. On contrary he was a rhetorician and indulged at times in "elegant" language which lent itself to the verdict of "brilliance." Thus he was "easy reading" and "convincing" to persons who were in a hurry to learn what was known about the laws of England, including the common law. When he declared, for instance, that by marriage "the husband and wife are one" and that "she performs everything" under his wing and cover, he was using metaphors; he was not speaking in any exact terms but in the sparkling fashion that intrigues readers who detest "dry facts."

Is Blackstone's statement true or what is its real nature? For the moment it may be said that there are some truths in it, that it contains a great deal of misleading verbalism, and that in upshot it is false. We must remember, moreover, very distinctly, that he was, at this point in his *Commentaries*, dealing solely with the rights or rightlessness of the married woman only, with her position, as he said, "in law." Now the words "in law" actually meant in common law. Blackstone so understood it and understood it as a qualification on all the passage. So did his readers who were trained in law.

The common law was, however, only one branch of English law, one of the laws of England, or bodies of law. Other bodies of law were acts of Parliament often drastically modifying the common law and old customs left undisturbed by the common and statutory laws; and, as Blackstone remarked casually, "over and above" these laws was Equity, "frequently called in to assist, to moderate, and to explain the other laws."

It was Equity administered by a special court, having no jury, that provided, in the name of justice, remedies for wrongs for which the Common Law afforded no remedies. Equity enforced trusts and other understandings that assured to married women rights of property denied to them by the Common Law. . . .

Besides, there were the private practices and agreements of men and women in the ordinary affairs of daily living, which as a rule prevailed undisturbed unless perchance they became involved in actions before the courts and were declared illegal, contrary to law or good morals. Only when such practices and agreements were notoriously contrary to law or good morals or the men or women who were parties to such practices and agreements were entagled in litigation was any kind of "law" applied to them. In fact the number of human actions and understandings which ever come before courts of law is small in comparison with the vast number that make up the complex of family and social life. . . .

In this highly restricted and technical sense, and subject to reservations he did not set forth and explain in detail, Blackstone's statement on husband and wife contained several correct sentences. But of all the men and women who for generations cited his statement as evidence of women's subjection, few were well trained in the technicalities of law. Most of them were unable, therefore, to comprehend the severe limitations imposed on it in fact and the exact sense in which the statement could be regarded as true, particularly in view of the metaphorical style which Blackstone used.

Did Blackstone willfully intend to mislead his readers into believing that the legal status of married women in England in 1765 was correctly and fully described in his statement on husband and wife?

Whatever his intentions Blackstone could have avoided the charge of distortion by including in his chapter on husband and wife another statement correctly presenting the rules of equity jurisprudence under which the wife could be fully protected in the enjoyment of her separate property rights.

*   *   *

Through the long legal struggle between the common law on the one side and statutory and equity law on the other ran the eternal struggle of life—not of individuals, but of men *and* women united by their inexorable relationships—to survive and provide safeguards for each other and for their children, under the law or in spite of it. Here the strength and permanence of the family was an objective. In legal essence this struggle, amid every variety of being and experience, involved conflicts with the precision, rigidity, and certainty of common-law rules, which were ceasing to fit the ever-changing conditions of life and economy, and with the strivings for more freedom to make adjustment to the new necessities and aspirations. And in England, Equity was the jurisprudence, or branch of law, in general to which men and women could look for relief from the "wrongs" inflicted by the common law. Blackstone was aware of this and did not wholly neglect equity.

Thus through Blackstone's selective jurisprudence and his treatment of equity, thousands, perhaps millions, of men and women in England and the United States were led to accept the idea of women's historic "subjection" into "civil death," as the whole truth. That is, they adopted a fiction about human behavior.

* * *

To the vogue of the Blackstonian doctrine, respecting the nothingness of women, Mary Wollstonecraft contributed, perhaps unwittingly. . . . In 1792, and twelve years after the death of Blackstone, while the strife over his legal conservatism was raging in England, when the "rights of man" was challenging all restrictions on human freedom, she published her *Vindication of the Rights of Woman*.

In arguing for the rights of woman she made use of the writing of philosophers, moralists, educators, and agitators rather than the works by lawyers. She depended most on Rousseau for the doctrine of "natural" rights. The objects of her special aspersions were customs and opinions, not specific provisions of law affecting women, married and single. . . . In her portrayal of the alleged social tyranny exercised by man over woman, she helped to vitalize the doctrine that married women were civilly dead, members of a subject sex in effect, nothing in history save perhaps obsequious playthings or furtive intriguers trying to make their way out from under man's domination.

* * *

Leaders of the woman movement in America formulated their own statement on the subjection of women at Seneca Falls in 1848, in terms more economic and political than Wollstonecraft's effusion and definitely in accord with Blackstone's legal thesis. Subsequent formulations at other women's conventions merely amplified and enlarged upon the Seneca Falls declaration of their historic servitude and their will to independence. And there is good reason for believing that American statements of this kind helped to crystallize insurgent opinion in England along similar lines and to bring the Blackstone creed forcibly to the attention of English feminists and their friends among men as the warrant for adopting the theory of total subjection on which to base a demand for freedom and equality.

At all events the following facts have a distinct bearing on the acceptance in England of the Blackstone formula of subjection as the starting point for the feminist argument. First, Blackstone never acquired in that country the tyranny over the legal mind which he exercised in America; from the very beginning powerful critics, led by Jeremy Bentham, assailed his underlying philosophy with devastating effect and English scholarship made inroads upon the soundness of his treatise in detail. Second, the first great textbook for the English feminist movement, written by John Stuart Mill, in cooperation with his wife, and published in 1869, was entitled *The Subjection of Women* and was based on the acceptance of the Blackstone formula as an irreducible datum applicable not only to married women but to all women. . . .

To the doctrines of Blackstone, American feminists, and the Mills, pertaining to woman in law and history, Marxian Socialists added a revised version near the middle of the nineteenth century. What Blackstone had done for British patricians in respect of law and order, what Wollstonecraft and the Mills had done for the bourgeoisie in respect of manners, law, and history, the Marxists did for the proletariat in their interpretation of woman, law, and history.

In two fundamental respects the Socialist thesis of woman's status differed from that of Wollstonecraft and the Mills. In primitive times, it asserted, women had not been subject to men: they had either governed the community or been equals of men in it. Once dominant or equal, women had been driven, however, into subjection by the appearance of private property and the beginning of capitalism. "The overthrow of mother-right," wrote Friedrich Engels, "was the world-historical downfall of the female sex." Since the subjection of woman has been due to the rise and tyranny of private property, not merely to man's lust of power over woman, it follows, the Socialist thesis concluded, that woman's emancipation lies not in the equal competition of women with men for wealth and employment but in the socialization of the instruments of production and in the provision of employment for all.

* * *

It is clear that the full-fledged thesis of woman's historic subjection to man was grounded on the belief in Blackstone's doctrine. Older than that doctrine, of course, were the preachments of many theologians, clergymen, and moralists to the effect that woman is evil and *ought to be* subject to man, but Blackstone afforded sanction for the feminist manifesto that woman had been *in fact* subject to man throughout the long history of Anglo-American law—and, indeed, of all law. Here was the original construct that was to give forms and twists to endless writing and speaking, even that alleged to be scientific, and to bedevil women and befuddle men in years to come in all parts of the world.

* * *

The dogma of woman's complete historic subjection to man must be rated as one of the most fantastic myths ever created by the human mind.

Leaders of the woman movement at some times and in some places stood fast by the contention in the Seneca Falls Declaration of Sentiments that the overweening object of man had been to hold woman in servitude to him and that the "history of mankind" is a history of "man's repeated injuries and usurpations," at least as far as women are concerned. At such times and places they represented women as rightless in long history and passive in that condition. Yet at other times and places, confronted with the question as to how a creature who had been nothing or nearly nothing in all history could suddenly, if ever, become something—something like man, his equal—a few leaders in the woman movement used history to show what force women had displayed in history.

This contradiction is manifest in the volumes of the huge *History of Woman Suffrage* put together from the archives of the campaign for woman's enfranchisement from 1848 to the 1880's by Susan B. Anthony, Elizabeth Cady Stanton, Ida Husted Harper, and other workers in that movement. In the first volume the dilemma is disclosed. The first chapters of that volume deal almost entirely with the great "achievements" of women in times past, from the Abbess of Whitby in the ninth century to George Sand, Florence Nightingale, and Clara Barton in the nineteenth century. The second chapter is devoted entirely to women in journalism and it presents historical facts about important women editors, publishers, and writers from colonial times in America to the very moment when the very doctrine of subjection was being stoutly asserted in the best Blackstonian style. In Chapter IV, so closely following the accounts of women, single and married, who were not mere victims of men's "tyranny," occurs the Seneca Falls Declaration against man the tyrant and the attendant Resolutions of resistance to his mastery. Yet throughout the mammoth volumes of this *History of Woman Suffrage*, a record setting forth women's labors in this cause, are scattered extensive references to women as writers, speakers, agitators, business enterprisers, doctors, teachers, and other types of non-domestic activists, most of whom were wives and mothers living on good terms with their husbands and sons.

*   *   *

In summary, what does modern critical scholarship find in the long review of English legal history prior to 1765? It finds men and women, in many fundamental respects, on a similar footing with regard to their property holdings under the requirements of a strong feudal State. It finds men and women making powerful efforts, individually and together, to protect their families against the encroachments of that State. It finds an early and persistent recognition, especially with the development of Equity, of justice as the ideal for adjusting and determining the relations of men and women as members of families and communities, and as individuals.

This is not to deny that there were discriminations between men and women in the feudal law—civil and criminal—which were in various cases carried forward through the centuries. There were many discriminations against women in both branches of the law; but many responsibilities, which may in some instances be called "unfair" discriminations, were imposed on men, independently and in connection with discriminations against women.

*   *   *

FROM CHAPTER IX: WOMAN IN THE AGE
OF FAITH—'JUDGE OF EQUITY'

Just as women took part and carried full loads of work in agriculture, domestic industries, and trading, just as they participated in the activities of craft, trade, and social gilds or corporations, so they shared and expressed themselves in all the forms of social life in town and country. In everything human their qualities and force were expressed—from religious and secular festivities, sports, games, and riots to the discussion of religious and moral questions and the management of charitable undertakings. In castles and cottages, in fields and in gild halls, on village greens and in churchyards, in towns and on city streets, in taverns and at market fairs they sought release from the rigors of earning a livelihood, from burdens of domesticity, or responsibilities belonging to the status of their class, whatever it was. . . .

Like many men of the time, many women were muscular and tough. In speech and deeds they were often libertarian, if not libertine, as the documents clearly show. . . . Although the word "emancipation" was not in vogue, liberties were taken as the mood dictated. . . .

That husbands were allowed by common and ecclesiastical law to beat their wives cannot be gainsaid. Although numerous cases of wife-beating appear in the records, the actual extent of the practice is unregistered and it is certain that priests often tried to mitigate the abuse. Men were frequently punished for cruelty to their wives.

The origin of the custom and law as to wife-beating is obscure. But from glimpses of mediaeval society afforded by documents, family life was commonly rough and boisterous. Women, as well as men, were free with their fists, assisted by their children and relatives. Miracle plays, pageants, and village tales with striking frequency depict women as outwitting their husbands by shrewdness, if not shrewishness, and it often happened that men resorted to their ancient device, violence, when their psychological resources were not equal to the occasion. Nor is it to be overlooked that wives were sometimes aggressors: Chaucer's Wife of Bath tore three pages out of her clerkly husband's book and clouted him on the cheek with her fists.

* * *

Closely related to marriage, inheritance, descent, and wills, all through the middle ages, were practices connected with the ownership, use, and disposition of property under or outside the law. In respect of property neither men nor women stood alone. As to property in agricultural land, little or none of it was held outright, save as far as the highest lord or king could be said to have owned a principality or realm. Landed property was everywhere as a rule subject to feudal services, whether nominally in the hands of men or women. And, as we have seen, women, married and single, had extensive rights in property under the law of England in the middle ages. . . .

Legal records even reveal women of those distant times selling men and women, as men sold men and women, into forced labor. . . .

In these, as indeed in other evidences from social and economic life in the middle ages, class lines are sharply marked. But sex lines, such as there were, if prescribed in law, were abundantly defied in practice and in any event cannot be brought within the scope of any single formula on the "status" or the "function" and "role" of women.

FROM CHAPTER XI: MEDIAEVAL EDUCATIONAL AND INTELLECTUAL INTERESTS

In the Protestant world, where the "rights" of women were first formally proclaimed in manifestos, it has been generally assumed, at least until recent times, that the Catholic Church was absolutely opposed to the education of lay people, and that the education of women in convents and by nuns is to be viewed as of little or no import in the development of Western civilization. How did this misunderstanding occur?

To some extent it was due to the fact that formal education in its upper ranges, particularly in mediaeval universities, was confined largely to the training of men for the priesthood and that men who enjoyed that privilege wrote so many treatises, chronicles, and works on theology. Apart from the tendency of Protestant critics to paint the "dark ages" as blacker than they really were, this conception was also due in no small measure to the neglect of woman by historians, both Catholic and Protestant, and their persistent habit of publicizing men as if they had made all the history worth noting. In these circumstances it is difficult to see the tree of women's education in the forest of controversial and masculine literature. . . .

Whatever was the weight of Church authority against the education of women and their right to an intellectual life of their own, records of the middle ages, though as yet meagerly explored for this particular kind of information, certainly reveal women, high and low, receiving an education by some process, pursuing intellectual interests, reading, writing, expounding, and corresponding with one another and with learned men. Voluminous writing was done by women, particularly those associated with the mystics.

* * *

In the rural families the men and women lived and worked together in almost uninterrupted association from season to season, from year to year. There the husband and wife each had heavy obligations connected with the economy of household and field; and when the man was away in wars, so often the case, the woman assumed responsibilities for keeping the family going by managing its land and household economy.

. . . In the royal and the aristocratic families which governed most of Europe for centuries, women displayed great force, directly and indirectly, in the affairs of state and in the management of the underlying economy which sustained the monarchy.

Not until the commercial and political revolutions, accumulating full force in the eighteenth century, actually disrupted the solidarity of royal and aristocratic families founded on a landed wealth did women alike with the great families to which they belonged lose most of the power which they had so long exercised in the affairs of State and Society. Not until then did the state pass to the control of parliaments composed of men and elected by men. . . .

The date, 1789, when the French Revolution opened, dramatizes this transfer of power. Yet the acquisition of political power by men-at-large came slowly and tediously in the opinion of men seeking enfranchisement, that is, the right to help make laws and hold offices of government. Nearly a hundred years elapsed before all the adult men of France definitely won full parliamentary suffrage. It was not until 1871 that all adult males in Germany were granted the suffrage for members of the new imperial Reichstag; and this right amounted to little, owing to the power retained by the imperial and royal families of that country up to the débacle in 1918. The extension of manhood suffrage in Great Britain, begun by the reform bill of 1832, was not completed until the close of the first world war. Even in the United States the struggle of white men for the vote was long and hard; the general victory did not come until more than fifty years after the Declaration of Independence had asserted that "all men are created equal"—and not full victory, at that, in view of poll tax and other qualifications then or later imposed in parts of the United States.

Furthermore, the period between the dissolution of woman's political power in royal and aristocratic families and the general enfranchisement of women was relatively short as measured against the long centuries of royal and aristocratic rule. When the movement for woman suffrage was formally launched near the middle of the nineteenth century, millions of men were still striving for enfranchisement throughout the continent of Europe. Women were winning the suffrage in the more progressive societies years before manhood suffrage had been won in other societies.

All things considered, men's monopoly over politics under systems of manhood suffrage, never complete, was brief, compared with the ages in which royal and aristocratic women exercised power in affairs of State and Society. Moreover, when women's campaigns for enfranchisement are contrasted with the violent and often bloody contests which masses of men had to wage for their enfranchisement, it is patent that women won the right to vote by men's consent with relative ease, including as case a smaller span of time. To the women who spent their adult years in agitating for the ballot, the contest seemed so severe and so prolonged as to try their souls to the uttermost. Nevertheless man, the "tyrant" and "usurper" of 1848, yielded the suffrage to women quicker and with more grace than women of royal and aristocratic families had bowed to the tempest of rising democracy, with its cry of "votes for men."

*   *   *

Despite the barbaric and power-hungry propensities and activities in long history, to which their sex was by no means immune, women were engaged in the main in the promotion of civilian interests. Hence they were in the main on the side of *civil*-ization in the struggle with barbarism.

If this phase of woman's force in history is to be capitalized as against barbaric propensities and activities, then an understanding of women's past history in both connections must be regarded as indispensable to the maintenance and promotion of civilization in the present age.

But this is no "woman question" alone, as social philosophers—women and men—have understood from the dawn of reflective thought. It is a human problem—a problem of knowledge, intelligence, and morals—for individuals, families, communities, and states. For centuries, judges of equity in the Anglo-Saxon world and makers of enlightened legislation everywhere have recognized it as such. So have all the men and women arrayed on the side of civilization.

Upon the truth of this matter and the uses made of it will depend forevermore the power of men and women to control themselves and the instrumentalities at their hands in the struggle *against* disruptive forces of barbarism and *for* the realization of the noblest ideals in the heritage of humanity.

8. *Woman–the Pioneer*[1] AND *What Nobody Seems to Know About Woman*[2]

NOTE: *"To know woman merely as a subject of man in long history is to know no history,"* said Mary Ritter Beard, at the age of seventy-four, in a nationwide radio broadcast. *"What Nobody Seems to Know About Woman"* was an NBC address delivered in June, 1950.

In the eleven years that separate that talk from "Women–the Pioneer," a radio address, presented in 1939 on CBS, one can observe that changes in Beard's mode of expression over time as well as the consistency of her themes.

In the earlier address, which is simple and straightforward, she reminds her listeners that "the arts of life began in the minds and purposes of women," and that the real revolution is this realization, which is, at last, "slowly penetrating the consciousness of both sexes." Still challenging "the women called 'feminists'," Beard notes that their efforts to achieve for women the right to study medicine and law is a struggle to re-enter professions women had once practiced and had been excluded from relatively recently. The desire of today's women to "express their wills and purposes" is "as old as women."

The 1950 radio address is considerably more complicated in style and substance. In describing the varieties of activities women have participated in, Beard returns to her familiar theme that women are not naturally lovers of peace and haters of war, but are participants in all aspects of life. While she did vacillate on this question throughout her life, she seems to give less emphasis to the positive view of woman as essentially creator and nurturer as a result of the experiences of World War II.

Aware that efforts were under way in 1950 to restrict the education of high school girls and college women to "home responsibilities," Beard exhorts women not to "take this restriction lying down." If women accept their place without a struggle, then women themselves will be responsible for denying their own history.

These are appropriate final selections for this section because they combine the form—nationwide radio addresses aimed at a general audience of men and women—and the content—an overview of woman's historic role through time—that well represents her thesis and its implementation, a thesis that was in many ways the organizing principle of her life.

1. "Woman—the Pioneer," a radio address broadcast in 1939, jointly sponsored by Columbia Broadcasting System and the Women's National Radio Committee.
2. "What Nobody Seems to Know About Woman," a radio address broadcast June 3, 1950, over NBC.

RADIO ADDRESS, 1939

It is commonly supposed that women were never in business or the professions until the nineteenth century, and that a great intellectual, economic and moral revolution drew them into these occupations for the first time. This view of life and labor tends to make jittery the women in business and professions, in the fear that the occupations considered so new to their sex be snatched from them at any moment.

But this is not sound history. In truth, the very professions of medicine, nursing, obstetrics, domestic science, budgeting, cooking and other basic professions were launched by women whom we call primitives. Medicine men came late upon the human scene. Even the first farmers were women. Business itself began when the commodities produced by women—pots and textiles, for example—were exchanged in a system of barter with people possessing grain and other foods. And they were exchanged either by the women manufacturers or by their men folk who could go on the errands of barter because they were not manufacturers themselves. Among peoples whom we call "backward" now, this first type of business enterprise may still be seen.

Yet the realistic and dynamic function or role of women was never understood until about seventy-five years ago. It was not until our modern age of anthropological research into the most ancient of times that men or women grasped the significance of women in the making of social life, including its business and work now known as "profession." This greater wisdom about the place of women in the world is the true revolution, and the assumed revolution in respect of women in a machine age out in public life for the first time is merely a pseudo-revolution by comparison.

Businessess and professions constitute important arts of life. The arts of life began in the minds and purposes of women. And the significance of this is slowly penetrating the consciousness of persons of both sexes. The significance is the fact that where we start our thinking about human affairs is the place where we come out; the place where we frame our opinions about human beings; the place where we make our judgments relative to women and men.

If, then, we trace the lives and labors of women up through the countless centuries, we find women always playing a realistic and dynamic function, or role, in society—not only in the home by the hearth with husbands and children, but also in public affairs, even in business and the arts of life now called "professions."

Nuns of the middle ages, for example, were remarkable business women. They were outstanding doctors and surgeons. They were great educators. They were feudal lords operating self-sustaining estates and directing the manifold activities involved in producing goods, settling controversies as lawyers and judges settle them today, governing and participating in all the arts of social living. We have only to recover our knowledge of colonial women in America, on these two continents to which Europeans began to come in the 16th century, Catholic and Protestant and Jewish women, with their long traditions of skills and wills, to appreciate the fact and admit the truth that public affairs are no new role for women.

Skills display themselves in new forms, of course. Better training in medicine, cooking, surgery, law and jurisprudence, educating and governing seem to have produced positively new women. It should also seem, however, to have produced positively new men. But this training is in fact a steady development in the career of women rather than a freakish relation of women to the universe. The battle of women in the nineteenth century—women called "feminists"—for a "professional" status, for the licensed right to practice medicine and law, for instance, was merely a battle for the up-to-date training and the ensuing license which were to carry these divisions of labor to greater heights of perfection in adaptation to modern life and social forms of managing it.

Men and women alike are now helping to build up the story of women throughout the ages. Men have rendered invaluable and perhaps incalculable service in digging out the origins of civilization, the invention of the industrial arts by means of which civilization exists in pre-recorded times. Their investigations reveal the first women as the major sources of creative intelligence. Women have rendered comparable service in tracing the work of women in historic times. Dr. Kate C. Hurd-Nead, for example, has published the result of her long researches concerning women in medicine, and her volume opens with the picture of a queen-doctor in the fourth century before Christ.

Women in colonial America were engaged in the management of great Southern plantations, notably Eliza Lucas Pinckney, who kept an elaborate diary of her experiences and ideas about this business. Women in colonial America were engaged in every kind of commercial enterprise in which America was involved, notably Margaret Hardenbroeck Phillips, who launched what is thought to be the first packet line between our new world and the old world; she traveled with her cargoes to England whre she exchanged them for goods which colonial Americans did not have and wanted. Women owned, edited and wrote in the colonial newspapers and were women of the press from the start of the press in America.

Thus, the women of today—domestic women and women in public affairs—are moved by an urge to express their wills and purposes which is as old as women. Why be jittery, then, about their hold on business and the professions? An urge so primordial and an enterprise so persistent cannot be suppressed by mere men. Or by parasitic-minded women either. If some women seek to escape the heavy exactions of the marketplace by retreating to complete dependence at the hearth in an age which is controlled productively by the machine, other women will continue to seek and find work and satisfaction amid the exactions of business and professional life.

RADIO ADDRESS, 1950

Remembering the amount of attention paid to woman since human beings learned to walk, draw, paint, model, sing, worship gods, or wail, isn't it time to drop this subject? Has it not been completely covered? Well, novelists do not think so. Their fiction floods the book market. Moreover in the political upheavals of our day, the role women have or should have in public life is a burning issue in many parts of the world. After all, What is woman?

The highest and widest, deepest and truest statement about her was Shakespeare's. He said: "All the world's a stage and all its men and women are the actors." He knew that it was not merely a man's world in Elizabethan days. Nor had it ever been just a man's world. It is not just a man's world today.

On the world's stage, throughout the ages of the past, in its human dramas women played major roles and great supporting roles. Every economic, political, and social structure of history women helped to build.

They erected themselves, or helped to erect, feudal dynasties. Countless queens and empresses ruled such dynasties long before and after the advent of Christ. Women were lusty and gusty participants in overthrowing governments ruled by such families of noble blood. They were also powerful agents in substituting military dictatorships. Yet women have helped with might and main to destroy military dictatorships and restore royal monarchs. Furthermore, by their industrial manufacturing and selling enterprises, business women helped to undermine feudal states, products of an agricultural economy, and establish the culture of cities which are essentially trade centers. At this present hour of history Communist women and girls strive with like-minded masculine comrades, to create a world revolution for the destruction of the bourgeoisie everywhere, amid the resistance of both sexes.

Among the things that nobody seems to know about woman is that she is not, by her very "nature", a lover of peace and hater of war. Long history is crowded with the names and records of warlike women who initiated wars of aggression, lined up their armed vassals to defend their kingdoms, and often fought side by side with men. In World War I, Russian women formed a "Battalion of Death" and did as much killing of the enemy as they could.

After Bismarck with his German troops had conquered France in 1870, a French woman, intensely patriotic, bent all her mind and strength to revenge. She knew France must have an ally for punishing the Germans. Failing to win Britain, she turned to Russia and was a major architect of the French-Russian alliance. Her name was Mme. Juliette Lamber Adam.

Yet women have been clever diplomats in ending wars. In 1529, Louise of Savoy—mother-regent of François I—and Margaret of Austria—guardian of Charles V—in positions of such authority during the murderous combat between France and Austria, met at Cambrai and procured a treaty of peace. It stands on the record as La Paix des Dames (The Peace of the Ladies).

Nor have women escaped in long history the experience and power attached to the direct ownership of wealth. Hatasu, high-priestess-queen of Egypt, about 15 centuries before Christ, like her maternal ancestors, had control of all the wealth of their great kingdom. She used it largely in building mammoth monuments. In old Sparta, many women acquired wealth in gold and silver coins when Spartan men brought this portable loot back from their wars and gave it to their women. Thereafter Spartan history was to a high degree the history of what women did with their money.

Feudal societies rested on landed wealth and women owned huge areas of lands in the feudal economic system.

Women also earned wealth, from primitive bartering to mercantile enterprises with money as goal. Women traders in Europe in the 14th Century have had a special write-up. In the 17th Century, three English women had government monopolies: one over the silk trade; another over the biscuit trade for India; the third over the import of iron. One of the immense, but scarcely known at all, phases of woman's history, is such relations to wealth with the power and influence wealth carried.

To view woman merely as a subject of man in long history is to know no history, if the subjection of men to women is to be ignored. Some women have been subjects of some men or of some women. But some men have been subjects of some men and of some women. The enslavement of war captives has known no sex discrimination. The buying and selling of slaves in the slave markets knew no sex inequality of rights as slave traders; nor did the slaves themselves belong to one sex.

Among the numerous things that nobody seems to know in our land of liberty-to-know-or-not-to-know, is that civilized women have always had an education which had to do with the arts of living that they had invented and with domestic economy which they inaugurated. Prehistoric women acquired by their own initiative, and transmitted to their young, the first distinctively human education.

As long ago as the sixth century, B.C., Greek women of the Pythagorean Order of philosophers, laid a strong basis for the seven Liberal Arts by their writings and teaching. In the revival of Greek and Latin learning in Italy, women with the highest possible human (not just feminine) distinction taught the liberal arts at the University of Bologna and were still doing that in the 18th Century. To their nurture of the liberal arts and from their high positions on the faculty of that university as educators, they sustained and promoted the liberal arts as a great tradition in education. Isabella of Spain introduced classical learning in her country and put her court to work studying it. She brought Italian women to Spain to help in the teaching.

In the sweep of religious movements women were always activists. In the age of goddesses, women served as priestesses on all the levels of priestcraft. Women managed the rituals of goddess worship for both sexes. Wars were fought by hard-hitting men to capture and recover shrines to goddesses. In fact it was exceedingly difficult for men to divert religions and rituals to the management of men.

Roman women were heavy contributors to the financing of the Christian Church and Roman women led the way to monasticism when Roman power was obviously decadent and the Teuton barbarians were thronging into Rome to assert their power. Women were influential in the selection and support of Popes and not to be forgotten in the selection of creeds for the Christian folk. They carried the gospel to the ends of the earth as missionaries and this they still do wherever Christianity can penetrate. In all the reform movements directed against the Vatican's dictation, women were active and determined. On the inside of all religious movements, everywhere, in all ages women have asserted their leadership, agitated, preached, written on religion, converted unbelievers, and offered themselves as martyrs when that was their spiritual imperative.

In the militant middle ages of Europe, nuns and laywomen launched social work among the poor, the sick, the helpless, in the spirit of Christ's teaching. Social work in our country today is an expansion of that medieval humaneness and not an original enterprise.

Unquestionably action has been a mighty force in history. But ideas about life and its values have also been a force in history. Social philosophy has figured importantly in the human drama as a play of minds reflecting on things good, beautiful and true. Greek intellectual women, companions of intellectual men, developed together principles of personal and social virtue. But scientific knowledge was not far advanced in ancient Greece.

By the 18th Century a great body of scientific knowledge had been accumulated and then in France social thinking rose to a height of rationality never before attained. Then and there associated men and women constructed and proclaimed a revolutionary trinity of social ideas: (1) the idea that human progress could go forward in the infinite future for the improvement of the human life on earth, by means of the new science and the use of reason; (2) the idea of civilization directed to the substitution of the civilian way of life for the ages-old military life; (3) the interpretation of long history as the struggle between barbarism and civilization. These philosophies of a better life than humanity as a whole had ever known are testaments to the vigor of women's as well as men's minds in the modern age.

I am giving now over the air to my invisible audience just a skeleton of woman's great historic meanings, but the muscles, tissues, and blood for completing women as potent makers of all history can be procured from documentary sources and books.

Lack of such knowledge by our women of woman's historic force is now giving play for educators, in increasing numbers, to cry for the restriction in the education of our American high school girls and college women to home responsibilities. If women should take this restriction lying down, then it would be women themselves who, in their ignorance or inertia, would shut themselves off from their own history—to become little women on the mental age level of children. If ignorance is bliss, surely it is not folly to be wise.

III.

FEMINISM AS A WORLD
VIEW—PRACTICE

As did most intellectuals of her generation, Mary Beard believed that knowledge derives from our actions on the world. By the early 1920s she had withdrawn from the political activism which had consumed her energies for years. She turned to a study of women in history in an effort to develop a theory of feminism. But she never lost her belief in the organic connection between ideas and actions. Armed now with her developing theory of feminism, she sought to apply that theoretical knowledge to practical, usable ventures. She wrote books and articles, gave lectures and radio addresses. At the same time, she was also putting her ideas into practice with three major projects.

The first was a carefully thought out syllabus for a Women's Studies course, which she wrote in 1934. It embodies her ideas on what constitutes an authentic study of women in history. She was less concerned with the sex of the student body than she was with the content of the education. Men, as much as women, needed to learn about the history of women, she believed.

The second project was the World Center for Women's Archives created in 1936. Mary Beard was its leading spirit. The purpose of the archive was to assemble *all* data on women everywhere in a massive effort to demonstrate the existence and force of a collective woman's world.

In 1941 Mary Beard, aided by a staff of three, undertook a feminist critique of the *Encyclopaedia Britannica*, the third project. Eighteen months after they began, the four women submitted a bold report exposing the male bias that permeated the selection and substance of the *Britannica*'s articles.

Beard's works on these projects constitute the first three selections. The book closes with a selection from an article about the impact of the unmarried adult on history and politics. In this piece, written in 1934, she examines the misogynist implications of Fascism and the appeal of the Nazi party for a particular kind of rootless, undomesticated bachelor. Mary Beard illustrates, by this analysis, how her special concern with the history of women widened her vision and provided her with an amazing facility to look at the world in new ways.

1. A Changing Political Economy as It Affects Women[1]

NOTE: *This imaginative and ambitious fifty-six-page syllabus for a Woman's Studies course was written by Mary R. Beard in 1934 for the American Association of University Women. She proposes a creative alternative to the prevalent notion of equal education for women as a simple extension to women of men's education.*

"Man's education of himself and of his female understudies," she says sharply, "has become so rigid, so scholastic . . . that to parallel it with the same woman's education of herself . . . would count for very little in the stimulation of social intelligence." A genuinely equal education would not simply demonstrate that "women were also there" but would examine the ways it is both a man's and woman's world with the purpose of understanding better how "their destinies are bound together and why."

The syllabus is designed to demonstrate that women were neither eternally oppressed nor always relegated to restricted domestic roles, but were engaged in every vital part of the human struggle, often in ways quite different from that of men.

Because college education provides so little understanding of the reality of women's pasts, "university women, like all other women," she says, "face the world insufficiently equipped to do much more than complain about sex discrimination." They are unable, for instance, to recognize that women frequently were able to "enjoy the liberties of the disinherited."

In an effort to provide women and, hopefully, men too with a true view of the past, Mary Beard wrote this syllabus. It is divided into four major areas: the history of the idea of sex equality and the actual status of women in the United States; the impact of international forces on the position of women; the role of nationalism in theory and practice; and the "feminine determination of feminine destiny," which today would be called woman's autonomy. Each section is further subdivided, and concludes with a sizable and impressive reading list and a series of proposed discussion questions.

With her firm belief that theory and practice need constant interaction, at the end of each chapter she suggests activities to link the classroom with the outside community. For example, in connection with the discussion on

1. "A Changing Political Economy as It Affects Women," 56-page syllabus published by the National Headquarters, American Association of University Women, 1934.

the history of the idea of sex equality, Beard suggests that students begin by analyzing their own knowledge and belief about the history of women, then survey their friends' attitudes, and, finally, go to others in the community. Students are advised to trace the origin of attitudes about women: do they rest on reading? on college learning? on business or personal experience? on observation? For the corresponding section on the reality of women's experiences, she suggests a study of the conditions under which the women of their community live and labor: the number gainfully employed, their occupations, their wages and opportunities for promotion as compared to those of men; their reasons for working.

In Part IV, "Feminine Determination of Feminine Destiny," under the subtopic entitled "Clarifying Our Minds," she urges students to "make a genuine effort to free your minds from their present burden of tradition . . . and draw up an ideal plan for our country to provide [adequate] . . . incomes to supply [necessities] for . . . health . . . decency . . . and beauty. . . . Have no shame in the doing. Remember that the Founders of the Republic . . . deemed it their highest privilege in a time of social chaos to draft plans for a new nation."

I have found no indication that the syllabus was ever used.

The excerpts reprinted here are from the Introduction.

All American attention is now focussed on the "New Deal." What it means for women or what it might mean for women becomes the major interest of all women who are concerned about their relation to the State, just as it is a prime concern of all such men.

Every woman in the United States is actually affected by the sweep of economic and political events. University women have been trained to be more or less consciously awake to the significance of such events. But it is one thing to watch passively the making of sex history, another thing to feel victimized, and something else to share competently in the making of sex history. University women are not always alive to the creative opportunity.

Hitherto in America the colleges have implied, through their emphasis on the history of men, that women have been so minor a factor in economic and political leadership that all history is but the story of the "man's world." "Equal education", for which women have clamored, has brought no change in this point of view. It has meant merely the extension to women of men's education in their own history and judgments of themselves. It is true that "women in industry" sometimes creep into courses of instruction but in that case only as subsidiary phases in the development of men's machines and men's economic arrangements. Women in industry remain women in the man's world alone.

Women are thus a lost sex as far as collegiate education goes, except with respect to home economics. And even home economics is taught in the narrowest possible way. It is very gingerly in its treatment of the general economic and political situation in which households have to operate; that is, it holds aloof from a frank examination of the principle on which wealth is distributed among the households which compose the nation. It subordinates the ethics and politics and esthetics of income to lessons in cooking, bed-making and marketing which may all be very well as useful adjuncts to a flourishing economy but which seem exceedingly inadequate as major values when homelessness and public charity are the plight of untold millions of our people. A comprehensive home economics study would presumably start with the integration of the home into the system of political economy which is functioning or which is suffering decay. In other words, it would start with the financial foundations of the home—with its securities and perils, with its meaningfulness in the State, and with the State's recognition of that value. But it would make equally significant women's historic responsibility for transforming raw materials into the "refinements" of all life, and treat of all life as it has been changed by the drastic separation of women from raw materials as their master. It would cover the government agencies which today in the United States assist women in their role of home-makers and uncover the gaps in assistance which render home-making on any broad cultural scale a farce. In short, the obligation which women first assumed voluntarily and creatively for enriching life would be studied in relation to modern life in an effort to get at the meaning of home economics in terms of a rich modern life.

To appreciate what it signifies to have no history, let us try to imagine what it would be like to know nothing even of men's past! "Workers' education" is a recent undertaking designed to teach a labor movement what it has tried to achieve, the methods it has employed, and wherein it has failed or triumphed. "Communistic" Russia, at last, after eliminating history as a "bourgeois" danger, is taking up its slack owing to the fact that it cannot thrive in a society of nations among whom it must make its way, without more historical knowledge of itself and of them. Women alone are supposed to be able to manage without knowing themselves; with knowing men only.

The result is that university women, like all other women, face the
world insufficiently equipped to do much more than complain about sex
discriminations in a "man's world", if they enter the trades and professions. Or to strive for the removal of these discriminations as they affect
women in industry, by throwing the burden for the same upon men. The
highest degree that a "seat of learning" may bestow does little, if
anything, to provide a woman who earns it with an appreciation of the
strength and weaknesses of her own kind. She may have what Professor
Franklin D. Giddings called a *"consciousness* of kind." She has almost
no *knowledge* of kind. Competent as she may feel to teach child psychology herself, she turns to a psychoanalyst, usually of the masculine sex,
for help in her own mature difficulties and he or she has nothing to offer
her as far as her great potentialities are concerned, being just as unaware
of feminine history.

Both men and women in America are thoroughly imbued with the
notion that the female sex has been subject to the male sex throughout the
ages. The notion has largely flowered from treatises on law, as if the
public should accept the law of "prohibition" or the law of "repeal" as
the true picture of the liquor traffic under either form of legislation.
Blackstone, moralist rather than wide-ranging jurist, was the instructor of
feminism from its birth. But in painting society under statutory law,
Blackstone refused to color it with the hues of equity courts in which that
discriminatory legislation was so commonly adjusted on the complaints
of wronged women who demanded safeguards for their property. What is
even more, the casual reader of law is apt to forget that only the propertied
come into review there in any case. The great mass of the people
frequently enjoy the liberties of the disinherited. In the settling and
exploiting of the New World these liberties were excessively broad.

For lack of knowledge about women, the proposal to elevate the
history of women to a position of equal importance in the schools with
that of men—the only honest basis of "equal education"—has no warrant in the popular mind. Women professors, in fact, are sometimes the
most hostile to the suggestion. Having risen to posts of prominence and
importance by special adaptability to the existing curriculum and taking
for granted that they demonstrate by such adaptability the very equality
prized by feminists, members of the gild have been heard to declare with
heat that "the time has come to forget women" and eliminate sex from
thinking. Nevertheless, the "sexless" education upon which they insist

is not, after all, abstract to any great degree. It is basically a sex education—masculine in design and spirit.

Its tissue consists of threads instinctively selected from men's activities in war, business and politics, woven together according to a pattern of male prowess and power as conceived in the mind of man. If the woman's culture comes into this pattern in any way, it is only as a blurring of the major concept. For example, H. G. Wells, in his popular and highly commended "The Outline of History", makes this strange remark: "Of Amenophis IV we shall have more to tell later, but of one, the most extraordinary and able of Egyptian monarchs, Queen Hatasu, the aunt and stepmother of Thotmes III, we have no space to tell."

In other instances peculiar sex attributes are veiled under the generic word, "man," when the distinction between male and female initiative is essential to the understanding of culture and history. To illustrate, we may again cite Wells. Though anthropologists are almost unanimous in their belief that the female of the species launched civilization—that she had the first creative intelligence—Wells, using the general term, "man", implies that the male invented the basic industrial arts, such as spinning and weaving, cooking and sewing; the humanistic arts of doctoring and nursing; the administrative art of budgeting; and the discovery of agriculture as a creative climax. While less is known about early agriculture than about the industrial arts, many reputable anthropologists maintain that women were not only the first farmers but the first farmers because they first learned to till the soil. Taking women for granted in the term "man", really leaves them out of account.

The point is worth contesting—not for the sake at all of starting an intellectual sex war which has no underlying value—but for the purpose of acquainting a lost sex with its primordial talents. In humanity's worst crisis, when the forests had begun to recede, the water holes to dry out, and the means of subsistence to shrink until life itself was imperilled, women, according to authorities on primitive life, gave humanity its first "new deal." If man was ever a primate wandering naked through the woods, gnawing raw bones, or munching grasses and seeds, through the new deal connected with the original inventions, he merged with his inventive mate into a genuine human being. Even if Adam and Eve were created fresh as the first human couple, there is no evidence that they acquired in the Garden of Eden the knowledge of how to cook, clothe and shelter themselves like human beings. . . . Social history refutes that idea of sex. It reveals woman always at the center of action and of thought, helping to shape the military and political policies of time, even as they affect herself, and, as in the middle ages, on occasion turning to willful celibacy.

From outside the colleges has usually come the pressure for an enlargement of the curriculum to include something deemed essential for public enlightenment. Such history as is now taught crept into the colleges in that manner. In the late eighteenth century, republican idealists in the United States argued that history on new lines must be introduced into the American institutions of higher learning which were then getting it only in connection with the Greek and Latin classics. Some of them also maintained that history on a larger plan was as important for women to study as for men—indeed the basic requirement for a self-governing people. These idealists knew practically nothing of the specific records of any other women than those who had helped to make the American Revolution a success, those who had tried to defeat it in England or her colonies, and of the rash queen, Marie Antoinette, about whom the French Revolution of their day revolved. But these idealists understood very well indeed the vital relation of women to the cultural defenses of a republic, and, as they planned for its future, they proposed to educate its women too in history with that in mind. Yet it was many years after the republic was launched before the actual teaching of any history other than Biblical and classical was begun in any American college. And history in American colleges has always, in fact, been a fairly casual branch of learning. Consequently, we should not be utterly discouraged because, in its brief and haphazard career, it has not yet widened its perspective to the feminine sex.

There may in truth be some intellectual and social advantage now in this drag of thought. For man's education of himself and of his women understudies has become so rigid, so scholastic, notwithstanding its elaboration, that to parallel it with the same woman's education of herself, as could be done, would count for very little in the stimulation of social intelligence. But if equal education could now be undertaken, not merely with a view to proving that "women were also there" but with a view to discovering how far this is both a man's and a woman's world, both sexes might the better comprehend how their destinies are bound together and why.

That there are grave risks in longer postponing the drive for a genuinely equal education must be apparent to all women who watch the trend of events in Europe and Asia at this time. A few years ago the Americanization and feminization of the world were proceeding so swiftly that all nations had to reckon with this united phenomenon. Today the tide is running against civilization of that nineteenth-century model. Even in America, determinants of the economic and political status of women become increasingly difficult to define. It was long presumed that the sheer assertion of feminine will embodied in law was enough to effect equal sex opportunity. But in this post-war depression which America is now experiencing, the cordon tightens about women's work and aspiration as it has not done for a century. And this happens beside the progress in law.

Harsh problems reappear and in many respects these present new issues to women. If the difficulties are to be overcome, creative intelligence will have to be brought into play once more. Feminists cannot forever trail in the shadow of the women who in 1848 launched the movement for equality. Almost a century has passed since 1848. During that period feminists have adhered to a straight course, more or less blind to forces other than their own determination which control life and labor. "New occasions teach new duties." At any rate it seems imperative to consider the changed economic and political setting in which feminism from this time on must flourish or suffer defeat. The very right to be educated at all may be eventually involved in economics and politics beyond women's control unless they realize the dangers in plenty of time, and prevent their ravages.

Though there are very few, if any, teachers equipped at the moment to handle equal education along the lines here drawn, the need is great and a start should be made to meet it. Hence the American Association of University Women frankly pioneers in this field. It offers the following syllabus of study for women as a guide to groups within the Association who see the necessity of reaching out for a better understanding of social forces determining status, since status is life! It believes, too, that within colleges classes might immediately follow this syllabus and thus lay the cornerstone for a structure of *equal education* to be *in fact* what it is now *in name* only.

Admittedly, limitless research is required for a comprehensive knowledge of the subject in hand but there should develop, it would seem, a zest for such research out of this framework of interests and ideas.

2. The World Center for Women's Archives[1]

NOTE: *Mary R. Beard was the guiding force behind the World Center for Women's Archives (WCWA), which was created in 1936. The purpose of the organization was to demonstrate tangibly to women the value of their history by having women themselves re-create their past. The goal of the WCWA was to assemble and preserve all material about women everywhere, on the grounds that written history was without meaning, if women continued to be excluded from it. The governing principle was "the projection of woman's personality out of the shadows of time into the living force which is woman, in fact, into written history."*

The material was widely scattered, and so the call went out for women to forage "in the furnace rooms, attics and cellars, in fading heaps, crumbling with age," to discover the "source material pertaining to women's aspirations, struggles, achievements, contributions and failures."

As Director of Archives, Beard structured the organization's activities. The material was to be housed in one center, which was to serve as a clearinghouse of information for the history of women. Beard envisioned the WCWA ultimately creating an Academy of Women to provide an institutional base for women and to stimulate intellectual work about women. The Radcliffe Institute, which embodies much of this spirit, was inspired partly by the WCWA. The Center was determined to make visible the invisible, to put together the material that comprised a collective woman's world.

Its sponsors included: Eleanor Roosevelt, Ida M. Tarbell, Margaret Sanger, Mrs. Vincent Astor, Mrs. Louis D. Brandeis, Frances Perkins, Roy and Jeanette Nichols, Oswald Garrison Villard, Mary E. Woolley, Mary McLeod Bethune, Alice Stone Blackwell, Harriet Stanton Blatch, Alice Paul, Pearl Buck, Mary E. Dreier, and Lyman Beecher Stowe.

Although the WCWA lasted only five years before financial and other problems caused its dissolution, it was a conception of astonishing magnitude, a magnificent effort. It is easy to overlook ventures that fail. But those who study the history of women are indebted, whether or not they are aware of it, to earlier achievements, such as the World Center for Women's Archives, which led the way.

The excerpts below are from materials distributed by the World Center for Women's Archives to publicize its aims and needs.

1. Excerpts from publicity materials distributed by the World Center for Women's Archives. Source: The Schlesinger Library, Radcliffe College.

I

The World Center for Women's Archives was formed because of the need for collecting, classifying, and preserving documentary evidence of women's thought, influence and activities. The prevalent theory, especially in the Occident, that women, other than queens, had no history, until they got the vote, is not only an injurious theory for men and women, it is an unsound one. Yet it dominates the writing as well as the unexpressed thought of this age. That it should prevail is largely due to the paucity of accessible documents pertaining to women. Without this material, humanity's knowledge of itself must be severely restricted.

What this institution is concerned with, therefore, is source material—letters, diaries, manuscripts, speeches, notes and memoranda of women, and pertaining to women.

All materials in private hands are in danger of being destroyed. What is not destroyed wilfully may be lost to public knowledge in other ways: by fire and political hazards; from the lack of facilities for preservation; from the absence of an appreciation of their social value; through casual transfer from owner to owner; through the indifference of existing institutions more concerned with source materials on men.

There is no other organization engaged in the work of collecting materials on women according to a systematic program of values. Even women's colleges have neglected this task. There is at least one instance where a city library has allowed important documents relating to women to lie crammed in drawers, crumbling to dust. The few unprinted materials of women held by the Congressional Library are mainly political in character, as is most of its unprinted material; neither in origin nor continued support is that Library adapted to the building up of a great archive dealing with the broad history of women.

Therefore the World Center for Women's Archives has a definite and necessary function. The attached brochure describes its aims and needs in greater detail.

II
[Text of brochure]

The purposes of this organization are:

To make a systematic search for undeposited source materials dealing with women's lives and activities, interests and ideas, as members of society everywhere. Included in such source materials will be letters, diaries, speeches, pamphlets and articles, manuscripts of books in special cases, notes and memoranda, programs of work and publicity.

To reproduce important materials, already deposited elsewhere, by means of microfilming and other modern processes.

To become a clearing-house of information with respect to the location and character of source materials on women in other libraries and institutions.

To encourage recognition of women as co-makers of history.

Who would use such available material?

The social historian who deals with the history of countries, peoples, business, professions, labor, arts, and sciences.

The playwright and novelist who seek background in which to place the struggle that makes fiction as well as history.

The biographer who wants facts about a woman's life and her relations to the world in which she lived or lives.

The educator who has no basis for handling the woman's role in history, past or contemporary.

The journalist who, writing the news of today, must have the background of yesterday.

The clubwoman who wants to know what other women have done.

The woman artist, scientist, doctor, lawyer, teacher, farmer, industrial worker, business woman, who wishes to deepen her knowledge of women in her field of activity or in another field.

The student who has papers or theses to prepare on subjects relating to women, or in fields of endeavor largely carried on by women.

The general information seeker who needs to supplement emotional reaction with factual knowledge.

Why is a new center needed?

Because existing institutions—even women's colleges—tend to specialize in men's materials. Often they have very little source material of any kind.

Because women are inclined to destroy their own documents, while carefully preserving the letters and other materials of their fathers and brothers. The Center will try to secure a more balanced picture of humanity in the interests of historic truth.

Because the public at large does not realize the extent to which history eliminates the story of women. Special attention has to be called to women's work, ideas, observations on life, and ideals to give them the consideration that their value carries in fact.

But wouldn't the Congressional Library be the proper depository?
No. Though the Congressional Library contains a copy of every book copyrighted in America and a magnificent collection of other books on every kind of subject, its unprinted materials are mainly political in character. In this relation it possesses some important materials on women in the abolition movement and in the woman suffrage campaigns. Papers of Elizabeth Cady Stanton, Lydia Maria Child, Susan B. Anthony and Anna Dickinson are there. But neither in origin nor in continued support is the Congressional Library adapted to the building up of a great archive dealing with the broad history of women.

What about giving materials to a city library?
Twenty years ago, an eminent leader of the woman movement gave to a public library priceless documents concerning the movement for equal suffrage. Today, twenty years after, these papers lie crammed in drawers crumbling to dust . . . . in such condition that readers cannot use them without injuring them. The institution had so little interest in these records that an investigator found them only after much searching and enquiry.

Why not give them to a state institution?
The direction of all public institutions is partly political and therefore subject to men's control in the main. Women need to direct the collection, preservation, and guidance of readers in women's materials to correct the balance—until such time at least as it acquires stability, through natural cultural discipline.

What is also true is that infinite waste of time, energy, and money occurs where researchers and general readers must seek materials among 48 states and many cities. Economy of education with respect to women will be served best by the World Center for Women's Archives.

Furthermore, the materials of women from other countries logically belong only in such a Center.

The center could best serve international culture?
Not long ago an enquiry was made by the great Deutsches Museum at

Munich concerning American women's contribution to Science. But no American was found who could answer that question.

Such questions the Center would try to be able to answer in time.

What is the present support of the center?

At present it is supported by sponsors, membership fees and contributions. To date this income has merely covered minimum office expenses.

An annual income of $35,000 a year would provide proper housing of records and a technically trained staff which would collect, preserve and make available the material to meet demands for service which are increasing daily. Such provision for three years, at least, would allow for development, unhampered by the immediate need for fund raising and would give the Board of Directors freedom to work toward an endowment, thus insuring the future of the Center.

What is needed at once?

Fire-proof space and proper equipment for the care of materials as they come in.

A trained technical technical staff to handle the search for materials and to care for them when they are deposited.

Members and friends.

3. *A Study of the* Encyclopaedia Britannica *in Relation to Its Treatment of Women*[1]

NOTE: *In the spring of 1941, Mary R. Beard, then in her mid-sixties, enthusiastically began a new and intriguing project. She undertook a feminist critique of the* Encyclopaedia Britannica, *at the suggestion of its editor in chief, Walter Yust. She put together a staff of three: Dr. Dora Edinger, Janet A. Selig, and Marjorie White, a long time associate. The staff operated on a small budget, while Beard, as editor, chose to function as an unpaid supervisor.*

In November, 1942, after eighteen months of work, they submitted a bold and challenging report, ''A Study of the Encyclopaedia Britannica *in Relation to Its Treatment of Women.'' The forty-two-page report overflows with suggestions for further research, many of them still untouched. Many ideas that appeared in* On Understanding Women *and that would later be developed in* Women as Force in History *appear in the* Britannica *critique. For example, the report examines the development and significance over time of sexual differentiation, and argues that some powers which women once exercised were assaulted and reduced in modern society.*

In vigorous language the report assails the male bias that dominates the tone and substance of the Britannica; *it also points to frequent Protestant biases as well.*

The document is divided into three parts. The first and shortest part cites articles in the Encyclopaedia *that are deemed satisfactory. The second portion, the critical section, which is twenty-eight pages long, analyzes those articles that are judged unacceptable. The third section offers suggestions for entirely new articles or major revisions of old ones. One should remember that this report was not submitted for publication. It is written in an ironic, hard-hitting, loose style which is characteristic of Mary Beard's letters but not of her formal writing.*

In spite of Yust's expressed interest in the report, and his repeated assurances that later editions of the Encyclopaedia Britannica *would*

---

1. Report submitted to Walter Yust, editor in chief of the *Encyclopaedia Britannica*, November 15, 1942, and signed by Mary R. Beard, Marjorie White, Janet Selig, and Dora Edinger. No stylistic or grammatical changes have been made.

incorporate the recommendations, few changes were ever made. The "long neglect in the compendium" that Yust guaranteed would be "rectified," was not rectified in any succeeding edition including the present one.

In 1947 Mary Beard wrote to Anne Martin Grey that "Mr. Yust has never kept me in touch with one of the numerous sketches or anything else which he authorized me to collect for this compendium. . . . I am asking no more women to write" for the Encyclopaedia.

A few short sketches submitted by the women associated with the project may have crept into later editions, but in general, the comprehensive and encompassing assessment of the Encyclopaedia Britannica *prepared by Mary Beard and her staff was insultingly disregarded.*

Selections from the report are included here so as to give the reader a sense of the range of topics which Beard and her staff covered, and the quality and style of the criticisms they submitted.

FROM PART II: CRITICAL ASSESSMENT

Abortion. This is neither uptodate [*sic*] nor comprehensive enough. It is more than a moral question. It is a population, political, health, medical and social issue. The ancient attitude and practices in Greece and Rome should be noted. The Church attitude should be faced. The Bolshevik revolutionary attitude shook the world for a time. The "frightful toll of abortion", presented in a New Republic article of March 28, 1934, under the title "Wasting Women's Lives", could be utilized for a more comprehensive discussion of this old and continuous matter. The laws affecting its practice in leading countries and the practicing attitude of women toward the laws—a historical review—belong in a better article. It would require a lot of hard research but no issue transcends it in importance.

American Frontier. There is no hint whatsoever that there were any women on the frontier and thus it neglects to consider the civilizing domestic arts, mutual aid in community life, the cooperative enterprises which elevated the individualistic will to social prowess, amid the liberties of pioneering.

This is an extremely narrow and bigoted article, both because it excludes women and because it follows Prof. Turner[2] too closely, uncritically. It makes the frontier the "cause" of the Am. Rev. It makes the farmer the sole source of Jacksonian democracy, whereas the urban artisan was a powerful element also. The author of the article cites the Beard and Beard treatment of the frontier as if that treatment bolstered his, except for (in the author's mind) an excessive economic emphasis. This is not true in any respect.

The French observer and critic, Alexis de tocqueville [*sic*], was not so crude as the author of this article, in his discussion of the Am. Frontier. Tocqueville was deeply impressed by the role of women there as bearers of civilization.

Nor was Margaret Fuller as naive as Turner; she made a trip to the middle border from New England in the 1840s and had far more insight than Turner respecting its life and meaning for the nation. She was more like Tocqueville in her acumen.

The tight little, provincial little, masculine thesis of F. J. Turner has had a death-like grip on the historical guild and has induced such historical writing by laymen as that in James Truslow Adams'[3] treatment of the frontier which made it definitely barbarous—and made it men without women.

The American Frontier article should either be removed or treated more competently.

Cookery. A reader would scarcely suppose from this article that woman was ever in a kitchen! Catherine de Medici is credited with reviving the art in France and a couple of English women who wrote cook books come into it. Otherwise it is another case of men's assuming all the management and graces. The illustration of mediaeval cookery reinforces that emphasis. We think that it should start with a statement about the prehistoric beginnings—the purely creative first forms of boiling, broiling, baking, etc. and illustrate that with pictures readily available from American Indian collections. A picture might be used showing the outdoor bread oven of the Indian women of Taos still in use. The weight

2. In 1893 Frederick Jackson Turner delivered a paper entitled "The Significance of the Frontier in American History," in which he argued that the American frontier was the greatest determinant of American culture.

3. James Truslow Adams, a well-known American historian, was a contemporary of Mary Beard.

of research credits women with starting this business. Men came into it later. But of course men have never taken it all over. And of course women have developed it too and written more than five foot shelves on it. A New England kitchen might well be pictured. A greatly dramatic presentation of this fundamental art of life could be written with full scholarship.

Education. The tang of this article is too masculine. The effect is to represent women as uneducated except as students in recent public institutions. Great and definite harm is done to women and to the minds of men by the assumption here maintained that women never had an education until recent times. The harm lies in the falsity of his assumption. How the problem of a finer and truer article can be solved is a question. It may require a separate article on *Education, Women's*, treated historically. . . . However it is also true that men have not been all educated in schools and universities. Conceivably therefore this article could be entitled in such a way as to limit its discussion to formal schooling. But in that case the other ways of being educated might be grossly ignored.

King. Why not an article on *Queen* too? This is very British in character but implies no woman-king in Britain. It should be made more comprehensive on the two counts. Perhaps the title could be broadened to embrace rulers of that classification as a political phenomenon.

Language. Where there is strict exogamy, there is a "woman language." Dr. Edinger, one of our signers, stresses the fact that Hebrew for about 2000 years was exclusively a language used by men scholars, despite the fact that Jewish religious practices conformed to a domestic feminine religious cult.

The variation in men's and women's language, spoken and written, should be noted. It was especially a variation in the ages before formal schooling but it is still a large fact—variation not in toto but in large measure. Cicero learned linguistic grace from his mother-in-law whose fine Latin language was his intense admiration, he confesssed. Well endowed schools sometimes employ both men and women teachers of languages because of their different styles.

Medical Education. Since women were the original healers women should be taken account of in connection with medical education as a sex discriminated against. Women continued to be physicians and surgeons throughout the middle ages. Midwives were also doctors. But the rise of formal medical education threw that education mainly to men. This article, by its omissions, commits the error of assuming that there is no distinction of sex in training. The denial of interneships to women, for instance, as a climax to medical education, compelled women in New York to found a hospital where women could get that clinical experience. Other women had to force open the doors of medical schools or establish such schools of their own.

Medical education was originally and for ages acquired through apprenticeship and not in schools. Women doctors and surgeons of the middle ages had apprentices in their convent-hospitals. Etc.

Medicine, General. This is excessively English. Why is it started at 1910? Would it not be better to place it in the history section? If the present arrangements [*sic*] stands, the place would be excellent for describing the increasing role played by women in organized or "social" medicine, notably in Russia. But by "increasing role" we do not mean to imply or permit the supposition that woman's role in general medicine is a purely modern thing.

Social Anthropology. This subject has wide ramifications in the Encyclopaedia Britannica, running into Philology, Marriage, etc. Its treatment therefore is a major issue. Here Malinowski dominates with his extremely masculine conceptual thinking combined with his dogma about monogamy as the first form of marriage. He is discussing here the "most debated and most instructive of all anthropological problems" under the section on *Marriage and Family*. He insists upon a functional interpretation but it is his own functional interpretation and it rules out history and evolution. He refuses to be interested in the evolutionary "school" of anthropologists and sets up his own, boasting himself frankly, instead of presenting the varied theories of the matter which he admits is the "most debated and most instructive of all anthropological problems."

He makes Mother-right or Father-right descent the sole clew to group life—supreme over economic management which makes his discussion merely psychological sociology.

He is ultra-mannish respecting "primitive man." On page 864 he refers to "man who controls tropical colonies." But that is not always the case and "controls" may be too strong a word in any case, for there is and was more mutual aiding than he reckons with. Prince Peter Kropotkin, in his volume on *Mutual Aid*, sought to correct such a point of view as this and Kropotkin was a careful anthropologist.

Malinowski contradicts himself several times: i.e. in discussing Totemism. Under a heading, *The Supernatural*, he says: "Man's interest in his surroundings is primarily practical"—after making Totemism a psychological phenomenon. Under *Totemism*, he cites the distinguished English scholar, Jane Harrison, who associated it with crises as a religion, but Jane Harrison remembered women primitives as he does not.

A more competent, less bigoted, more enlightened review of Social Anthropology would first of all present the theories of all anthropological schools relative to social origins. No one can positively know social origins. New facts are discovered apparently from time to time. The debate must go on. Malinowski tries to close it.

Song. No woman sang in Europe, it appears from this review. The contributions of the nuns, in choir composition and singing, is not recognized at all. One woman is included in the Bibliography for this article but none in the article itself. Julia Ward Howe is not mentioned in the section on the U.S. though her *Battle Hymn of the Republic* shook the nation and for the North was comparable to the Marseilliase [*sic*]. Some American women after the civil war are named but the discussion closes with a masculine superiority bias to the effect that women are rapidly approaching the men in excellence. Madrigals were women's song; they are not so described, for instance.

We recommend a section on women and song to be written by the scholarly German woman musicologist, Käthe Meyer, and illustrated from her collection of pictures for reinforcement.

FROM PART III: SUGGESTED NEW ARTICLES

Bathing. It has both an amusing and quaint history from the standpoint of modern "bath tub mindedness" charged to Americans particularly. It was forbidden by Catholics in times and places. Some peoples, Russians and Japanese, have been accustomed to the sexes bathing together in pools or in the sea without the clothing of Occidental Victorianism. It has always been associated with architecture of course. It bears a peculiar relation to modern housing in the USA. See article, American Weekly, 1938.

If illustrated, it might show the Japanese steaming device with the place for the fire.

Bread-making. If space is needed, the article on "pig sticking" might give way to this staff-of-life manufacture. Goguet has written a history of it. It should open with early description and be a narrative of the historic business. Weigall in "Sappho and Her Times" gives luscious sentences to the beauty of Greek bread. Since so many peoples have lived on bread alone, really, the subject is of comprehensive importance.

The article could be handsomely illustrated, with a picture of an outside oven in Taos, i.e., and old communal ovens, and on up to our great all-machine plants.

Dyeing. It has been as important as Weaving. It was an early performance of women as the present article admits. It could be richer in its treatment by dealing with women's use of color for embroideries, carpets, textiles; by suggesting at least that available materials were a consideration.

Hospital. Unless a new section is inserted into this article which is now in the Encyc. Brit., a separate article should be written dealing with women and hospitalization. The single paragraph here on "The Origin of" is weak in its scant recognition of the women's hospitals of the middle ages—in their convents. Those were the great hospitals of those times. The discussion here savors to excess of Protestantism. We call attention again to the early women who were the first doctors and nurses and who kept up that doctoring and nursing to the point of founding hospitals and guarding them ever after—until for a brief time in the modern age, men entered this field of sick care, shut women out of hospitals, and forced them to make their way back to their age-old responsibility. The story could be told, in part, under monasticism, or under a new article on Nuns. But it might be told with enlightening effect here.

Hull House. Since Toynbee Hall has a separate sketch, we think that Hull House fully merits a separate sketch too.

Hunger. The historic story of this prime human (and all-biological phenomenon) is told in such a powerful, moving, and significant way by Ezra Parmalee Prentice in a book entitled "Hunger" that we propose a grand article on the subject, written along the lines of his treatise and by him if he is willing to undertake it.

Laundrying. Women's penchant for washing clothes is one of the strangest freaks of nature, in our opinion. It deserves a long and impressive narrative—article of a historical nature leading up to the use of the BENDIX machine in our day. Women have washed throughout the ages in streams, beating clothes with paddles if they could get the stuff for making paddles, otherwise by beating on rocks or rolling and rolling in their hands. In time they made pads on which to kneel and in Italy today, here and there, one may see a hood, no doubt made by a man, as protection over a woman washer's head. In Switzerland can be seen the tall cement tanks filled with ice cold water which makes the women washers' hands as red as beets and rawer than uncooked beets—almost frozen. The "achievement" of indoor tubs with running water and heated is a tremendous advance from pail-carrying from distant wells. From the old crude washing machines to the glorious Bendix is the latest advance.

Getting mangels and electric ironers should be in the story of advancement. Getting racks for drying is far ahead of the ropeless use of fences as one finds the custom in our South as well as in Italy. Without fences, the grounds were used.

Now we work for great cooperative laundries and laundrying is also a big business.

All this could be grandly illustrated.

Man. The lack of a generic word in English, other than *man*, for the human being, leads to such assumptions of masculine priorities and prerogatives as appears in the article on *Fire*—assumptions to which we have called attention in various parts of this Report. Men speak and write of "men" even in our democracy in commonly unconscious perhaps neglect of women—and despite of women voters—in many ridiculous ways. If attention were called to the restriction of the English language in this matter, more care might be exercised in speaking and writing. In the case of the aforesaid article on *Fire*, the author makes "man" do the cooking with fire when he probably did no such thing.

Nuns. In Vol. 16, p. 640 there are 2 lines dealing with *Nuns.* The cross reference refers to *Monk!* And to Monasticism. If the reference to *Monk* worked out helpfully within its 4 line treatment, that would be something, though we would suggest a reference in the article on *Monk* to *Nun* as equally helpful.

The reference to Monasticism is indeed helpful. But Nuns had a larger role than is recounted in that article. Owing to popular conceptions among Protestants to the effect that women entered convents involuntarily for the most part and owing to the popular ignorance respecting their role as physicians and surgeons, the scope of their education, their "spring into freedom" via the convent in Rome, England, and elsewhere in large reality, and their dramatic and scientific writing, etc., we incline to call for a new article on *Nuns.* So much more is known about Monks that this call seems warranted. Rich material on Nuns awaits the writer of the article.

Salons. The role of the Salon as an intellectual, political, and social implement or device was a powerful phase of woman's force previous to the rise of the democratic public forum. Wendell Phillips gave vigor to his support of the woman movement in his time by pointing out that tradition of feminine expression declaring in one public speech, for instance, that it was in the French salons that Frenchmen did their thinking. That was true. In Germany also the Salon became a center of intellectual, political, and social influence. It existed in America in the middle period, especially in New York. There are at least two powerful social salons in our national capital (or were before Pearl Harbor): Alice Roosevelt's and Mrs. J. Borden Harriman's.

The French Salon was the backdoor to the Academy. Its role as promoter of scientific interest is recognized in J. B. Bury's "The Idea of Progress." Much has been written on Salons which could be used as the substance for an article on a phase of history of such importance.

Social Implements. An article in the present Encyc. Brit. discusses *Weapons, Primitive.* They are reviewed as features of the male's fighting function or inclination. But primitive weapons for social construction are not even hinted at. Surely they were even more important. We suggest introducing an article on constructive implements (not calling them weapons), beginning with a section on *Primitives* and frankly acknowledging the leadership of women in this connection as inventors of cooking (with its implements), spinning, weaving, etc. The article could stop with *Social Implements, Primitive* or come on to the implements of today.

4. The Economic Background of the Sex Life of the Unmarried Adult[1]

NOTE: *Despite its titillating title, this unusual article examines the political, economic, and cultural effect that the unmarried adult has had on human history, and continues to have on contemporary politics. Concern in recent years with family patterns, Beard says, obscures the crucial social role of the unmarried mature population.*

She examines the Fascist movement in Germany–and note that the article was written in 1934–as "essentially a dynamic of unmarried males." After World War I, political power in Germany "went begging in the streets, where it was picked up by soldiers." Hitler has surrounded himself, she warns, with men "of sadistic temper, unaffected by the restraining influences which education, jobs, families and public obligations" exert. This handful of "undomesticated men" is supported by a "romantic youth movement, naturally violent, and composed of men just reaching manhood, all poor, all jobless . . . all resentful."

With the "rage of tigers [they] leaped over the barriers which civilized nations had erected for human behavior." They are "American gangsters armed with political power."

Bachelors may have formed the Nazi party, but they were supported from the start by unmarried women, Beard says, "spinsters, lacking homes and gainful employment," who also looked "wistfully to the 'glory' of war."

In the United States, too, in the face of economic chaos, there are "hordes of young men and women wandering about . . . like nomads, in search of sustenance and comfort." We should remember, she warns, "how thin is the veneer which civilization spreads over mankind's natural urges."

Beard then scans world history to isolate the historical importance of the unmarried. She looks at the meaning of celibacy in the Catholic Church, the misogynistic implication of Nazi homosexuality, the economic exploitation of girl workers in the textile industry, and she concludes that "husbands and maternity are essential to women's mental health just as paternity and wives are . . . vital to that of that males."

As the economic crisis grows at home, she writes in the midst of the Depression, people look to the "conventional escape from public

1. From *The Sex Life of the Unmarried Adult: An Inquiry into and an Interpretation of Current Sex Practices,* New York: Vanguard Press, 1934, pp. 155-185.

calamity—more war.'' But war settles nothing, says Mary Beard. Her hope rests with the thousands who are ''bent on errands of economic mercy,'' who seek a ''new economic deal'' to solve realistically and humanely the economic problems of our age. A strong supporter of Franklin D. Roosevelt and the New Deal at this time, Mary Beard, along with Charles Beard, would later become critical of FDR's foreign policy. Charles and Mary Beard feared that involvement in international affairs would lead to scrapping the New Deal domestic reform, which it did. As she says in this article, ''war seems to settle nothing.''

This article of Mary Beard's is valuable because it embodies many of the strengths and weaknesses of her work. She wrote it only months after the Nazis came to power in Germany, which makes her analysis all the more impressive and, at the same time, partly explains some of its shortcomings. She demonstrates how her special perspective provides her with tools to deepen her understanding, not of matters involving women alone, but of questions of politics and ideology which affect society as a whole.

The idea that one should look at the unmarried society as a group is extraordinary. Her overriding political objective in writing the article, however, kept her from developing more fully many of the fruitful ideas that are implicit in her approach. She uses the Nazi example to illustrate the threat to social stability that is inherent in those outside of a family structure, but she does not extend that analysis to examine under what circumstances the family plays a negative role precisely because it supports social order. In general, in this article she draws upon the more conservative implications of her remarks to buttress her political critique and to endorse a position of domestic social reform.

An observation is in order concerning Beard's description of Nazi homosexuality as ''perversion,'' her holding single men and women in German society responsible for Nazi power, and her assumption that mental health for both sexes rests on marriage and parenthood. Mary Beard, as was characteristic of most of her contemporaries in the woman's movement, was not comfortable with questions of sexuality; indeed, the entire aspect of sexuality is absent from her analysis of women in history. Beard's distaste for Nazi male homosexuality should also be viewed in the context of her general assessment of Nazi criminality, and as part of the point she was making concerning Nazi hostility to women. She also well knew that support for the Nazi party came from the married as well as the unmarried, but the theme of the book in which her article appeared dealt with unmarried adults, and so that aspect of Nazi support was unduly stressed. Beard's style, in general, was to use overstatement to emphasize a point. As for her conclusion that men and women need marriage and parenthood, one should not view her statement of 1934 with the perspective of the present. The question of homosexuality was not on the agenda in the 1930s. What is significant in Beard's statement is her insistence that men, as well as women, need roots and domesticity.

Mary Beard did not systematically develop many of the invaluable insights that flowed from her historical analysis, but the creative ideas remain as a powerful demonstration of how she was able to look at familiar material in new ways. Above all, in this article she illustrates how she used her intellectual skills to defend humane social values.

An old economy is passing. A new economy is in the process of becoming. The status and character of unmarried adults within the order-that-is-to-be will mirror the culture of the new age as the status and character of the unmarried adult have reflected the culture of all former ages. The recorded history of human relations early displays concern with the problem of the unmarried and it remains a consideration of prime importance throughout recorded history. . . .

Unfortunately there has been a tendency in recent years to fix attention on the family, to the exclusion of genuine interest in the mature population that is more or less adrift. For example, a habit has been formed of thinking about women without husbands mainly in terms of sex deprivations and of thinking about men without wives largely in terms of their vocations. This inclination is responsible for the unabashed statement in the United States Census of 1930 that, since "the marital status in relation to occupation is so much more significant in the case of female workers than in the case of male workers," the aforesaid Census restricts its attention to the marital status of females alone. If such was the American mental horizon of 1930, four years later, in 1934, even a statistician could scarcely escape counting undomesticated men, too, for they have a large section of the world by the throat.

The unmarried do not live in social isolation. . . .

Their struggle for existence and the claims which nature makes upon their bodies and minds are not wholly individual affairs; nor can the modern family guard them in every respect if they dwell at home. The unmarried constitute aspects of a total situation which embraces both the economic setting in which they may try to earn their own daily bread . . . and the attendant ideas as well which set for them standards of conduct. That has been true for the unmarried since single blessedness or single woe became conscious of itself or a matter for social observation.

Today with untold millions of men and women uprooted from the soil, dismissed from industry, shut out of the professions, footloose, unemployed, resentful of the fate life has meted out to them, but still dynamic and driven forward by irrepressible hungers, the slightest attempt to comprehend their significance, even to themselves, compels consideration of the economic matrix to which they are bound like a composite Prometheus and of the currents of ideas which circulate in the air they breathe.

Throughout the economic background of the generations of unmarried adults who are seeking to solve their personal problems today runs the fact of world depression combined with the ideology of war. Interests and ideas are inseparable partners. Such prosperity as came to America between 1914 and 1929 may be traced largely to her advantage as a manufacturer of arms and as a creditor of nations at war. That prosperity provided work and extraordinary pleasure for American citizens irrespective of their marital status, unless they happened to be ex-soldiers and shell-shocked. But its duration was brief. Within ten years after the World War the gloom of panic settled down on the American scene.

And the good fortune of America, even on a transient frame, was not shared by nations less fortunately placed in the world economy. Germany, for instance, steadily crumbled into a condition of general misery after the World War. . . . In the circumstance, political power went begging in the streets, where it was picked up by soldiers.

The Fascist movement in Germany, as in Italy and Japan, is essentially a dynamic of unmarried males. If strong and desperate men are not helped by the State to sink roots into civilian enterprise and if they cannot do it unaided, they turn invariably to fighting—man's oldest and most enduring trade. The case of Germany is a glaring illustration of the menace to the State inherent in a large citizenry of unoccupied celibates.

Adolph [*sic*] Hitler, a bachelor like the majority of the thirty or forty leaders of the Nazi party, is a rover, a veteran of the World War, undomesticated and unused to the responsibilities connected with public life in a time of peace. He gathered around him in the hour of economic chaos men like himself of sadistic temper, unaffected by the restraining influences which education, jobs, families and public obligations are wont to exert. A number of the prominent Nazis are men with records of sex perversions as well as of military daring. They were supported in their rise to power by a romantic youth movement, naturally violent, and composed of men just reaching manhood, all poor, all jobless, all energetic, all resentful. These battalions of idle bachelors, with the rage of tigers, leaped over the barriers which civilized nations had erected for human behavior, and hurled themselves upon their prey, snarling and clawing, snatching posts and emoluments from private persons and appropriating state and other property wholesale. The Nazis suggest American gangsters armed with political power. Having seized a State, they reveal the fact that their sole conception of statecraft is that of a bellicose bachelor. The republic, fathered and mothered by democrats, they immediately scrapped. In its place now stands a war machine such as the German State did not represent even under the Prussian Junkers who, as men of family and great estates, regarded war with less light-hearted insouciance than these newcomers into politics who have little to lose by going on a rampage.

The Third Reich is perhaps the first example of a nation dominated by convinced bachelors. In the past, warring males, merely aggressive on foot and on horse, when they were victorious simply seized native women and carried them home to their lairs. The Nazis, on the contrary, are men trained by modern trench warfare, in an isolation from women unknown to a Tamerlane, a Wallenstein or a Pizarro. They are anti-woman in a new sense. They propose to ignore the sex completely. Their case was set forth by Ernst Roehm, as chief of the Storm Troops and Reich Minister without portfolio, the man who organized the Army of the Brown Shirts.[2] In his autobiography (1928) he gave vent to the hostility of the modern veterans toward the opposite sex; he showed how men in the late war were more aloof from women than warriors in former times who marched or rode from town to town altering the racial stock as they passed. To borrow a title from Hemingway, these Nazis are "men without women.". . .

Roehm never denied the accusations of perversity made in 1932 by the *Welt am Montag*, which published sensational letters of his addressed to boys. His attitude toward the family is revealed in these words,

2. Beard wrote this article only a short time after the Nazi party came to power in Germany. A ruthless struggle had already taken form within the Nazi party, with Hermann Goering and Heinrich Himmler united against Ernst Roehm, chief of the S.A., or Brown Shirts. There was also a rivalry between the S.A. and the German Army. The charge against Roehm and his followers of sexual perverison, which Beard voices, was widely circulated in Germany. The political struggle between the S.A. and its enemies was settled when Roehm and several hundred of his followers were murdered under Hitler's orders in June, 1934.

repeating the remark of the wife of one of his Captains: "In the heart of my husband stands in first place his Captain, above whom is nothing; only after that come his mother and myself." And Roehm highly approved this "comradeship of the soldier, cemented by blood" which, he declared, can "never be expunged from the heart."

This rebellion of the undomesticated, un-civil-ized males of contemporary Germany—surplus males—has been accompanied by manifestations indicating the presence of surplus women as well. The first group of women to join Hitler and the Nazis were nationalist and bellicose, a group which had issued a manifesto, just before the Armistice in 1918, demanding that women be called to arms as well as men. As the mothers of Germany were not united in a peace movement, the spinsters, lacking homes and gainful employment themselves in a peace period, reverted wistfully to the "glory" of war which, as Guida Diehl, their leader, says "took them out of themselves." This need of unmarried women to be "uplifted" by a Cause, even by a holy man, is made painfully clear in Diehl's *Deutsche Frau*.

She calls Hitler a messiah: "In a holy state of divine possession, Hitler serves the mission of God!" She summons women to ally themselves with the messiah and his war band. For their inspiration she offers not the "weak-yielding" Gretchen but "Brunhild, a heroic woman, with whom men must fight" and "Krimhild who takes over the blood-feud and never rests until she has wiped out her whole tribe of kinsmen." Guida Diehl and Hedwig Foerster and other female Nazis mirror the unmarried woman's yearning to forget herself in admiration of weaponed males and in "service" to the "boys" at the front. If bachelors formed the Nazi Party, they were pushed toward power from the very start by women whose votes for Hitler out-numbered men's in the final reckoning.[3] The craving of these women for homes was frequently laid bare. Hitler explicitly promised this at least: "A good German husband for every good German woman." But the women did not realize, it seems, that they would be marrying German soldiers. Now that they understand, they are increasingly horrified.

The economic interregnum has not come to a violent end in the United States, it is true, and may not end violently. But signals flaming from the

---

3. In this reference it is clear that Beard realizes that the support given the Nazi party by women came from both unmarried and married women.

pages of the past and world events in the present warrant the gravest assumptions with regard to the effect of economic and emotional hardships on the spirit and designs of mankind. It is generally taken for granted that women lose ground in such circumstances. There may be no exact figures respecting the size of our own unmarried adult population, we may only presume concerning its numbers, we can merely guess at the emotions which sway it. . . .

Note the hordes of young men and women wandering about the continent, like nomads, in search of sustenance and comfort, as the aborigines were doing when the Europeans arrived on the scene in the 17th century.[4] This 20th century migration of homeless, tool-less and landless persons bears no resemblance to the activity and optimism which settled and exploited the continental domain. Older generations carried cattle and plows with them, staked out claims upon public land and carved out states for a nation. This generation of rovers looks forward to no independence, individual or familial. Its highest reach in hopefulness is the winning of a chance to labor for someone already established, secure, and in need of employees. If the vigor of these Americans gone nomad is praiseworthy and their initiative commendable, if, in other words, they refuse simply to squat beside closed mills and mines, offices and shops, in the event that their quest for work proves futile, their very determination not to be utterly defeated may sweep them into the party of any magnetic personality, however demagogic, who offers them a program. The risks of a national relapse into banditry and savagery may be minimized. . . . but it is surely well to remember how thin is the veneer which civilization spreads over mankind's natural urges.

"What is the source of this man's rage? Of this woman's fury?" asks an outstanding columnist. And no query is more important. Resentment at society, coupled with the economic chaos which provides exercise for malcontents, is the source material of every known dictatorship. Unemployment, every investigator nowadays reports, is an unmistakable compulsion to crime. Knowing this, the War Department has made full preparation for handling "eventualities," in the form of organized rebellion, by its own expertly organized and well-equipped force. And not only does the present Secretary of War, George H. Dern, call for a

---

4. Reference here is to the enormous number of jobless, poverty-stricken wanderers created by the Depression. Most of them were young people.

strengthened standing army but in that plea he is joined by an ex-secretary of War, Newton D. Baker, who felt assured while he was in office that not even for America did the World War end in 1918. While the Treaty of Versailles was being penned, he was insisting that the United States must take more lads into its army. All men and innumerable women think in terms of rioting and fighting. Can they think in any other terms?

The signs and symbols of social havoc inherent in economic chaos shoulder up in other ways above the plane surface view of peace and order lightly held by the complacent. They appear in the resurgence of prostitution, open and clandestine, in the cities; in the dearth of positions awaiting college graduates and the steady sinking down of the white-collar classes into the ranks of the proletariat, or, lower, into the ranks of the paupers. They are evident in the bankruptcy of trust funds set aside for the care of the "well-born"; in the weakened capacity of parents to provide for their daughters that ancient and long-enduring encouragement to matrimony, the "dot"; in the sex segregation attending efforts to relieve the needy when the unmarried are being succored; the comparative neglect of single persons in schemes for charitable or work assistance. They are manifest in the wretched hovels where "hoboes" foregather; in the free-loving of the free; in the raids on the national treasury by veterans of the late war; in the hunger marches on the Capital; in the closure of opportunities for mature individuals with experience and capacity to apply their knowledge and talents in public life. They are mirrored in the mounting insanity and suicides; in the community efforts to amuse the forlorn that they may be at least mentally occupied; in the increasing number of clinics for the psychopathic; in the propaganda among the well-circumstanced for the sterilization of the "unfit"; in the assemblies of the young debating ways out of youth's tragedy; and in the violent solutions offered for this riddle of the universe—bread and a full life for all.

No picture of a civilized society every conceived by the mind of man or woman would tolerate in any particular this starvation of brawn and brain, this narrow channeling of the human spirit, this confinement of thought and action, this peril to human stock, this menace to a democratic republic erected in a New World in an age of abundance and still faced with the potentialities of plenty. Men and women cannot be made social outcasts with impunity—to themselves or to the commonweal. Yet the number of pariahs in the United States at this hour mounts to uncalculated millions. Their interest lies in economic security and a rounded personality. The dominant idea in their times is violence. Interests and ideas flow together.

When we consider the problem of celibacy and the State, we must consider how often the European nations have been wrecked by unmarried hordes. The conclusion seems inescapable that, if husbands and maternity are essential to women's mental health, paternity and wives are as vital to that of the males. The rulers of societies in the Far East in days gone by connected marriage and political stability as an inseparable affair. The family system was deliberately linked to statecraft. As early as the 6th century B.C., Confucius prescribed the family system as a remedy for the feudal anarchy of China, and monarchs adopted this philosophy in order to consolidate their centralized power. Thus when the Japanese shoguns took over Confucianism in the 17th century, A.D., it was with the conscious determination to base the State on the family. And today the unique national cohesion of the Japanese is in a striking measure due to the Shinto (the national religion) emphasis on the family. In ancient India, too, although Buddha taught celibacy, he had first tried marriage, and the Hindus still marry extremely early. Not until their full maturity, after their families are founded, do the men feel justified in entering holy orders.

This exaltation of the family has never proceeded so far in the Occident. While Church and State united to consecrate marriage, the feudal economics defeated marriage on a vast scale, for the eldest son inherited the family estate and the younger sons were obliged to enter the Army or the Church. Europe was continuously filled with restless throngs of unmarried adults, footloose as well as family-loose. They provoked much of the turmoil as well as much of the progress in the West. Thus the old French Monarchy was led to economic ruin partly through its effort to finance the vast aggregation of religious celibates in its midst. Many revolutions occurred as the consequence of revolts by the married against the claims of the unmarried for support. The separation of Church and State in France eventually reflected this dispute.

Slavery, war and prostitution absorbed their share of the responsibility for surplus men and women, and effected a gigantic combination, in fact, for carrying out the task. Indeed, this alliance remains active in Japan, where hapless youths serve Mars and hapless girls serve Venus, the latter generally sold in childhood to the brothels. In Germany the new social prescription reads that no damsel must divert a soldier from his course of "raw brutalism" through the agency of feminine wiles. Prostitution is *de rigeur*, with emphasis on the rigor. But if ethical perceptions are equally lacking in Japan under a revived State-as-War, esthetics holds a tighter rein. In Japan even the warrior is expected to take his sexual pleasure with artistic delight. The military officer of the Japanese race is apt to be a poet. He has been trained in the appreciation of art. He enjoys music and he esteems dainty food. Not so long ago he actually drank his tea ritualistically. His one true god is a female—the Sun Goddess— ancestor of his race, a benign agricultural deity, chiefly disturbed because her brother's piebald colts have been allowed to ramp over her rice fields. In her distress the goddess retreated to a cave but she was lured forth again to bless mankind through the medium of the dance. She is thus no Brunhild, no Teuton deity wrecking even her kinsmen in her fury. She is a genial creature permitting human graces. And the geisha girl, with her religious affiliations, is noted for her graces—her posturing, singing, dancing and elegant costuming. Since interests and ideas move along in a united front, possibly their feministic religion stamps sex manners on the Japanese. At any rate, the sexual slave is an adjunct of Japanese politics and a conspicuous feature of every new community which the race establishes in the world.

Baroness Shidzuè Ishimoto[5] would check the supply of prostitutes at its source by birth control, but, while that movement makes some headway, the enormous birth rate meanwhile makes the mass production of sexual slaves so preposterous that all the politicians can devise are schemes for migration and imperialism.

The sing-song girls of China and the nautch girls of India are more manifestations of the economic alliance—slavery, war and prostitution. Infanticide was the more primitive way of balancing mouths and the food supply, and infanticide is not unknown nowadays in China. It lingered in the highly sophisticated Greek societies beside prostitution, as a means of handling overpopulation and at that stage of birth control knowledge, Plato was unable to eliminate it from his social planning. Greece, however, contributed high ethical values to thought about life. Granted that she erected free-loving into a cult of beauty worship, her courtesans served as models for immortal works of art. . . .

Through companionate liaisons with thoughtful men, unmarried

5. Baroness Ishimoto was a leading Japanese feminist.

Greek women perhaps more than wives extended the reaches of intellectualism. Single women had the run of the Greek islands. They possessed
keen minds. They had wit as well as curiosity. They were members of all
the academies and, indeed, were heads of some. The roots of the Stoic
religion which finally mastered Rome may be unearthed in Megara,
where the teacher of Zeno, founder of Stoicism, studied under the
woman, Euklides. . . .

But it was Roman destiny to distribute Greek culture even further
afield than Alexander had done. While unmarried Roman males joined
married men in the wars for empire, a new profession appeared for men in
Rome, a civilian pursuit known as the law, and it became an obsession
rivaling sex and pugilism. While young children, especially girls, continued to be exposed to death or slavery, unmarried women, surplus
women, Roman as well as Greek, rose to prominence in the professions
of medicine and nursing, acting, teaching, painting and merchandising,
among others. Sex was thus repressed by public interests and ideas, by
opportunities to earn a livelihood in unwonted ways, and by more wilful
spending as wants enlarged or multiplied.

But such liberties collapsed with imperialist enterprise. And in this
crisis the cult of celibacy swept all else before it. . . .

That the rigid doctrine of virginity made such growth among the
Romans was due in part to the propaganda against intermarriage with
Teutons and to the desire to preserve Roman blood from barbaric con-
tamination.

*   *   *

Virgins helped matrons to create the ideology of sex as sin and the
celibate practices of the long monastic era. In so doing they were heir-
esses not only to Roman wealth but of Roman devotion to the phenomenon of sex—the core of the varied cults that one after the other inundated
the Eternal City. Their grip was not relaxed by the Christian monastic
movement, for the consciousness of awe, pain, gratitude, hunger, peni-
tence, hope, love and mercy still found no satisfactory application that
did not involve sex.

Monasticism, however, was varied in its offerings to the unmarried.
Through the priesthood, males escaped military service under barbarians.
They likewise escaped family duties without having to be total abstainers
in the matter of female society. Could they not lecture the ladies to their

hearts' content, consult with them, pray with them, hear their confessions, and be as fathers and brothers to them? Be their holy men? If single blessedness had its price, though it was increasingly the purpose of the Papacy to prevent family interests from penetrating into the monasteries so that the whole attention and revenue of these institutions might serve the interests of the Vatican, though the celibates of both sexes had to serve the Church materialistically, yet monks and nuns achieved economic security in the form of food, clothing and shelter as well as protection from military service in a turbulent age, and by asceticism simple folk could reach powerful offices.

While monasticism provided for Roman women a flight from financial panic and mental bewilderment to sheer ecstasy, no doubt, it was also a spring into freedom in many ways.

* * *

For five or six centuries after the collapse of the Roman Empire the energies of celibates went into pioneering on a tremendous program. Thus they claimed the forests of Germany and Britain for civilization. Monks and nuns went forth to found towns, for example, Bremen, and to carry books to the Irish bogs; they conquered the wilderness and baptized the heathen. For many a generation, as Dopsch shows, religious celibacy had an activist motive *par excellence*, reaching around the globe with its enterprise.

By turning from conquest through marriage to direct conquest over land, English noblewomen attained an economic independence of feudal proportions and a freedom to dare and to do which court life would only have hampered.

* * *

The Crusades represented a mass movement of devout celibates, in addition to an excursion of married men and female hangers-on. But one must not forget the fighting orders of knights—*Ritterorden*—which held back the Slav waves from overwhelming Prussia and, indeed, the whole of Europe. One of these orders, the Knights Templar, was supposed to have been more inclined than the others to tolerate perversity, symbolized, it is maintained, in the order's heraldic bearing—two men on one horse. So in our own historical moment, a new Nazi professor at Berlin University, Alfred Baeumler, is one among many men working at a celibate philosophy for the Third Reich. He declares that the military

State cannot be founded on the family but only on the close association of men and boys. "Not the home and salon, but the male-assembly and the field-camp are the symbolic realities." He makes exceedingly plain what scores of writers are saying, namely that the Prussian State, with its heritage from the medieval *Ritterorden*, is akin to the ancient Greek State—military and male. The Nazis have chosen for their bard the poet, Stefan George, who hymns the love of man for man.

*   *   *

Guilds of laymen and their wives, as time advanced, took control of commodity production and the market in which goods were sold. Then the ascetics, once able to find release for their emotional vitality by hard labor on the soil, through their handicrafts, processions and singing, by fasting and praying, with their brushes and quills, were thrown back upon meditation more and more. In their plight, mysticism captured monasticism, visions supplanted toil and prophets and prophetesses appeared as the sensational phenomena of changed economic operations.

*   *   *

Luther proposed to solve the celibate problem of Europe by marriage. But Columbus, unknown to him, had found another way to dispose of surplus energies. The discovery of America opened a fresh theatre in which unmarried adults could play their various roles.

*   *   *

And when all was as a tale that is told, by the 19th century, when the last blood-letting directed by Napoleon had temporarily settled the celibate problem, a new solution loomed—the mechanical. The Industrial Revolution was on the calendar of history. In Japan, as in England and the United States, the early stages of the Industrial Revolution were marked by a kind of industrial monasticism. It was in the secular retreats of a machine age that this latest phase appeared. Girl workers in the textile factories were housed in company dormitories and a watch and ward was kept on their liberty of movement. But this scheme did not last. Profiteering potentialities reduced the plant owners' anxiety about their personnel; nor did the working women long accept their jails. Only in the detail of wages did sex retain much identity with labor; women were regularly paid less than men.

To retrieve the merest vestige of their former recognition as human beings, which was their lot under the old household economy, or to go forward into a day of such regard, women working away from home sometimes had to fight with the strike as their aggressive weapon. Thus, romanticism about the machine economy died away. It was understood in its stark reality— not as public service but as service to profiteers. Unmarried adults of both sexes who were gainfully employed toiled for money rewards—not for direct consumption of the things they produced. Pleasure was thus an affair of good fortune; it was no longer an affair of creative labor. Everyone in need—and that meant more than ten million women alone, in 1930, in the United States—was out in the big world as an individual at work, and unless he or she could combine with his fellows and bargain collectively, he or she was operating according to a philosophy of grab-as-grab-can. Humanity was moving back to a primitive tooth-and-claw mode of life and labor. . . .

Under the capitalist economy, occupation for both sexes ranged from a central type where work and a complete life were intimately related, as they had been in the preceding household economy, to a distant periphery where they bore no relation at all and where every degree of sublimation was necessitated for the maintenance of working efficiency.

* * *

While the conscientious and ambitious woman strives to fix her attention as closely as may be on her work and to derive her satisfaction by trade or professional achievement, the more volatile and perhaps the less gifted woman is sadly immune to the facts of low wages, bad conditions of labor and the absence of opportunity for advancement. This type of unmarried adult waits for a miracle to happen. She expects marriage eventually to lift her out of her struggle for existence on its lonely plane. She does not accept the dogma that work gives more satisfaction than wedlock. And yet marriage under modern economics rarely solves her problem of want and rarely proves a substitute for hard labor, whatever solace it may bring to the soul.

* * *

In this crisis the cry grows stronger in America, as around the world, for the conventional escape from public calamity—more war. The potentialities of peace in a technological time demand for their realization the play of social, constructive talents—brains, in short—which mankind has been slower to develop than the cruel, destructive skills. Rather than sink disgracefully down into a pauper's grave, surplus men tend to revert to the rigid concepts of heroism that they may at least perish glamorously. And young women, impressed by the futilities of their lives, dally with the idea that war offers glory for them, too.

Amid such economic conditions and such mental bewilderment, facing such passions and such dire needs, explorations are being made by the rational into ways and means of abolishing the raw brutalism of war as an answer to the riddle of the universe, particularly in view of the fact that war seems to settle nothing. Up and down the long corridors of office buildings in Washington, the capital of the American Republic, move today intelligent young men and women by the thousands, bent on errands of economic mercy for married and unmarried alike. They are devoting the maximum of their physical and mental energy to the task of solving, not mystically, not sadistically, but realistically and sensibly, the economic problems of this latest age. A secular philosophy competent to the new economic deal conceivably may be achieved in these corridors of time.

Bibliography

Books Written by Mary R. Beard Alone

Woman's Work in Municipalities. New York and London: D. Appleton & Co.,
    1915.
A Short History of the American Labor Movement. New York: Workers Educa-
    tion Bureau of America, 1930. Reprinted by Greenwood Press, Pub-
    lishers, New York, 1968; second printing, 1971.
On Understanding Women. New York: Grosset and Dunlap, 1931.
Woman as Force in History: A Study in Traditions and Realities. New York: The
    Macmillan Co., 1946. Reprinted (paperback) by Collier Books, New
    York, 1962; second printing, 1971; third printing, 1973.
The Force of Women in Japanese History. Washington, D.C.: Public Affairs
    Press, 1953.
The Making of Charles A. Beard. New York: Exposition Press, 1955.

Books Edited by Mary R. Beard

America Through Women's Eyes. New York: The Macmillan Co., 1933.
Laughing Their Way: Women's Humor in America (with Martha Bensley
Bruère). New York: The Macmillan Co., 1934.

Books Co-Authored with Charles A. Beard

American Citizenship. New York: The Macmillan Co., 1914.
History of the United States. New York: The Macmillan Co., 1921. (Later eds.
    have subtitle: *A Study in American Civilization*.) Rev. ed., 1921; 2nd rev.
    ed., 1932; 3rd rev. ed., 1934.

The Rise of American Civilization. 2 volumes. New York: The Macmillan Co., 1927; college ed., 1930; revised and enlarged, 1933.

The Making of American Civilization. New York: The Macmillan Co., 1937. Reprinted with additional material, 1939.

America in Midpassage. 2 volumes. New York: The Macmillan Co., 1939.

The American Spirit: A Study of the Idea of Civilization in the United States. New York: The Macmillan Co., 1942.

A Basic History of the United States. New York: Doubleday & Co., 1944. Revised edition under title *The Beards' New Basic History of the United States*, by William Beard, 1960.

Pamphlet (Co-authored with Florence Kelley)

Amending State Constitutions: A Study of State Constitutions which Lack Suffrage Amendment, June, 1916, no publisher cited.

Articles and Speeches

"An Appeal to the Reader," *The Woman Voter*, November, 1911, Vols. 1-2, p. 21.

"Mothercraft," *The Woman Voter*, January, 1912, Vol. 3, pp. 12-13.

"Votes for Workingwomen," *The Woman Voter*, September, 1912, Vol. 3, pp. 3-5.

"The Campaign for a Federal Amendment," *The Woman Voter and Newsletter*, June, 1913, Vol. 4, pp. 18-19.

"Woman's Work for the City," *National Municipal Review*, 1915, pp. 204-205.

"The Legislative Influence of Unenfranchised Women," *The Annals of the American Academy of Political and Social Science*, November, 1914, Vol. 56, pp. 54-61.

"The Congressional Union," *The Woman Voter*, January, 1916, Vol. 7-8, pp. 14-15.

"The New Japanese Women," *The Woman Citizen*, January, 1924, pp. 10, 28-29.

"American Women and the Printing Press," *The Annals of the American Academy of Political and Social Science*, May, 1929, Vols. 143-145, pp. 195-206.

"Women and the War Habit," *The Women's Journal*, May, 1930, pp. 12-13.

"University Discipline for Women—Asset or Handicap?" *Journal of the American Association of University Women*, April, 1932, Vol. XXV, No. 3, pp. 129-133.

"A Test for the Modern Woman," *Current History*, November, 1932, pp. 179-183.

"The College and Alumnae in Contemporary Life," *Journal of the American Association of University Women*, October, 1933, Vol. XXVII, No. 1, pp. 11-16.

"The Economic Background of the Sex Life of the Unmarried Adult," in *The Sex Life of the Unmarried Adult: An Inquiry into and an Interpretation of Current Sex Practices*. Ira S. Wile, M.D., ed. New York: Vanguard Press, 1934, pp. 155-185.

"Is Collectivism the Answer?" *Independent Woman*, March, 1934, Vols. 13-14, pp. 69, 92.

"Women and Social Crises," *Independent Woman*, series of three articles: November, 1934, Vols. 13-14, pp. 347, 362-63; December, 1934, Vols. 13-14, pp. 376, 400-401; January, 1935, Vols. 13-14, pp. 8, 30-31.

"In Justice to the Supreme Court," *Independent Woman*, June, 1936, Vols. 15-16, p. 164.

"Memory and Human Relations," *The Key of Kappa Kappa Gamma*, December 1, 1936, pp. 308-311.

"The Direction of Women's Education," address to the Alumnae Luncheon at the Centenary of Mount Holyoke College, May 7, 1937. Reprinted in *The Centenary of Mount Holyoke College*. South Hadley, Mass.: Mount Holyoke College, pp. 44-61.

"The Raw Materials for Thinking," address to Business and Professional Women's Association, 1937, copy in Schlesinger Library.

"Society's Interest in Human Resources," *Proceedings of the Seventy-fifth Annual Meeting of the National Education Association, June 27 to July 1, 1937*, Washington, D.C.: National Education Association, 1937, pp. 80-91.

"American Traditions in Art," *Magazine of Art*, June, 1938, pp. 326-331.

"In Pioneer Days," *Independent Woman*, September, 1939, Vols. 17-18, pp. 288-290.

"Woman—the Pioneer," *Talks*, Columbia Broadcasting System, Inc., 1939, Vol. 4, No. 4, pp. 37-39.

"What Do Women Want in the 1940 Democratic Platform?" *The Democratic Digest*, March, 1940, p. 6.

"Changes in the Intellectual, Ethical, Spiritual Climate," address to Woman's Centennial Congress, November, 1940, New York City, copy in Schlesinger Library.

"Feminism as a Social Phenomenon," *Woman's Press Magazine*, November, 1940, 5-10.

"The Historical Approach to Learning About Women," address to Radcliffe College, May 22, 1944, copy in Schlesinger Library.
"Woman's Role in Society," *The Annals of the American Academy of Political and Social Science*, May, 1947, Vol. 251, pp. 1-9.
"Mirrors Held Up to Women," *The Delta Kappa Gamma Bulletin*, Fall, 1947, pp. 5-12.
"What Nobody Seems to Know About Woman," *Independent Woman*, April, 1950, Vols. 29-30, pp. 103, 124.
"What Nobody Seems to Know About Women," National Broadcasting Company, June 3, 1950, given to author by Dora Edinger.
"The Teacher as Teacher," *The Delta Kappa Gamma Bulletin*, undated, pp. 13-15.

Miscellaneous

"A Changing Political Economy as It Affects Women," syllabus for a Women's Studies Course. Washington, D.C.: American Association of University Women, 1934. Mimeographed.
"A Study of the *Encyclopaedia Britannica* in Relation to Its Treatment of Women," dated November, 1942, signed by Mary R. Beard, editor, and Dora Edinger, Janet A. Selig and Marjorie White. Copy given to author by Dr. Edinger.

Unpublished Articles and Speeches

"Have Americans Lost Their Democracy?" October, 1913, Woman's Party papers, Library of Congress.
Deputation to Senator Musgrove Calder, January, 1917, Woman's Party papers, Library of Congress.
"Woman in Long History," undated, late 1930s?, Schlesinger Library.
"What No College Teaches Young Men or Women," November, 1948, Smith College Library.
"New Social Content for Education," undated, copy given to author by Dora Edinger.

There is no significant body of Mary Beard papers. It is the extensive published work that constitutes the major bibliographical source for an understanding of her life and work. Still, there are some archival collections that were of value in the preparation of this book. The Woman's Party papers in the Library of Congress have some information relating to Mary Beard's early activist days. The Schlesinger Library of Radcliffe College contains transcripts of her radio addresses, many articles, papers relating to her efforts to establish and direct the WCWA, and correspondence, including some with Mrs. Arthur Schlesinger. The Sophia Smith Collection at Smith College also contains Beard material, including correspondence concerning the WCWA, and a series of letters from 1941 to 1956 with Margaret S. Grierson, former Director of the Sophia Smith Collection. The DePauw University Archives hold a file compiled by the Beards' children that includes some speeches, newspapers clippings, photographs, data about family backgrounds, "everything, really, that is in our possession about mother," said Miriam Beard Vagts. The University of Wisconsin Library has some Beard material deposited by Merle Curti, after his preliminary efforts to write a biography of Charles Beard proved futile.

Index